D1602720

YORTY
Politics of a Constant Candidate

YORTY
Politics of a Constant Candidate

JOHN C. BOLLENS
GRANT B. GEYER

PALISADES PUBLISHERS
Pacific Palisades, California

Library of Congress Catalog Card No. 72–95289

International Standard Book No. 0–913530–00–X

Printed in the United States of America

PREFACE

This book is a political biography of Samuel W. Yorty, former California state legislator and congressman and more recently the longtime Mayor of Los Angeles. It also is a study of his political style and campaign techniques and tactics. But why, you may ask, a book about Yorty and not about any one of the great number of other politicians? Because apparently he has been an announced candidate (and an almost announced candidate) more times for more different kinds of elective governmental offices than any other individual in the annals of American politics. In addition, since Yorty has been an indefatigable Los Angeles-based political campaigner for practically all of his adult life, an analysis of the record of his campaigns and near campaigns reveals much about the contemporary politics and the recent political history of Los Angeles and California.

Various people have helped along the way during the many months of work, and we are pleased to express appreciation to them. John Goldbach furnished sage advice in his pre-publication review, and James Kubeck was consistently patient in responding to inquiries about production details. Howard L. Feinberg, Thomas McGuire, and Gordon Francisco assembled important data on certain topics. Robert Vosper and James Mink extended permission to quote from materials in the valuable Oral History Program at the University of California, Los Angeles. People who were interviewed increased our insights, and we have respected their desire to remain anonymous. Our special thanks go to T. K. O'Brien of Loyola University Law School, Los Angeles, for his editorial comments and contributions.

J. C. B.
G. B. G.

CONTENTS

1

POPULIST SAM GOES WEST

Samuel William Yorty was born in Lincoln, Nebraska, in
1909 to German-Irish parents of modest means. They were
members of the strong Populist movement that included
many midwesterners of that era. Andrew Jackson and Abraham Lincoln were among their Populist heroes, but at the
time of Sam's birth the star that shone most brightly in
Lincoln was that of William Jennings Bryan. Sam's early
reminiscences are replete with references to the life of the
great liberal orator. Bryan's words were probably a strong
influence upon Yorty's early political thinking, as he has
said that his father was actually a personal friend of Bryan's.[1]*

Another early model for Sam was President Woodrow
Wilson, and from the liberalism of Wilson and Bryan, Yorty
seems to have developed, early in life, a strong sense of iden-
tification with the little man's struggle for equality. Ed
Ainsworth, a highly sympathetic biographer, has described
Sam's plan of action:

> From his early high school days, Sam's goal was to work his
> way up in politics until he [could] . . . exercise all his powers
> in the social and economic betterment of everyone. . . . He
> believed he possessed certain qualities which could be em-

* All source notes appear after the final chapter of the book.

ployed, in catalytic fashion, to contribute to human progress.[2]

Sam was forced to begin his catalytic career right in Lincoln, selling clothes. But Lincoln was not a big urban center at the time (official 1920 population: 54,934), so about the most catalytic action involving Sam there was the sale of a pair of socks to Knute Rockne of Notre Dame football fame. The authenticity of this anecdote is not in question since Sam retold the story during one of his successful campaigns, the courting of his wife, Betts, in 1938.[3]

At the age of 18 Sam decided to look for a bigger pond. He bought a ticket on the Union Pacific Railroad and arrived in Los Angeles in 1927. With the aid of a letter of recommendation from his previous employers in Lincoln, he almost immediately found a job selling clothes. A salesman by day, he attended law school by night, at Southwestern University, alma mater of a number of prominent Angelenos. He also took correspondence courses from Chicago's LaSalle Extension University.[4] Many years passed before he earned his law degree, which he finally received from LaSalle in 1939.[5] What took away much time from his studies was not only the clothing business, but another interest that had long been gnawing on his mind and now began to move more fully into his life. Acquaintance with a group of men prominent in the early activities of the Los Angeles Department of Water and Power stimulated his interest in California politics. According to Ainsworth, Yorty noted that the government and politics of California were replete with traditions, feuds, and conflicting patterns that formed:

> a flowing river of political continuity . . . [and] down deep there was a basic current which could be followed by those with the proper set of sounding tools. . . . He was determined to acquire a set of those.[6]

Probably more significant in his early entry into the political wars, more important than any professed life-drive, ideal plan for humanity, or the like was the Yorty voice. In a time when dependable public address systems were not yet prevalent, a would-be politician needed a strong voice to reach and convince the doubters at the rear of the meeting hall. "I wear a 15½ size collar and my vocal chords and throat are abnormally large so that I never have trouble being heard in the largest places. It's a wonderful asset for which nature is to be thanked. I would rather give a speech than eat."[7] This statement may explain Sam's success in keeping his waistline under control over the years; he certainly has made many speeches.

Yorty became increasingly in demand as a speaker in Los Angeles public power and Technocratic circles in the early 1930's. (Technocracy was a blending of certain semi-scientific engineering principles into theories of public administration. Technocrats, among whom E. Manchester Boddy, later a prominent Los Angeles newspaper publisher, was an early southern California leader, wished to turn over government to scientists.[8]) Yorty spoke on behalf of many candidates, one being John Baumgartner, president of the city Water and Power Commission, who was making his initial race for City Council in the downtown 12th district in 1933. This was Sam's home district, and he "attained a little local fame as a young man who could speak directly to the point and impress an audience."[9] During the campaign, Yorty's stepfather was a precinct worker for Baumgartner. After his election, Baumgartner secured for the stepfather a job with the Department of Water and Power. Soon Sam left the clothing business and took a position as a supervisor with that department. His duties included not only supervising the installation of a part of the power line from Hoover Dam to Los Angeles, but also making speeches and writing letters in support of various matters of interest to

the department. Sam was getting his feet wet in many sides
of politics.

Sam Yorty was a liberal, but a special kind of liberal. In
his embrace of Technocracy and his espousal of some radical
"share-the-wealth" proposals, he displayed his ultraliberal
leanings. But it is typical of Sam that even at this early date
he would appear one way in his actions and another way in
his thoughts. To the observer in the 1930's, Sam was quite
left of center, but he maintained in his own mind during
this period the belief that his ideas were moderate, saying:

> Those who stamp a label of Socialism or Technocracy are
> merely dodging and befogging the issue . . . that our deluxe
> citizens are facing the dilemma of returning some of their
> wealth through charity and taxes on the one hand, or of
> accepting a more judicious distribution of wealth on the
> other. . . . Wealth is not a criterion of true worth and
> ability. The urge for acquisition is, according to Veblen
> and Spencer, the outgrowth of the honor attached to the
> savage collections of skulls and ancient trophies.[10]

Although the above passage reads like a cross between
Upton Sinclair and Norman Thomas, Sam strove to remind
his listeners that he was an American patriot who did not
subscribe to any alien philosophies. But what he truly seems
to have been was an ultraliberal who wanted to keep a moderate appearance. Sam must have sensed around him the
despair of the depression, with its bread lines and apple-
sellers. He must have watched the national landslide of
Franklin Roosevelt in 1932, followed by the defeat of erstwhile socialist Upton Sinclair, the E.P.I.C. candidate for
Governor in 1934. Sinclair changed his registration to Democrat, but many Democratic voters were frightened off by
Sinclair's earlier socialist connections, voting for the Republican, Frank Merriam. Yorty's opposition to Sinclair
was probably due less to ideology than to practical politics;
the publicly-owned city water and power department was

incongruously among Sinclair's most vocal opponents.[11] Sam also must have seen that the people of California were interested in electing liberals who spoke most of the anti-poverty words of the socialists but were not closely aligned with them.

The mood of the mid-1930's invited a political candidate who was patriotic yet ultraliberal. And this is what Sam became.

2
THE CATALYST GETS HIS START

Frank Shaw, a candidate for Mayor of Los Angeles, was another man, besides John Baumgartner, for whom Sam campaigned in 1933. Sam had applied on his own volition to speak in the Shaw campaign and had been accepted. He made speech after speech lauding Shaw and castigating his opponents. But although Shaw won the election, all Sam got afterward for his efforts was a raspy throat. It then may have occurred to him that he had more to gain from supporting a man for whom he had never campaigned: Samuel William Yorty.

As early as 1934 Yorty had talked about running for public office. He wrote back to Nebraska that he had almost run for the Assembly (the lower house of the California legislature) in this year, but the only support he could drum up was from the theater interests, which naturally wanted some legislative returns on their investment. Sam refused to run, he said, because he would only go to Sacramento with a free hand.[1]

Different reasons for his reluctance to seek state legislative office may be suggested, however. First, this was the year of the race between Upton Sinclair and Frank Merriam for the governorship, and the opinion takers believed it was a Republican year. Second, and seemingly more important, the incumbent assemblyman in Sam's district, John D. Mc-

Carthy, an aging, red faced, white haired individual, was running for reelection.

But in 1936 word got around that McCarthy had decided to give up his seat in the Assembly in favor of making a run for a seat in Congress. Yorty went to him in hopes of getting an endorsement for the Assembly post, but McCarthy pointed out that 11 candidates were vying for the seat, and what Sam wanted would hardly be fair. So Sam had to run his first campaign practically on his own. Little financial backing was available, and Yorty could not hope to take out a loan. After all, even if he were elected, his Assembly salary would only be $100 per month, a sum only half what he had been earning with the Department of Water and Power.

The 64th Assembly district had been redrawn after the reapportionment of 1931 and took in much of the northwest section of downtown Los Angeles.[2] It was not a wealthy district; its homes were mostly of modest size, apartment houses flourished, and businesses were generally small. The district had a long Republican history, but the latest reapportionment and the Franklin Roosevelt landslide in the next year had considerably improved the Democratic prospects.

Harry Lyons was a Republican who had represented the district from 1917 until his defeat by McCarthy in 1932. A practicing attorney who had resided in the district for 32 years, Lyons was running as a Republican but also, under the cross-filing system, as a candidate for the Democratic nomination. The Republicans were also cross-filing a man named Frank McCarthy, who may have represented a Republican attempt to fool Democrats who remembered the incumbent's name.

In addition to Yorty, two other Democrats were leading contenders. Walter Winebrenner was a lecturer whose son wrote for Manchester Boddy's *Los Angeles Illustrated Daily News*, the only large circulation Democratic newspaper in the city. The son also contributed regularly to the *United*

Progressive News, a Democratic weekly tabloid. The other major protagonist was Allen T. Richardson, a public school teacher who had backing from education interests as well as from local units of the American Federation of Labor.

Even this early in his career Yorty was displaying, privately at least, the kind of personal, cutting rhetoric for which he one day would be well known. In a letter he wrote to his father in Nebraska shortly before the start of the 1936 Assembly race, Sam noted, "I am in a hot spot all the time because of jealousy. . . . I certainly wish I was financially independent so I could cut loose on these petty political figureheads [the local councilman and congressman]. . . ."[3] It is hard to know whether Sam really believed he was being persecuted politically at this early stage when he represented a political threat of dubious strength, but it is evident that he was not financially independent yet.

The Republican press endorsed Harry Lyons; the Democratic tabloids favored Winebrenner. The bulk of Yorty's campaigning was carried out by his sister, Enid, and her friends, who went door to door with a picture of Sam, showing the new mustache he had grown in an attempt to counteract his far too youthful appearance. They were accompanied by Enid's little black dog, "Flash," who carried the proper "Yorty for Assembly" sign.[4] The girls would tell the prospective voters that despite his youth, Sam would be a strong campaigner for progressive legislation when he was elected to the Assembly. This was during the great depression, and such talk was what many voters wanted to hear.

The campaign strategy had two major elements. First, Sam had learned through his five-year apprenticeship in local politics that in a race such as this, a wise campaigner avoided spending much time or money on the residents of the apartment houses, who had a high turnover and tended to be apathetic at election time. Because Sam's major battle appeared to be in the primary election, this avoidance of the numerous apartment houses seemed to be a good shortcut to enable him to spend his skimpy campaign resources where they would do the most good.[5]

The second aspect of the campaign plan involved much busy work. It occurred to Sam that many people, out of politeness, might be quick to agree with him or with the young girls who were going door to door, but they would not necessarily back up their endorsement if and when they went to the polls. Sam therefore decided to get as many of their names as possible on petitions of support. The girls would get everyone who showed the slightest receptiveness to their arguments to sign the petitions. When Sam had the names and addresses of all the voters who seemed to be leaning in his direction, he laboriously wrote personal notes of thanks to each one, thus further cementing the relationship.

As a final tactic, Sam received the aid of the publisher of a small throwaway paper. Sam wrote some glowing endorsements of himself and paid for their printing in the newspaper as editorial matter.[6] Those writeups, along with the glossy prints which emphasized Sam's mustache maturity, went door to door with the female campaigners.

The primary campaign of 1936 drew to a close and Sam had trouble sleeping on election night. But at 4:30 A.M., when all the results were in, he was the winner. It was very close, but no matter how small his margin of victory, Yorty was in a great position. He was the Democratic nominee, in a Democratic district, in a very Democratic year. Here are the percentages computed from the official returns:[7]

Republican Ballot (5,230 votes)
Lyons	49.3%
F. McCarthy	31.5
Others	19.2

Democratic Ballot (8,927 votes)
Yorty	20.1%
Winebrenner	18.2
Richardson	16.5
Lyons (R)	11.7
F. McCarthy (R)	10.6
Others	22.9

As soon as the results were certified, Sam took off for a short, restful vacation on Catalina Island. When he returned he began to harbor some doubts about his chances of winning the general election. After all, in the primary, thanks to the cross-filing law, Harry Lyons had outpolled Sam in total votes by more than a two-to-one margin.

Sam sought some advice from another Democrat, the state senator from Los Angeles County (and later Governor) Culbert Olson:

> This little note is to let you know that I am a candidate for the office Assemblyman McCarthy is vacating; You may remember me as having invited you to speak on the "Power Bureau Bonds" a short time ago, at which time I also introduced you over the radio. Any counsel or assistance you may see fit to give me will be greatly appreciated.[8]

According to Ainsworth, the confident Olson's reply was, "Forget it. You're on the ticket with FDR!"[9]

Such unguarded optimism was not out of line. Sam's victory was a safe assumption to make. The turnout for the primary had been very low, and the estimate was that the general election would bring out twice as many voters. This was the year that Roosevelt would "surprise" some pollsters and bury Alf Landon. In a Democratic district like the 64th, it would be a tremendous upset for Harry Lyons to escape the FDR landslide. In addition, Sam had managed to get the supporters of the defeated Democratic candidates to join him; he even got nominal backing from labor groups. Sam was such a new face that he had made very few enemies. The *United Progressive News* said that Sam was a "young Roosevelt Democrat" and would be a "credit to the 64th Assembly district."[10] The election showed that his worries had been unnecessary; Sam had won in the FDR landslide:[11]

Yorty (D)	17,791	60.9%
Lyons (R)	9,564	32.7
Barnes (Progressive)	1,835	6.4

The catalytic reaction would now get its chance. Young Samuel William Yorty, his liberal ideas, his mustache, and his golden throat were on their way to Sacramento.

3

AN ULTRALIBERAL
IN THE LEGISLATURE

Unlike many first termers, Sam Yorty was not content to sit
back and be a hard working but silent observer of government in action. Sam had decided to take the Assembly by
storm.

Yorty's biographer, Ainsworth, admits that some observers thought Sam must have been introducing new bills with
a shotgun. Most of these bills eventually died, but it is not
their fate that is significant here but their character. Almost
all of them were far-reaching, liberal bills. They called for
reform of the state laws regarding divorce, labor arbitration,
and unemployment compensation. They pleaded for more
aid to the needy and blind, for lowering the voting age, and
increasing the protection of civil liberties. At one time in
1937 Yorty joined in a moving declaration against capital
punishment:

> As we declined to vote two years ago on the bill which sub-
> stituted the gas chamber for the gallows, so now we decline
> to vote "aye" or "nay" on A. B. 54 to substitute the option
> for the condemned man to choose the gas chamber or the
> firing squad, and for the reason that now, as then, we de-
> plore any action of the State in murdering its murderers.[1]

The eradication of the State Senate, one of the two houses
of the California legislature, was another of Sam's proposals
for change. It may be that the basis for this stance was his

familiarity with the Nebraska system (Nebraska, then and now, being the only state with a unicameral legislature). Yorty spoke on the one-house system many times and wrote a series of articles in the *United Progressive News* expounding his feelings on the subject. In the modern era of one man-one vote the actual arguments Sam put forth are insignificant. But the Populist rhetoric that Sam employed helps indicate how far to the political left he stood by standards of those days. The following passage from one of his articles denotes the underlying theme of the common people being fooled and robbed by the wielders of economic power:

> One of the most effective means [of checking the law-making power of the people] is the spreading of propaganda which arouses racial, social, religious, or petty political prejudice, thereby dividing the common people into opposing groups, which bicker about transitory matters with much emotion, but which disregard entirely the common problem of eradicating those evils in our economic system which cause so much needless suffering, insecurity, hardship, waste, and injustice. . . . It has so happened that through the ages some have labored, and others have, without labor, enjoyed the fruits of labor. This is wrong and should not continue. To secure every worker the full product of his labor as nearly as possible is a worthy object of any government. . . . This fear of the power of the people increases as the intelligence of the citizens increases, because the growth of tolerance and greater enlightenment herald the end of prejudices that divide the workers of the nation. Those who possess undue economic advantage sense the injustice of their position, but outwardly disclaim it and rationalize it, by assuming themselves to be superior to and different from the average citizen. . . .[2]

The similarity between this and certain passages from *Das Kapital* is remarkable. But this is not the writing of Karl Marx. It is not even that of Norman Thomas or George McGovern. The writer was Samuel William Yorty, who owed a literary debt to Abraham Lincoln.

During his initial term in the legislature, Sam also spoke at some meetings convened under the auspices of very liberal organizations. On July 12, 1937, for instance, he was advertised as a guest speaker at a forthcoming mass meeting sponsored by the American League Against War and Fascism, which was held in support of the communists who were then fighting in Spain against the forces of Franco.[3]

Sam was thus extremely liberal politically when he first served in the Assembly. He was a Populist by birth, and at this time he must have truly believed that the rich, the powerful, and the Republicans controlled the fate of the worker. But then again, Sam himself was prejudiced; he was a Democrat, was not powerful, and did not have the financial resources to control his own fate!

There was another freshman assemblyman from southern California, Jack Tenney, who shared part of the spotlight in the legislature with Yorty. Tenney had come into California politics through a side door. In the 1920's he had been variously employed as an organist in a silent film theater, a band leader, and a piano player in dozens of clubs and dives from San Francisco to Ely, Nevada, and even south of the border. During his long engagement as a bar pianist in a popular Mexicali club he composed his famous song, "Mexicali Rose."

Because of this long career as an itinerant musician, Tenney had become intricately involved in the musicians' union, and by the early 1930's he had found himself spending far more time as a union official than as a musician. He began to study law to strengthen his capacity for directing union affairs, and he eventually managed to be elected president of his local.

After passing the bar examination in 1936, Tenney needed an avenue of publicity to build a law practice. Even though he knew he would probably lose, he filed for the

Assembly race in a district which included Inglewood, Manhattan Beach, Redondo Beach, and Santa Catalina Island, hoping to get his name in the newspapers. But fate smiled upon him in the guise of Arthur Samish, the powerful California liquor lobbyist. The incumbent assemblyman had incurred the disfavor of Samish, who was in Los Angeles casting about for a wheelhorse with whom to pester his legislative foe. He had been unable to find the appropriate person and was in a quandary when he happened upon the feisty Tenney at a rally for the incumbent. The rapport was instantaneous and thanks to Samish's support Tenney awakened the morning after the election to find himself in more than print. As newspaper publicity had been his constant objective in the campaign he had reason to be pleased, but to his surprise he found that his name was listed as the successful nominee. Tenney was not the first unknown that Artie Samish had put in the legislature. Once before he had entered a skidrow resident in an Assembly race as a practical joke; but the campaign was so well done that the man was elected and served eight years in the Assembly.[4]

Tenney and Yorty were constant companions in Sacramento during the 1937 session of the legislature. They even shared the same Sacramento apartment until Tenney moved his wife and daughter up to Sacramento.[5] Their similar ultraliberal political colorations as well as the geographical proximity of their home districts made them natural partners. They shared authorship of several bills, including one which would have thrown out California's criminal syndicalism law, which liberals saw as an infringement on civil liberties.[6] Their careers continued to run on parallel tracks for almost 15 years.

The story of Sam Yorty and his companions as ultraliberals in the 1930's could be considerably expanded. But we think a sufficiently full picture has been presented of the man as he thought and acted in this part of his long, winding career. Besides—the more significant story is yet to come: What did this ultraliberal stance get him, and how, why, and when did it disappear?

4

THE FIRST LETDOWN

After his election as Mayor in 1933, Frank Shaw had had an eventful four years in office. Constant rumors of corruption and inefficiency emerged, far more than were usual even in that wild era. The rumors centered upon Mayor Shaw, his brother, Joe, whom he had appointed as his executive secretary, and the Shaw police chief, James Edgar Davis (not to be confused with later Chief Edward M. Davis). Joe Shaw was reputed to spend most of his time selling city jobs. Chief Davis was best known for having his underlings set up an unconstitutional "bum blockade" at various Colorado River points of entry to California, denying entry to any man whose economic status did not measure up to Davis' arbitrary examination.[1] Davis was also alleged to be spending so much time persecuting anti-Shaw forces that he had allowed vice to flourish in Los Angeles. The 1937 grand jury was presented with evidence of 1,800 bookie establishments and 600 brothels said to be operating in the city.[2]

But rumors were rumors, nothing more, and Shaw did not need to answer them. He had ample backing from the Republican establishment. It was not until an odd combination of outraged bluenosed eccentrics, political opportunists, and stable concerned citizens could coalesce around a viable candidate that Shaw would need to worry. And even then his foes would need either unimpeachable proof of their allegations, or at least some outrageous scandal with which to stir up the apathetic voters. Until then, Shaw had nothing to fear.

When Frank Shaw came up for reelection in 1937 his major opponent was County Supervisor John Anson Ford, a Democrat. (True, it was a nonpartisan race, but Shaw was known to be a Republican, and partisan politics were in reality very close to the surface). In the campaign, the almost endless claims of graft and corruption politically wounded the quiet, unassuming Shaw, but not to a decisive degree. Although forced into a runoff election, he emerged as the victor because his opposition had been disorganized, underfinanced, and unable to prove any of its charges.

When the *Los Angeles Times* claimed that the Shaw reelection proved the city a "white spot" among large American cities,[3] the irate accusers began to organize in earnest for civic war. One of the leading knights of the reform movement was Clifford Clinton, son of a Salvation Army family.[4] A successful restauranteur who opened his cafeterias to all patrons, regardless of their ability to pay, Clinton had been a member of the 1937 grand jury that had sought to prove dishonesty in City Hall. Clinton had been incensed at the blatant Shaw misrule and decided to finance from his own funds an independent investigation of the City Hall regime. Several conservative clergymen joined with Clinton to form an investigating organization and christened it with a perfect acronym: C.I.V.I.C. (Citizens' Independent Vice Investigating Committee).

Reuben "Rube" Borough, an ultraliberal writer and unsuccessful City Council candidate, formed another group, the Federation for Civic Betterment. It attempted to get cooperation between liberals and conservatives united only in their opposition to Shaw. This group contained such liberals as Don Healy of Labor's Non-Partisan League, and young Stanley Mosk of the Workers' Alliance (who was later

Attorney General of California and a justice on the state Supreme Court).

Chief Davis' predeliction for spying on so-called "radical groups" (meaning labor organizations and any groups hostile to the Shaw regime) had spawned the formation of still another organization, the Committee for Political Unity. It had among its leaders Congressman Lee Geyer and Assemblymen Jack Tenney and Sam Yorty.[5] Chief Davis had instructed his subordinates William Hynes and Earle Kynette to compile a blacklist of "dangerous radicals," which included Ford, Borough, and Clinton.[6] Also on the list was Sam Yorty. When asked about Yorty's presence on the blacklist, Chief Davis told the grand jury prosecutor, "He's a radical assemblyman."[7]

The various reform organizations were dedicated in their activities but belittled by the establishment, and the burden of proof was on them since the guilty were clever and highly placed. To bring a recall action against the Mayor, they needed the signatures of 20 per cent of the voters who had cast ballots for that office in the preceding city election.[8] Such a task was considered beyond the reach of the well meaning citizens' groups, because the voters were complacent. One significant turn of events would be enough to catapult the reformers out of the doldrums, however.

On January 14, 1938, Harry Raymond, a private investigator working for C.I.V.I.C., was severely injured when a bomb exploded in his car. It was alleged that a prominent police official, Earl Kynette, who was Davis' confidential aide as well as a captain in the Police Intelligence Squad, was responsible for the explosion.[9] The subsequent lengthy investigation disclosed that City Hall had been dragging its feet in the matter, and also that Shaw forces had been using dictaphones for the political surveillance of certain important anti-Shaw citizens.

The bombing and the resultant revelations provided all

the emotional push needed by the reformers, who began to circulate their petitions for the recall of Frank Shaw. They gathered far more than the required number of signatures, and to the surprise and chagrin of the *Los Angeles Times* and the City Hall establishment, the petitions were declared valid and a recall election was set for September 16, 1938.[10]

The major battle seemed to be over at this point, but aside from the actual recall election, one tremendous problem was yet to be settled. With the incredible diversity of interests involved in the campaign, how could the coalition ever hope to agree upon one candidate to put up against Frank Shaw? The details of the city charter's recall provision (which have since been changed) made it extremely important that the groups agree on a single candidate; otherwise the odds were that Shaw would lose the recall but be re-elected on the same ballot. Voters would, in effect, have to vote against Shaw twice, first on the question of recalling him, and then for a person on a list that included Shaw's name. On that second portion of the ballot, the winner needed only a plurality, which clearly meant that any splitting of the reform vote would return Shaw to the office.

More than 20 names were mentioned as potential candidates, but John Anson Ford was the first choice of nearly the entire coalition. At one of its first meetings, the coalition tried to draft Ford, but he was not anxious to accept the invitation; he had just been defeated by Shaw the year before, and he also felt committed to the race for County Supervisor for which he had already filed. Nevertheless, Ford's supporters in the recall movement were so adamant that they once awoke him at midnight and kept him "shivering, clad in his pajamas for half an hour with their pleadings."[11] Evidently the real reason for Ford's reluctance was that he believed Clinton was lukewarm about his candidacy. Although Clinton had joined the Ford draft movement, he had two strong reservations about Ford as a candidate. First, Ford had close ties with labor and other liberal political factions which Clinton felt might alienate many reform-minded conservatives. Second, Clinton observed that Ford had been defeated by Shaw a year ago and if he ran again Shaw would point out that the people's wishes (as shown in the 1937 vote) were being thwarted. At last Ford appeared before the coalition and withdrew his name from consideration.

Superior Court Judge Fletcher Bowron, the conservatives' second choice, was also reluctant to accept the nomination. Bowron had been quoted as refusing "consent to be drafted as a candidate, [for] I do not know anything that could induce me to become a candidate for Mayor."[12] Liberals were vociferously opposed to the candidacy of the judge, and the coalition meetings dragged on for several days, finally adjourning temporarily. During the six day adjournment, the liberals, led by Healy, Borough and Mosk, decided to put forth a new choice: It was none other than Samuel William Yorty.

Meanwhile the Shaw forces, led by the *Los Angeles Times*, were happily deriding the inability of the reform groups to agree upon a standard-bearer. Shaw scornfully said at a press conference, "It is not true that I have been endorsed by the so-called C.I.V.I.C. committee!"[13]

The final day of reckoning came August 8. Sam Yorty and his friends awaited the news at the Alexandria Hotel, fully expecting to hear good news. A meeting of the 25 executive committee members was being held at Clifton's Cafeteria, and Clifford Clinton had made it known that if no decision was forthcoming in favor of Bowron, he would pull his faction from the coalition. Bowron had by now assured all factions that he would be willing to run, if chosen.

When it became apparent that no agreement was forthcoming, several key defections went in Bowron's favor. Switching from support of Yorty to Bowron was Don Healy of Labor's Non-Partisan League, who said:

> I'll probably get my head chopped off for what I'm about to say. Distasteful as it is to me to support Judge Bowron, I want you to know that I have made such a decision because I know that Sam Yorty could never be elected.[14]

Healy then urged his followers not to inject any candidate's name into the discussion but that of Bowron, but his request was in vain. Stanley Mosk of the Worker's Alliance insisted on a minority report:

> I want to tell you how the [coalition's executive] committee voted today [in private session]. There were 13 votes for Judge Bowron, 7 for Sam Yorty, and 3 did not choose to vote. The remaining two were absent. I say that Yorty merits support and that your delegates should have a chance to vote for him.[15]

Mosk then attempted to place Yorty's name into nomination but was blocked by parliamentary rules. Speakers rose from the floor and discussed the merits of both men, but thanks to Healy, Yorty's formerly strong left-wing and labor support was split. A final vote was eventually taken, and a show of hands gave 121 to Bowron with 67 opposed. A motion to make the vote unaninimous was declared lost when a small coterie of voters heckled and shouted loud "noes" in opposition.[16]

The long drawn out battle was over. For Sam Yorty, what was significant was that he had been let down by the leftists, despite his constant espousal of their causes. What was even more surprising was the Communist party's radio editorial endorsement of Bowron:

> He is an honest conservative, a man of unquestionable personal integrity and principles. . . . [He] typifies in his person the social and political character of the recall move-

ment which is comprised in the main of middle class conservative minded people and of religious, reform, and good
government groups. The people are primarily motivated
by the desire for clean, honest government, a desire that
we Communists fully share with them. All honest, civic-
minded people who want to have clean municipal government in Los Angeles, who want to rid our city of the dis-
credited Mayor Shaw, have only one practical course open
to them, and that is to rally behind the candidate of the
Federation. . . . Only in this way can Shaw be defeated.[17]

At the recall election Bowron defeated Shaw by almost
two to one. Two other candidates managed only a sprinkling
of support. The reform coalition's quest for unity had been
successful.

The obvious conclusion was that Yorty had the wrong
political stance to ever rise above the Assembly. Even his
communist supporters realized that he was too liberal to
have beaten Frank Shaw. And the campaign itself served to
prove them correct, especially the violent condemnations
which emanated from Shaw as he attacked the moderate
Judge Bowron:

He [Bowron] must be prepared to be judged by the company he keeps. He is now the official apologist for an un-
holy alliance of bigotry, communism, and rule-or-ruin de-
featists.[18]

We can only imagine what Shaw might have said of some of
Sam Yorty's political connections!

Sam's losing out for Mayor because of being an ultraliberal must have planted seeds of doubt and puzzlement in
his mind. But the seeds would remain undeveloped for a
while longer.

5

A SEARCH FOR AN ISSUE

The statewide elections of 1938 posed no great threat for Sam Yorty. He was the incumbent this time and did not have strong opposition in the primary election for his Assembly seat, although he was again opposed by Allen Richardson, the teacher who had been one of his adversaries two years earlier. Yorty easily won the Democratic nomination and even picked up considerable Republican support by cross-filing.

In the general election Yorty's Republican opponent was Roger Alton Pfaff, a young attorney who later would be appointed to a judgeship. Pfaff had had an earlier career as a foreign correspondent in China and as a lecturer on various political subjects.[1] One of his favorite speeches was "Thinking American," a collection of glittering patriotic exhortations that may have sounded good to Yorty. The connection cannot be proven but later Yorty speeches contained considerably more patriotic appeals than the pre-1938 variety.

Sam really did not need to worry about losing to Pfaff. Californians were about to elect Culbert Olson as the state's first Democratic Governor of the century. Olson's coattails would prove both strong and crowded. Sam's backers built a cardboard locomotive on an old truck chassis and drove it around the district, ringing its bell. Jack Tenney dispatched bands and orchestras from his union local to enliven Yorty parades and rallies.² Sam was reelected with almost 60 percent of the vote.

As soon as the clamor of the post-election celebrations died down, Sam began to stick close to the side of Governor-elect Olson. He had a long-standing desire to be named to the state Railroad Commission (now the Public Utilities Commission) because of his association with public Utility advocates such as leaders in the Los Angeles Department of Water and Power. Yorty understood Olson to have agreed to appoint him to the commission. The appointment was not forthcoming, however. According to some of his colleagues Yorty was supremely disappointed, and this disappointment was one reason for Yorty's estrangement from the Olson liberal block in the Assembly.³

The loss of the Railroad Commission appointment, coming after the loss of the mayoralty in 1938, must have given Sam second thoughts about his ultraliberal philosophy. Then that same philosophy caused a third disappointment. Yorty's name had often been mentioned for speaker of the Assembly, but once again in 1938 the complaints were voiced about his "leftist leanings," and the speakership went to another man.⁴

As Yorty looked upon his career it must have been apparent to him that his political chances were hindered by several debilities. First, he was evidently too liberal for his own political good. Second, he was young. He was only 28 years old at the time of the Shaw recall. And as if being too liberal and too young were not enough political handicaps, Sam was also virtually anonymous. Few people outside of his own Assembly district had ever heard of him.

Still another problem was the driving ambition that was so important a part of Sam Yorty. It is certainly normal for a young politician to be ambitious, but he may have been extremely opportunistic even for an office seeker. One possible reason for this was the noisy aftermath of the Bowron selection as Frank Shaw's opponent, when Yorty supporters had refused to join in a unanimous resolution of support for Bowron.[5] Although the behavior of his supporters was out of his control, some had inevitably interpreted their performance as an indication that Yorty was more interested in his own advancement than in municipal reform.

Another incident that some considered evidence of opportunism was Yorty's part in exposing an Assembly bribery scheme during the 1937 session of the legislature. Sam had been concealed in the men's restroom of the Assembly chamber when two men had entered and, believing themselves to be alone, had openly discussed the availability of some funds for assemblymen who "voted the right way" on a certain oil regulation bill. Yorty almost immediately brought the bribery scandal out on the Assembly floor and said that he could identify the two men by their voices. Subsequent investigations implicated several lobbyists and assemblymen.[6] None openly questioned the propriety of Yorty's bringing the bribery offer to the attention of the authorities, but many feelings were hurt because the revelations were gauged more for headlines than for a quiet settlement.

Another incident occurring later involved a meeting between Yorty, Tenney, and two high-ranking California communists. Ed Ainsworth and Jack Tenney have written two diametrically opposed versions of the meeting. Ainsworth saw it as an illustration of the dangers a young liberal risks in trying to deal with political extremists. Tenney called it an example of an ambitious young lawmaker's willingness to use others for his own political motives.

According to the Ainsworth version Yorty was under harassment from communists and was trying to expose them via a small Democratic tabloid newspaper when the paper's editor offered to arrange a meeting between Yorty and two individuals involved in the harassment. Yorty agreed to the meeting on the condition that he could bring Jack Tenney as a witness. Ainsworth maintains that Yorty only later learned that the men in question were top echelon communist officials.[7]

According to the Tenney version of the story, Yorty asked Tenney, his former roommate, to drop by the Yorty apartment after the Assembly adjourned one evening, saying there were a couple of men he wanted Tenney to meet. Tenney accepted the invitation and wondered aloud who they might be, but Sam was noncommittal.

When Yorty and Tenney reached Sam's apartment that night, the two visitors were already waiting at the door. Sam introduced Tenney to William Schneiderman and Paul Cline, and then he wandered into his kitchen to get himself a cold beer, while the other three men got acquainted. But when Schneiderman explained to Tenney that he was the California state secretary of the Communist party, and that Cline was the party's Los Angeles county secretary, Tenney was unable to believe his fast-reddening ears.

Sam was still busy out in the kitchen opening his bottle, so Tenney was on his own. He pointedly asked the two communists what business they had with him, to which they replied that they thought they might be able to help him out. At this point the insulted Tenney grew irate and excused himself from Yorty's apartment.

As soon as Tenney felt sufficient time had passed for the communists to have departed, he called Yorty on the telephone. He was still angry and demanded to know why Yorty had led him into a meeting with two functonaries of the Communist party. Sam told him that he was very surprised at his show of temper. Sam said, according to Tenney, that he knew Jack had been experiencing severe difficulties within the musicians' union due to pressure from communist organizers, and he thought Tenney might have been able to deal with Schneiderman or Cline, thus removing some of the pressure on the union.

Tenney writes that he next pointed out that he could not

conceivably commit himself to any such "deals." Sam asserted that one did not have to worry about honoring com-
mittments made with communists, since "everybody knew"
they were dishonest. Thus a legislator could make deals with
them and later doublecross them without feeling culpable
in the least. Tenney writes that Yorty was satisfied to let the
matter drop.[8]

During this period Sam Yorty first became involved with
the major oil companies of the state, a relationship that began on a sour note but eventually harmonized into one of
the sweetest political love affairs on record. Sam had first
gone to Sacramento as a legislator who stood with the small,
independent oil producers in their fight against heavy
odds to remain competitive with the giants of the industry,
such as Standard Oil. In early 1939, a bill was introduced in
the Assembly that many felt might spell the end of independent oil production in California. The Atkinson oil bill, as
it came to be known, produced one of the most heated legislative battles of the 1939 session. Yorty was originally vi-
olently opposed to the measure, because he considered it to
be a giveaway to Standard Oil. At the previous session, in
one of Yorty's frequent moments of dry humor, he had introduced a facetious resolution which might have accom-
plished the same purpose as the Atkinson bill but in less
time:

> . . . Said lands are hereby granted to the Standard Oil Com-
> pany of California for their development and the produc-
> tion of the gas and oil contained therein in such manner as
> said company shall determine shall be for its best interest.
> The Director of Finance is authorized to accept from said
> Standard Oil Company of California such part of the pro-
> duction of oil, gas, and other hydrocarbon substances from
> said land as said company deems advisable for the best in-
> terests of its stockholders.[9]

When the final vote came on the Atkinson oil bill, however, Sam Yorty voted in favor, thus siding with the large oil companies. The bill passed but was held up for referendum. The anti-Atkinson campaign slogan was "Stop Standard Oil Political Dictatorship." At a special election the bill was decisively defeated.[10] Yorty had guessed wrongly about the popularity of the large oil companies.

Because of his youthfulness, his liberal record, his reputation as an opportunist, and most of all his relative anonymity, Yorty needed a course of action that would lessen some of his political liabilities. Shortly after the 1939 Assembly session convened, he introduced an issue which he may have hoped would help. He would proclaim his patriotism, gain headlines, and draw stronger labor support, all through a single bill.

6

THE OTHER JAPANESE ATTACK

A few months after the Japanese attack on Pearl Harbor in December, 1941, the Japanese residents of California, citizens and non-citizens alike, were ordered from their homes and into relocation camps. There have been numerous after-the-fact condemnations of the internment policy but, in truth, it was a product of the most emotional of times and, at that, its popularity was virtually unanimous. But what is not nearly so well known is that for decades before Pearl Harbor, some Californians had been attacking the Japanese and other Orientals.

The first Oriental Exclusion Act, passed in 1882 by Congress, had been aimed at Chinese immigrants. The Emperor of Japan had only in the late 1800's lifted a traditional ban on the emigration of his people.[1] Soon their importation had been encouraged by American merchants who sought a new source of cheap labor. But Japanese could only become citizens by being born on American soil; there was no naturalization.

Two other factors worked against Japanese assimilation in the early twentieth century. First, the mother country had displayed surprising military strength when she had soundly defeated the Russians. Second, and more important, the Japanese in California had widely adopted truck farming as their livelihood and were outproducing the other farmers, thanks to their family labor and intensive farming techniques. Strong resentment of the Japanese arose. Attacks at first were only on their farming methods, but the aim was gradually lowered until the racial background of the Japanese became the major issue and clamor arose for legislation against their right to own land and their children's right to attend school with white children.

The strength of this anti-Japanese feeling was far stronger in California than in any non-Pacific states.[2] It was also most prevalent around election time. Dozens of California congressmen were repeatedly reelected through their support of anti-Japanese legislation.[3] A politician could even use the issue for votes regardless of whether any Japanese lived in his district.[4]

After the passage of the last alien land law in 1924, the level of anti-Japanese feeling had tailed off temporarily, but with the increasing militarism of the Japanese Emperor in the 1930's it began to surface once more. A fascinating and illuminating example is the strange story of the two famous Oriental movie detectives, Mr. Moto and Charlie Chan. Both were very popular in the 1930's. And although Chan (as portrayed by various Caucasian actors) played cleverly on into the 1940's, Peter Lorre's character was mysteriously less fortunate. Such a totally sympathetic Japanese character was suddenly out of touch with the reemerging "yellow peril" imagery. Late in the 1930's the film makers felt forced to abandon the successful Mr. Moto series because of the rising anti-Japanese feeling.[5] It was right about this time that Sam Yorty decided to hitch a ride on the Japanese.[6]

Many of the earliest Japanese settlers on the Pacific Coast had been fishermen in their native land. Some of them had tried and failed at farming and had turned in desperation to their old livelihood. Through hard work, good fortune, and an uncanny ability to catch fish, many of them had thrived, brought over wives, and settled in various "fish harbors" up and down the coast. They had formed their own communities and raised children.

Sam Yorty's bright idea was quite simple, as contained in Assembly Bill 336 (1939). In short, it said that all commercial fishermen must have a valid commercial fishing license, and that no individual could be issued such a license unless he was a citizen of the United States, or was eligible to become a naturalized citizen.[7] It was not necessary to include the word "Japanese" in the bill because alien Japanese were not permitted naturalization. Thus alien Portuguese, Italians, and Germans, for example, all eligible for naturalization, were not affected by Yorty's bill; only Japanese fishermen would have been deprived of their livelihood.

Yorty got many headlines as a result of the bill. He claimed that Japanese officers were masquerading as fishermen, and that they were really spies.[8] Other supporters of the Yorty bill claimed that some of the Japanese fishermen were taking soundings all along the coast so that the depths would be known for eventual submarine attacks; these depths, however, had long been available from the U. S. Coast and Geodetic Survey for a nominal fee.[9] Sei Fujii, in his own newspaper, the *Japan-California Daily News*, scoffed at Yorty's reasoning, joking that "[Yorty] believes that Japanese fishermen could swim out to submarines and man them into San Pedro harbor." Fujii was far from a planted Japanese propagandist. It was he, a great believer in "the system," who years later initiated the test case that would finally establish the unconstitutionality of the alien land laws in a 1952 decision of the U. S. Supreme Court.[10] In 1939, Fujii further claimed that most of the alien fishermen had either died of old age or were by this time over 50 years of age, and that they had resided in California for over 30 years.[11] Surely, he implied, Yorty did not believe the Japanese emperors had the foresight to have sent their spies over so far in advance of the attack. Fujii's claims were backed up by scholarly work on record concerning the Japanese community.[12] And later work by U. S. government experts has shown that Japanese living in America were amazingly innocent of sabotage both before and after Pearl Harbor.[13]

In addition to its impact on Japanese fishermen, another potential effect of A. B. 336 involved organized labor. The American Federation of Labor had unionized the majority of the fishing boats in California, and its rival, the Congress of Industrial Organizations, wanted a piece of the action, too. Yorty's bill, while it brought him headlines as a protector of the nation's security, would have made available the Japanese-owned boats and their established fishing grounds for a C. I. O. takeover.

In Ainsworth's book Yorty maintains that he had proof that the alleged spying was truly taking place, and that he was receiving "information from the United States Navy" that Japanese naval officers were involved, but he was "unable" to reveal his sources of information.[14] Yorty evidently believed that he was protecting his country from an insidious plot.

But the bill was unpopular in Sacramento. Colleagues scoffed at Yorty's spy stories and declared the bill discriminatory. It was in and out of committee several times, and finally died.[15]

Other theories exist about this bill besides that of the labor battle. Yorty at the time may have already been sizing up Senator Hiram Johnson, against whom he would run in 1940, and may have been trying to show himself as even more of a Japanese-fighter than the aging Senator. The latter had a long history of anti-Japanese action, which may have been derived from his father's attitude. The elder Johnson had written in 1909 during a controversy over the right of Japanese to attend white schools:

> I am responsible to the mothers and fathers of Sacramento
> County who have their little daughters sitting side by side
> in the school rooms with matured Japs, with their base

minds, their lascivious thoughts, multiplied by their race, and strengthened by their mode of life.[16]

Johnson himself was a member of the Native Sons of the American West, a group which had begun by preserving historical landmarks, but which later had descended into anti-Orientalism.[17]

Sam Yorty was disappointed that A. B. 336 had died, and he railed for weeks against the fish canning interests, whom he claimed were responsible for its defeat.[18] Although the bill had failed to pass the Assembly, it had been a partial success for Sam Yorty. It had gained him more publicity throughout the state than he had ever enjoyed before.

7
FOILED AGAIN

All during the months of publicity about the anti-Japanese fishing bill, Sam Yorty was involved in his second attempt to move into the Los Angeles municipal political scene. Los Angeles municipal elections always come in odd-numbered years. In 1939 all 15 members of the Los Angeles City Council were up for reelection. As now, most incumbent city councilmen were heavily favored to retain their seats, because campaign funds were scarce and voter turnout was low, especially if (as in 1939) the Mayor was not up for reelection.

But Mayor Fletcher Bowron was determined to make this election year an unusual case. He had become the city's chief executive the year before and found his effectiveness severely hampered by the opposition of several councilmen who had been allied with former Mayor Frank Shaw. In the 1939 election, Bowron set out to "purge" the body of unfriendly councilmen by campaigning openly for a slate of "approved" councilmanic candidates.[1]

The incumbent in the 12th Council district was John Baumgartner, for whom Yorty had campaigned in 1933. He had been unopposed for reelection in 1937 but Sam Yorty decided to run against him two years later, despite the fact that Sam would be occupied in Sacramento during most of the campaign. The headlines were flying as his anti-Japanese bill was being debated in the Assembly, and he may have felt that he was being sufficiently publicized to outmaneuver Baumgartner.

Clifford Clinton wanted to oppose Baumgartner, too, but he was still adamantly opposed to the liberal Yorty. Clinton filed papers for conservative businessman Ralph Gray, thus putting a third candidate into the 12th district race.

Gray had the unusual distinction of having worked for the reelection of Frank Shaw in 1937 and for his recall the next year. When Harry Raymond's car was bombed in January, 1938, he was working closely with Gray who was trying to get Shaw to repay some funds he owed Gray.[2]

Considerable speculation developed as to whether Baumgartner would be on Mayor Bowron's "purge list," for he was neither an outright foe nor a consistent ally of the Mayor. Clinton, as one of Bowron's strongest backers a year before, might have been expected to await the Mayor's move, but he went ahead and backed Gray. Then when Bowron took to the radio waves and began his "purge" campaign, he completely ignored the 12th district contest.[3]

In the primary, Baumgartner finished first but did not receive the necessary majority of votes, and the race to be second (and thus qualify for the runoff general election) was close. Yorty defeated Gray by a margin of 70 votes. Clinton was incensed and demanded a recount, hoping that Yorty would lose out when the ballots were tallied again. Clinton paid $1,000 for the expenses of the recount, but it merely upheld the earlier result; Sam had won the right to a runoff with Baumgartner.[4]

During the general election campaign, Yorty for the first time was subjected to harsh journalistic criticism. In 1936 he had not had enough of a record to provide his critics with much ammunition. Here are some excerpts from stories and columns about Sam in the then-conservative *Los Angeles Times:*[5]

Samuel W. Yorty is the Assemblyman from the district, around whom all the radicals have rallied. Yorty's ego reached its flower last fall when he described himself as "THE LITTLE GIANT." At Sacramento he loudly advocates the extreme in legislation but has recently let his legislative schemes fend for themselves while he campaigns here. . . .

A Roosevelt elector in 1936, Baumgartner has been challenged by the ultra-left of his party which is running Sam Yorty. . . . Yorty's "liberalism" at Sacramento this year appears to be a brand too stout for even the Olson administration to stomach. Yorty is regarded as the spearhead of the C.I.O.-Municipal League aggregation in its effort to control city government. Yorty's estimate of himself as "The Little Giant" in his campaign literature last autumn caused considerable ridicule to be aimed at him, without disturbing his self-opinion in the least. He has set himself up as a sort of ambassador-at-large for California. . . .

Usually he has devoted his legislative efforts to harrying businessmen and taxpayers. . . .

What was even stronger medicine for Sam was that most of his former opponents, Republicans and Democrats alike (including Harry Lyons, Roger Pfaff, Allen Richardson, Walt Winebrenner and Ralph Gray), saw fit to endorse John Baumgartner. The A. F. of L. endorsed Baumgartner, while Clifford Clinton refused to endorse anyone.

To make matters worse, Yorty was continually forced to race north to the Assembly and could not manage a systematic and well-organized campaign. Then, at the last minute he was the victim of his liberal background as Gray mounted a write-in campaign, saying that Yorty had communist backing.[6] The *Los Angeles Times* published a photo showing that the communist newspaper, *Peoples' World*, had endorsed Yorty and several of the Bowron candidates.[7] The final results showed that Yorty had come close, but not close enough:[8]

Baumgartner	10,564	51%
Yorty	9,766	47
Gray (write-in)	402	2

When added to the string of Yorty setbacks (the 1938 recall campaign, the loss of the Assembly speakership, and the Railroad Commission appointment), this councilmanic defeat shows that Sam Yorty was definitely handicapped in running for office and in seeking preferential treatment. He had lost these contests because of his expanded ego, youth, opportunism, and liberalism.

Yorty has never done anything about his ego, and a number of people still distrust him as an opportunist, but he was about to make an amazing change in his fundamental political philosophy: He was to be a liberal no more.

8

COMMUNISTS ARE
EVERYWHERE, EVEN
ON THE FRONT LAWN

In the hungry, struggling days of the depression of the 1930's it was not incriminating politically to be seen as an ultraliberal. The New Deal had taken proposals that some called socialism and had put them into law. On the international scene, Stalin was seen less as a communist than as a benign and popular leader, and the similarity of the Russian nation-building task to that of our own country in her earlier days was a fixture in the public mind. The eagle and the bear were friends. The real villain of the world political scene was Adolf Hitler, whose armies had begun to menace the nations of Europe and the peace of the world.

But when the meetings between Hitler and Stalin were adjourned on August 23, 1939, the political situation was altered throughout the world. By signing a non-aggression pact with Hitler, Stalin had almost overnight diminished the popularity of the leftist political stance in the United States. Anti-communism as an issue rose to an unprecedented intensity level on the radio waves and speakers' platforms across the land.

Two leaders of the anti-communist movement were Congressman Martin Dies of Texas, chairman of the House Un-American Activities Committee, and Father Charles E. Coughlin, a radical right-wing Catholic priest whose most familiar pulpit was the radio microphone. Dies got tremendous publicity with his claims, which were always made as dramatic as possible. In a Hollywood Bowl speech in May, 1939, he told his enraptured audience that 8 to 10 million people were involved in subversive groups in the United States.[1] This would have been more than 10 percent of the adult population!

Sam Yorty had been the victim of such claims before, especially during his recent attempt to win a City Council seat. The Clinton candidate, Ralph Gray, in his last-minute campaign for write-in votes, had made allegations that Yorty's communist support was more than a coincidence. The charges grew so harsh that Mayor Bowron was moved to make a radio speech decrying the injection of anti-communism into the campaign. Interestingly, the words used by Bowron to castigate Gray would, soon afterward, fit Sam Yorty even better:

> When Samuel Johnson made the statement that "patriotism is the last resort of scoundrels," he implied that flag-waving was done for ulterior and selfish purposes in the England of two centuries ago. Unfortunately, it is true in America today. Calling names cannot distract the attention of voters from the issues. The charge of finding communists is ridiculous. There is not one candidate who is seeking to oppose an incumbent councilman at tomorrow's election who has any communistic leaning.[2]

There had been another large-scale instance of Yorty victimization by anti-communists. In the days immediately preceding the 1938 general elections allegations had been made that Assemblyman Yorty, as well as the entire Olson ticket, were communists. The attack came from purported testimony before the Dies committee and was front-page, headline news, although subsequently it proved to have been without a factual basis.[3]

Sam did not need a weatherman to tell him which way the wind was blowing. He was tired of not making headway in

the pursuit of his ambitions. It was not impossible that
he himself might have become caught up in some anti-
communist persecution. But still more fundamental, Yorty
had seen that his leftist support had more than once deserted him when the going had become difficult. He was
tired of being on the "wrong side," and it was typical of this
impulsive young man not to sit back and let things tran-
spire, but to pitch in and take the initiative. All he needed
now was an opening, some vehicle he could use, both to announce to the people of California that Sam Yorty was not
a communist, and to keep him in the forefront of the news
for as long as possible. Such a vehicle was available.

In California during the 1930's, welfare was administered
in Sacramento, through the State Relief Administration
(SRA). Then, as now, there never seemed to be sufficient
money to finance welfare. As a result, no one was ever satisfied with it, neither the liberals who wanted more money for
the poor, nor the conservatives who wanted less money for
the "dole" and felt the poor were all loafers who simply did
not want to go to work.

Dewey Anderson had been state director of the SRA, but
liberal organizations, including the Workers' Alliance, had
clamored for his removal on grounds that he was starving
the poor.[4] Governor Olson fired Anderson and appointed
Walter Chambers as his replacement. The conservatives
viewed this as a concession to the leftist side of Olson's political support and warned that no increases in funding
would be granted. At the time, the Democrats had a narrow
majority in the legislature, and the Chambers appointment
stood.

In 1939, as today, the people who tended to become interested in social problems, such as the feeding and housing
of the poor, came more from the liberal side of the political
spectrum than from the center or the right. Also, sympathy
with some communist and socialist doctrines was nothing

unusual during the period, and therefore it was not surprising that the SRA would have some employees who had records of communist involvement. So for Samuel Yorty the SRA represented nothing so much as a giant plum tree, almost begging to be picked.

Sam Houston Allen, a liberal, was Los Angeles County director of the SRA. On December 19, 1939, Sam Yorty fired the first loud blast in his new war on communism and the "radical elements," by declaring in a press conference that Allen was under communist influence.[5] Yorty railed against the involvement of politics in relief and said that past Republican mistakes in this field should not be made by Democrats. "We promised a better performance," said Sam.[6] Allen had been widely supported by both liberals and moderates alike. A moderate independent weekly that had only reluctantly endorsed the highly liberal Olson in 1938 said about Allen:

> It is certain that his [Allen's] exceptional talents, courage, and honesty will be utilized, Governor Olson has made this clear. His appointment ranks among the best made by our Democratic Governor.[7]

Sam Yorty disagreed with the appraisal. He was later quoted as stating that "California was in mortal peril from a Communist plot to disrupt the state through the virtual conscription of relief recipients by Communists in state positions."[8] Sam took his complaints right to Governor Olson. On December 29, when Olson was in Los Angeles on SRA business, Yorty waited outside the Governor's office while Olson conferred with Allen and Walter Chambers. Yorty had said that he would present the Governor with a list of the radicals in the Los Angeles SRA and would then demand the dismissal of Allen. However, no such list or demand, according to Olson, was given him at that time.[9] But without doubt, Yorty was out to get Allen, his employees,

SRA people throughout the state, and ultimately Walter Chambers.[10]

Sam Houston Allen was quick to respond in detail to the Yorty charges. He published a list of his top 64 staff members and employees, 44 of whom were holdovers from the Republican administration of Frank Merriam. Allen said that his employees were loyal and professional. He said that Yorty was "blaming everything on us [the SRA] except earthquakes and the European War."[11] Olson remarked:

> If any communists are found in any relief office they will be discharged. The people of California did not elect a Communist administration. But they did not elect an administration controlled by the state Chamber of Commerce, either.[12]

Under normal conditions in the 1930's, which were rife with scandals, claims, and counter-claims, the Yorty allegations probably would have enjoyed their headlines for a short time and then faded into obscurity. The people were hardened from constant exposure to this type of political news. But the issue did not fade away because it coincided with another problem of the SRA which had come to a head at the same time. The State Relief Administration had finally run completely out of funds; it was broke.

As a part of his emergency measures to rescue the SRA until he could wring from the legislature more money for its support, Governor Olson, with the approval of Chambers and Allen, closed down the giant Los Angeles County relief office and eliminated many jobs. From that time on, the county operation was handled from Sacramento. Although this action was really forced by economic necessity, some observers, possibly including Sam Yorty, believed that it was a concession to them by Olson and Chambers.

Regardless of what he actually believed, Yorty quickly took advantage of whatever momentum this coincidence could offer him in his drive for publicity. The anti-communist line was becoming stronger and stronger. By this time, Finland had temporarily held off and beaten back giant Russia, and with Russian arms at that. Such a romantic development added to the emotion of the anti-Russian and anti-communist movement of public opinion. There were Sibelius benefit concerts at the Hollywood Bowl, the proceeds to be sent to Finland, and resolutions were passed in statehouses across the country deploring Russia as the world's most brutal and degraded tyranny. On February 1, 1940, following the passage of such a resolution in Sacramento, Sam Yorty took the floor of the Assembly. In an impassioned, hour-long speech, he declared that the communists were attempting to disrupt the state, had forced the removal of Dewey Anderson and the appointment of Walter Chambers, and were trying to dominate the Democratic party.

In his speech, Yorty vowed he would "lead the Communist 'Trojan Horses' out of SRA headquarters."[13] He went on to accuse the head of the Los Angeles County Young Democrats of being a "registered Communist." He attacked his earlier backer Don Healy as worthy of a red tag. He said that Governor Olson was no communist but was inclined to take the word of those who were using the Democratic party as a mask to cover their communist affiliation. "When Don Healy speaks," said Sam, ". . . the Governor thinks it is the voice of Labor's Non-Partisan League, instead of the Kremlin."[14]

Yorty next asked for a resolution to send a committee down to Los Angeles to investigate and expose the communists and the "radical element." The resolution was passed by a vote of 51 to 20; the small appropriation for the committee was $500. The Yorty speech to the lawmakers was over. Then began his speech to the reporters:

We're going to subpoena about 25 persons. Among them will be Sam Houston Allen, if he is in town. We want to find out why Communistic groups are threatening to oppose the Governor unless he rescinds his order [to close the Los Angeles SRA office]. This may be only the opening wedge. If we are successful here, we may get more funds to subpoena a lot of persons who do not expect it.[15]

Said Allen:

If Yorty comes to see me on official business he will be welcomed with all the respect due his official status. Such a visit will be interesting, because it will be the first time Yorty has come to see me without seeking personal favors. I'm quite sure Yorty already knows more about the Reds than I do.[16]

The approval of the appropriation was symptomatic of Governor Olson's difficulties. Although he still had a slender Democratic majority in the legislature, several conservative Democrats had begun to change sides and form a coalition with the Republicans on key issues, especially on legislation affecting funds for the SRA. Two other movements had begun, in and out of the legislature. First, a drive was on by Republicans to put the administration of welfare in the hands of county government. Second, a surprisingly strong movement to recall Olson was developing. The Governor was in a precarious position, and Yorty, his former ally, was one of his most strident detractors. Sam claimed that Olson was:

playing a dangerous game in failing to rid his administration of Communists. He is a veritable dictator. The last time I spoke to the Governor, he told me, "I believe in a dictatorship of democracy"; I replied, "Governor, I don't believe in any kind of dictatorship."[17]

The Yorty committee was originally composed of five

legislators, two Republicans and three Democrats. In addition to Yorty, the other important committee member was Assemblyman Jack Tenney. Within a few days of obtaining its appropriation, the Yorty inquiry moved into Los Angeles. Sam continued to claim a "Communist plot" was under way in California; he maintained that the Communist party was trying to increase the cost of welfare to the point where taxpayers would revolt. He also claimed that many of the communists working in the SRA were graduates of the University of California.[18]

According to the *Independent Review,* the "Yorty committee took one day to hear all the testimony against the SRA, then adjourned and returned to Sacramento without giving the other side any opportunity to be heard."[19] As Sam had predicted, the committee did secure new money, and it continued to travel up and down the state in 1940. It gained the nickname "The Little Dies Committee," due to its organizational and psychological resemblance to Congressman Dies' group. The biggest fireworks came in Stockton, where several SRA employees refused to cooperate with Yorty's investigation and were hauled off to jail in a paddy wagon.[20] Later the committee issued a sensational report that blistered Governor Olson, the SRA, and assorted radical groups of all kinds.[21]

The term "radical groups" is found throughout the Yorty rhetoric of this period, and some attempt should be made to ascertain whom he meant when using such an umbrella phrase. It was evidently merely a convenience to be employed if he could not prove a person or an organization to be connected with the official Communist party. The *Los Angeles Times* attempted to define the term as used by Yorty: "The 'radical element' was a phrase that took in more than just Communists—it also included liberals, radicals, the C. I. O., Labor's Non-Partisan League, the Young Democrats, and [Lieutenant Governor] Ellis Patterson."[22]

One day in 1940 as Tenney and Yorty were riding in a train from one of their committee hearings to another, the two men had a serious talk which clearly illuminates the Yorty political shrewdness. According to Tenney, who was a Democrat at the time, he and Yorty both concluded that they really belonged in the Republican party, but Sam said that a party switch would be politically unwise in a predominately Democratic state that permitted cross-filing. Yorty would, of course, heed his own advice and remain a Democrat (a nominal one, many would subsequently say), but Tenney spent most of his later years in the legislature as a Republican.[23]

When Yorty, Tenney, and their fellow detectives finally submitted their *Report of Assembly Relief Investigating Committee on Subversive Activities,* California red-baiters nodded approvingly. The report briefly referred to what it called a well-planned scheme to undermine the state government and warned that the communists were merely lying low, awaiting a crisis.

The report went on to describe the international character and organization of the Communist party, quoting extensively from party manuals and periodicals. Terming the party a "disciplined army of termites," the report delved deeply into its history anc briefly described the background and character of Karl Marx. Passages were quoted from official Soviet government publications and the west coast newspaper *Peoples' World* was called "the *Pravda* of California." Next, the Yorty–Tenney report examined international relations, discussing communist attempts to keep the United States from entering the European War. It even included a short treatise on the relations between Stalin and Hitler.

In short, like the Martin Dies–Joe McCarthy genre of anti-communist reports, the Yorty–Tenney report had great difficulty remembering its original purpose. Of the 150 paragraphs that made up the Yorty–Tenney report on communism and the State Relief Administration, in only 15 paragraphs was the SRA even mentioned![24]

Another event that made headlines during the same period involved jobless pickets who had begun a campaign of harassment of elected officials whom they pictured as being against relief appropriations. One assemblyman whom they picketed at his home was Norris Poulson (later a congressman and the Mayor of Los Angeles), who got rid of them by telling of a man he knew to be hiring workers that day. Soon Sam Yorty was in the headlines saying that the "Communists" (in reality, jobless workers) had threatened to picket on the front lawn of his mother's home.[25]

The "Little Giant" had by now become the "Little Dies," believing that he had found the philosophy, the issue, and the publicity needed to lift him out of the Assembly into higher office. But he was to be sorely disappointed.

9

LETDOWN NUMBER THREE

Senator Hiram Johnson, the patriarch of California politics, was up for reelection in 1940. The primary was set for August 27, and Johnson as usual had decided to take advantage of the cross-filing system and try for the nominations of both major parties. Johnson himself was an ideological puzzle at this late stage of his career. He had begun as a progressive Republican Governor and had succeeded in implementing many needed reforms. He had not been a straight party Republican, having lent support from time to time to some Democratic candidates.

Johnson's image as a progressive had suffered considerably, however, in the years that led up to this reelection campaign of 1940. He had grown increasingly reactionary, and his relations with the ever-popular Franklin Roosevelt had deteriorated due to Johnson's isolationism and opposition to certain parts of the New Deal. Johnson was a strong believer in defense, he said of himself, but not in intervention into the affairs of other nations. He commented about Franklin Roosevelt:

> This president of ours is so anxious to go down in history like a Napoleon or a Washington, or even a philosopher like Jefferson, that he would go to any lengths. . . . He thinks that he can make history, and, by golly, he is going to do it at all hazards.[1]

Johnson had been the major congressional roadblock to some of FDR's international policies. The President was through considering Johnson a progressive, and he made it clear that California voters should end the Senator's long career.

Johnson was also getting on in years. He was 73 in 1940, and he was something of an "old" 73.[2] How poor his health was, few people knew, as he seldom appeared in public.

Progressive Democratic forces in both California and Washington, D. C., wanted Johnson to retire. They felt he was a doddering old man whose irascible temper and well-nourished ego had gotten in the way of his desire to keep the state moving forward, and to keep its interests well represented in Congress. In the opinion of one Democratic journalist of that era:

> There is about to expire the term of that ancient and sometimes honorable Hiram Johnson. . . . Much shaken by the wind of political expediency, much swayed by his prejudices . . . a wobbling wobbler he has at last come to be; the aged occupant of that highest of representative offices in the gift of the people of our state.[3]

The first candidate to throw his hat in the ring in the race to keep Johnson from getting both nominations was the Lieutenant Governor in the Olson administration, the liberal Ellis Patterson. Patterson had started out as a Republican, but in 1936 he had become a victim of the cross-filing system, in one of its stranger twists. He had filed for his Assembly seat on both the major party tickets. He won the Democratic race, but he was nosed out by another candidate on his own party's ballot. According to state law, he was disqualified from the general election because he had not won the nomination of his own party. Patterson had then stunned the political pundits by mounting a write-in campaign and succeeding in becoming the first person ever to get elected to state office in California via write-in. His campaign trick had been the distribution of hundreds of pencils bearing the inscription "Write-in Patterson." Subsequently, Patterson had changed his registration to Democrat. As Lieutenant Governor, he had been one of the most liberal politicians ever to have held statewide office in California.

Patterson had several political liabilities in contesting Johnson. First, his liberalism was regarded as too strong for many California Democrats. Second, his political base was in northern California. Third, Patterson had recently run as titular head of an unsuccessful slate of delegates in the state presidential primary. (In 1940, the state held two primary elections, first, for presidential delegates, then for the regular state primary.)

Patterson had also been involved in some minor scandals that had harmed his image even though he had been proven blameless. (For example, he had been accused of giving his sister a state job for which she was unqualified.) Finally, Patterson had been damaged in the Yorty SRA inquiry, when he had been quoted as saying:

> We don't care whether a man in the SRA is a Red, a Communist, or a Republican. If he does a good job, he shouldn't be fired.[4]

California Democrats realized that it was imperative for them to put up only a single, strong candidate against Johnson in the Democratic primary. If they allowed more than one Democrat to oppose him, the anti-Johnson vote would more than likely be split, giving the Democratic nomination (and, in effect, the senatorship) to Johnson.

Hoping that Patterson would withdraw, moderate Democrats had talked John Anson Ford into seeking the nomination. In his second term as a Los Angeles County Supervisor, Ford was a much respected administrator of county affairs. Many were convinced he was the best qualified opponent for Johnson, although he was little known outside Los

Angeles County. The presence of two Democrats in the race all but guaranteed Johnson's reelection, in the eyes of the leading Democratic strategists. They urged Patterson to withdraw, but he refused.[5]

When Sam Yorty tossed his hat into the ring, it was generally thought by others to be a joke.[6] If neither Patterson nor Ford had a chance, certainly young Sam Yorty, despite his wild publicity campaigns, was an even less likely winner.

Several factors seemingly were involved in Sam's decision. Considerable concern had developed that his recent dramatic switch from ultraliberal to red-baiter had substantially eroded his base of support in the 64th Assembly district.[7] Furthermore, Governor Olson had launched a bitterly strong campaign of opposition to those conservative Democrats who had let him down and sided with the Republicans during the recent relief appropriations battle.[8] Some people believe that Sam had simply grown bored with the Assembly and was looking for a more prestigious platform, desiring at least one last grab for publicity before leaving public life for a more profitable career.[9] Still another reason is the most likely of all. With Hiram Johnson's increasing feebleness, an element of chance grew that he might die before the election, thus throwing the race for his seat into turmoil. Such a possibility was worth the chance of being embarrassed by a poor showing in case Johnson lived.

Johnson did live on, and by the time of the primary five men opposed him on the Democratic ballot: Ellis Patterson, John Anson Ford, Samuel William Yorty, Richard S. Otto (widely known as the "alter ego" of Upton Sinclair),[10] and James Meredith, a Sacramento attorney.

Johnson made only one trip to California during the campaign either because of his declining health or his feeling that extensive campaigning was unnecessary. He did make a series of radio speeches, mostly alluding to the fact that important things were going on in Washington which made it impossible for him to waste his time on partisan politics. He said, "We are too close to great events to waste time on futile and childish denunciations."[11] He evidently made no references to his opponents by name.

Patterson attacked Johnson for his conservatism, and Ford denounced him for his opposition to the New Deal and for what he called "Johnson's arrogant isolationism."[12] Franklin Roosevelt personally entered the campaign, in a vain attempt to rid himself of Johnson, his cantankerous opponent on Capitol Hill.

The Yorty campaign ran entirely on the issue of isolation, and Sam called for immediate entry into the European War.[13] His campaign slogan was "Stop Hitler Now!" But his main campaign activity was the Yorty anti-subversive committee. From March to August, Sam's committee raced around the state, making headlines and calling people names in a sort of mobile court. The committee provided a great deal of publicity. The "Little Dies" was constantly in the news.

It was widely believed that Johnson would win both party nominations. The *Los Angeles Times* at one point said that "John Anson Ford has about as much chance against Johnson as Luxembourg did against Hitler."[14] The *Times* had been a bitter enemy of Johnson in the past, due to his early reforms in California and to his occasional tendency to back Democratic candidates.[15] But this time the *Times* endorsed him. He also got considerable labor support, including the endorsement of the California State Federation of Labor.[16]

Hiram Johnson won the election decisively in the primary by successfully cross-filing. It was his last election campaign, as he did not live out his term in the Senate. Here are the official Democratic returns:[17]

Johnson (R)	507,389	50.3%
Patterson	206,479	20.4
Ford	175,110	17.3
Yorty	74,332	7.3
Meredith	26,425	2.6
Otto	18,191	2.1

Finishing a poor fourth was a severe setback to Yorty's plans for ascension. Since he had been unable to run for reelection to the Assembly (he could not seek two elective offices simultaneously), Yorty was out of a public job and no longer had his own committee. The leadership of the "Little Dies" investigation went to Jack Tenney. Sam Yorty was out of political office, and he would continue to be on the outside, looking in, for almost a decade. But he was far from being out of politics.

10

SLIPPING DOWNHILL
IN THE 1940'S

After making an unsuccessful race for the United States Senate, Sam Yorty entered or nearly entered several campaigns—for Mayor (twice), Governor, Lieutenant Governor, State Senate, and Assembly. In each there was the usual maneuvering for support as well as the customary name-calling and other political mudslinging, but Yorty was unsuccessful in all but the last of these campaigns. Either he lost out at the polls or circumstances forced him out before filing his candidacy. In every instance the deciding factor seemed to be that he had no real ideological constituency. His new anti-communism had alienated much of his former liberal base of support, and he could not gain extensive moderate and conservative backing because other candidates were already established. Of equal interest is the Yorty campaign vocabulary of the 1940's, which depended mostly upon drama, bombast, and the words "communist," "fellow traveler," and "mushroom group." The last term referred to Yorty's allegations that many small communist front organizations were popping up around the regular Communist party much as small mushrooms grow up around the base of a large one.

Yorty's first reentry into politics after finishing fourth behind Hiram Johnson in 1940 was another attempt to become Mayor of Los Angeles. Fletcher Bowron was making his first reelection bid in 1941 since the Shaw recall. By this time Yorty had gravitated to a political position to the right of Bowron on many issues, a far cry from the situation in 1938 at Clifton's cafeteria when Sam had been regarded as too far left!

Yorty had kept his name in the newspapers in late 1940 by campaigning for the reelection of District Attorney Buron Fitts. Sam claimed that John Dockweiler, Fitts' opponent, had been "fooled by Reds."[1] The Yorty mayoralty race began on January 31, 1941, when he took out a petition for Bowron's job. At that stage he stated that he had not made up his mind about running for the office, but would wait "to see whether a candidate offers himself who is willing to let the people of Los Angeles play and have a little fun instead of raiding their harmless evening pastimes as Bowron does."[2] Yorty was fishing for a constituency among the anti-bluenose voters in the city. This was the time when the pinball machines were banned, and Bowron was being pressured by conservative and church groups to increase the city's vice prosecutions. Yorty also stated that Los Angeles was losing many potential conventions because of the bluenose attitude.

Soon the race for Mayor was cluttered with men eager to try their hand at Bowron, including two who knew a lot about the office of Mayor: Frank Shaw and his predecessor, John C. Porter. Shaw had escaped relatively unscathed from the fiasco of his former administration.[3]

On February 5, Yorty made a loud denouncement of Mayor Bowron. He warned that the Police Department had become demoralized. He cited "demonstrations in front of the homes of legislators whom Communists disliked."[4] He said that the police stood by, afraid to interfere, for fear of losing their jobs from complaints by communist friends of the Mayor. He observed that he thought Bowron was fooled by communists into carrying out their wishes.[5]

On February 13 someone stole Yorty's thunder. Congressman Charles Kramer, a conservative Democrat who had been red-baiting long before Sam had, entered the mayoralty race. Then, four days later, still another conservative, Councilman Stephen Cunningham, decided to run.

After Yorty's hopes for conservative backing had wilted, he backed out of the fight with a harsh anti-Bowron tirade. He released to the press a manifesto of his opposition to Bowron, which was printed in the *Los Angeles Times* the following day:

1. Bowron refused to cooperate with defense interests.
2. He demoralized city government by petty bickering and unfair treatment and criticism of those serving under him.
3. [He fostered] appeasement of subversive groups by appointing their henchmen to city positions and curbing police investigation of their activities.
4. He attempted to gain campaign publicity by using the police force to raid beer parlors and penny-ante poker games while burglaries, robberies, and other major crimes increased.
5. He caused Los Angeles to be shunned by convention groups by advertising his bluenose policies.[6]

Mayor Bowron finally faced a field of seven candidates, including a midget, Angie Rossitto. Councilman Cunningham forced Bowron into a runoff election but the latter won another four-year term.

The next big event in Sam Yorty's life was Pearl Harbor. According to the Ainsworth biography, Sam was torn between entering the service and running for Governor in 1942. He had never tried the latter before. Yorty must have relished the thought of having another chance to castigate Culbert Olson, his former political ally, and he tentatively announced his candidacy for Governor. But on April 10, 1942, Earl Warren said he was a candidate. By this stage in

Warren's career it was clear that his star was rising in formidable fashion. Sam soon withdrew from the field, his
second dropout in a row. He next urged State Senator
Tenney to run for Warren's post of Attorney General, so
Sam could run for Tenney's State Senate seat, but Tenney
was too happy with his position as head of the "Little Dies"
committee, and he declined the offer.[7]

Yorty's backers filed his name in 1942 for his old seat in
the Assembly, but he had long since tired of the post. Sam
decided to go to war. The Assembly campaign was virtually
an absentee affair, won by Republican John C. Lyons while
Yorty was away studying to become an army officer. Sam
did have one consolation; at the close of his army training
he was elected valedictorian of his class at Officer Candidate
School.

What Captain Sam did in the war is not under examination here. But one of his activities in the Western Pacific
Theater was predictable; he organized off-duty officers into
political debating clubs.[8] Even though he served as an intelligence officer and later as a civil affairs officer on the
staff of General Douglas MacArthur, Yorty was unable to
keep his mind off politics.

One of the first persons Yorty met with upon his return
to California was Democratic party leader (and wealthy
oilman) John B. Elliott. Elliott believed that Yorty, as a
returning veteran, might be a promising candidate to run
against Mayor Bowron; Sam did not need much urging—
he filed for the mayoralty race. This time he remained in
the battle to the end. He said that one reason he should be
elected Mayor of Los Angeles was because he had helped
set up some civilian municipal governments during the
reoccupation of the Philippine Islands.[9]

One important facet of this 1945 attempt at City Hall
was the emergence into the Yorty retinue of a person who
would remain there for more than a quarter century. She

would become the engineer, brakeman, and conductor of the Yorty political train; her name was Eleanor Chambers. She had been a Los Angeles resident since the age of eight and had become the youngest member of the Jefferson Democratic Club while a student at the University of Southern California. In 1945 she managed the Yorty campaign for Bowron's job. She subsequently lost more often than she won, but she was nevertheless the "woman behind the man" until she died.

In retrospect it seems obvious that Ms. Chambers should have pulled Sam out of the 1945 race. There was no conceivable constituency for him. Bowron had become well entrenched, and by this time he even had the *Times* endorsement. He had strong labor support, and that portion of labor support that did not go to Bowron in the mayoralty contest went to Anthony Entenza, an attorney who had earlier worked for the A. F. of L.

Another factor working for Bowron's reelection was the war, which was still going on . Many opinion molders cautioned against deserting Bowron in midstream. Near the time of the election, a *Los Angeles Times* political cartoon featured a giant cannon facing outward in the direction of Japan with the caption: "A United Front in Los Angeles." The cannon was labeled "Mayor Bowron."

The race was crowded with 14 candidates. One was the quixotic Clifford Clinton, fighting to remove the man he had almost single-handedly promoted seven years before. Conservative County Supervisor and dairyman Roger Jessup was another of the strong candidates. During the week preceding the election the Allied armies were racing toward Berlin, and the race for Mayor was often only third-page news. The election drew one of the lowest turnouts in years. Bowron won in a walk, and Sam Yorty finished in sixth place; the drawing power of the "Little Giant" had slipped.

During the next four years, Sam sat out the political wars. At this time he appeared only occasionally in the news, once for being physically attacked along with Jack Tenney on Catalina Island (by a former Tenney purge victim), and on another occasion for his involvement in a controversy over what parking meters the city should buy.[10]

Ever since Yorty had lost in the Assembly election of 1942, John Lyons had stayed in power in the 64th Assembly district, but in December, 1948, Lyons died. In April of the next year Yorty won a mildly contested race to finish Lyons' term. By this time he had moderated his conservative stance somewhat, probably because he had his eye on Helen Douglas' 12th Congressional district, a liberal constituency.

Yorty and Tenney had remained close friends during practically all the 1940's, and Tenney had built himself into one of the state's leading political figures. He had taken over the Assembly Un-American Activities Committee from Yorty in 1940 and had managed to keep it intermittently in the headlines throughout the decade. Yorty and Tenney were such good friends that Sam had permission to use Tenney's Los Angeles law offices whenever the latter was out of the city.[11]

When Tenney heard the news that Sam had won back his old Assembly seat he was overjoyed. He had a series of loyalty oath bills prepared to be introduced in the legislative session of 1949 and had been searching for a likely ally to handle them in the Assembly while Tenney himself maneuvered them through the State Senate. He approached Yorty in Los Angeles and mentioned the bills. Tenney knew how much Yorty liked to fight subversives, and he knew that the loyalty oath issue would be sure to generate reams of publicity, which was another point of interest to the flamboyant Sam.

But Tenney was surprised at Yorty's answer when he was

offered the chance to present the bills in the Assembly. Sam told his friend that he found a completely different atmosphere prevailing in the Assembly than had existed during his previous experience there in 1940, and that he felt the bills would fare much better if another Assemblyman introduced them.[12] This was hard for Tenney to believe, since Yorty had shown himself to be a champion red-fighter in the past, but Tenney felt he could count at least on Yorty's support, and he got Assemblyman Harold Levering, of West Los Angeles, to introduce the bills.

Tenney later wrote that he noticed from this time on that Yorty seemed to be trying to avoid him during the session. He wrote that several times he tried to reach Yorty by telephone but was put off by Sam's secretary. He wrote of button-holing Sam in the Capitol hallway on various occasions, only to be told of "important meetings" that Yorty had to attend immediately. What Tenney did not sense was that he had become too radical politically for Yorty to be seen with him.

Tenney had not realized that Yorty not only would not present the loyalty oath bills to the Assembly, but that he would not even support them, and what is more, that he would be the man ultimately responsible for killing them. Much to the surprise of Tenney, Yorty moved for referral of the bills to the Assembly Rules Committee, virtually assuring their demise. The next day the *Los Angeles Times* carried the story, adding, "Tenney's old pal Yorty pulled a parliamentary knife from his legislative toga and sank it in Tenney's back with a swift stroke." The reporter who wrote the article remarked to Sam that his move was "pretty slick work." To this Yorty replied: "That's your two Uncle Sams."[13] (He referred to himself and the Assembly speaker, Sam Collins.)

What had obviously come to pass was that Sam had foregone the publicity of fighting for the bills because he knew he could get even more headlines for defeating them. At the same time he could cast himself in a new, more moderate political light, and put an end to any association with Jack Tenney, who was becomming more and more carried away with his incessant red-baiting. Soon after the Assembly incident Sam was quoted in the *San Francisco Call Bulletin*: "The communist menace is overrated. No communists are about to land on our shores."[14]

In one respect Yorty had not changed at all since 1936; he was still a lover of the big bill, the dramatic and unexpected legislative bombshell. But Sam must have been joking when he made one proposal late in the 1949 session. He wanted to appropriate funds for a series of three bridges to Catalina Island, at a cost of five billion (billion he said) dollars! The proposal was soundly defeated.[15]

During the 1949 session another bad day occurred in Jack Tenney's career, and once again Sam Yorty was involved. It was a municipal election year, and Mayor Bowron, seeking reelection, was again called upon to defend himself. Lined up to oppose him this time were former Lieutenant Governor Ellis Patterson, City Engineer Lloyd Aldrich, Tenney, and, believe it or not, Joe Shaw. Evidently Tenney was overconfident, and so was his personal secretary, Murray Stravers. In a passing remark, Stravers let Arthur Samish know that Tenney (who had become increasingly loud in his attacks upon the Samish lobbying activities) would soon be out of Samish's legislative hair, because Tenney was about to be elected mayor of Los Angeles.

Samish could not imagine such an event ever taking place and, being an energetic gambler, offered to make a small wager with the insistent Stravers. Samish has said that he always kept a roll of bills in his pocket in case he felt the urge to lay a small sum on the line.

But on this occasion the whimsical "Secret Boss of California" had in mind some more interesting stakes than mere dollars. Taking to heart the obvious overconfidence of Stravers, Samish suggested that the loser of the bet should first run 100 laps around the lobby of the Senator Hotel, and then push a peanut around the block with his nose. The two shook hands and waited for election day.[16]

Tenney later insisted that he only needed to finish ahead of Ellis Patterson in the mayoralty election for Stravers to win the bet.[17] Whichever version of the story is more accurate in this regard does not matter a great deal, because Tenney finished fourth, behind Bowron, Aldrich, and Patterson. Stravers owed Artie Samish a small debt either way. When the big day of the payoff approached all Sacramento buzzed with anticipation and excitement.

The Senator Hotel was the Samish headquarters in the capital. From his suite on the fourth floor, he carried on his legislative generalship, almost never having to venture into the hallowed halls personally. Still, if he needed to appear, the Capitol was conveniently located right across the street from the Senator.

On the big day, the stage was elaborately and imaginatively set for the now repentant Stravers. It almost seemed as though part of a circus train had been sidetracked for the entertainment of the multitudes. The Senator lobby was decorated with banners, crepe paper, and balloons. Spectators received free whistles, canes, and more balloons. A running track had been laid out around the lobby, and a man was conspicuously standing by wearing a white coat and a stethoscope.

The lobby was jammed with more than 500 guests and even more people were outside awaiting the second act. Inside, circus clowns, jugglers, and tumblers entertained the crowd with their pratfalls and stunts. A disreputable looking piano player sat in the center of the lobby, playing a sloppy version of "Mexicali Rose," over and over again, on a dilapidated piano. [18]

At the climactic moment, Murray Stravers was brought out to the delight of the crowd. He had been dressed in a suit of old fashioned long red flannel underwear, and he had a large gold hammer and sickle sewn on the rear flap. After some appropriate preliminary remarks from the master of ceremonies, a starter's gun went off and Stravers began to run around the lobby. After ten laps he "took a dive" and the "doctor" declared him unable to continue due to exhaustion. Samish excused him from the peanut push and the festivities were declared adjourned.[19]

It had been a signal day in the story of the 1949 legislative session. But probably the most interesting and revealing fact about the great peanut pushing payoff did not involve the clowns, the victim, or even the perpetrator, Artie Samish. It revolved around the identity of the former best friend of Jack Tenney who had recently deserted him in the legislature and had now led his public humiliation. The master of ceremonies that day at the Senator Hotel was none other than Samuel William Yorty.[20]

No one can say for certain that Sam Yorty's tactics in leaving Tenney's side were directly responsible for the persecution complex and political extremism that eventually dragged Tenney down to oblivion. But it is obvious that the loss of Yorty's support and the manner in which that support was withdrawn were devastating shocks to the sensitive Tenney. The longtime anti-communist felt that he had been sabotaged by the Little Giant and later said that the most disheartening aspect of the Yorty tactics was that they came not from a foe, but from a man who had been Tenney's close, trusted friend for many years.[21] And after these two 1949 incidents—the Yorty switch on the Tenney loyalty oath bills and his part in Tenney's public ridicule —the two former friends never spoke to each other again.[22]

11

THE LITTLE GIANT
GOES TO WASHINGTON

As the 1940's drew to a close, Sam Yorty once again was comfortably ensconced in public office and, as was his usual custom, he began to consider his next attempt at upward political movement. Many options were available to such an inveterate campaigner, who looked upon the potentiality of defeat with nonchalance. But he was most tantalized by a major office for which he had not yet run: a seat in the national House of Representatives. To better his odds, he knew he needed an opening, a vacant seat, for he had more than once been politically burned by the mistake of running against an incumbent. And he needed a solidly Democratic district. As luck would have it, his home congressional district, the 14th, satisfied one of these requirements: it was heavily Democratic. In the election of 1948, for example, the Democratic incumbent there had trounced her opposition by a margin of nearly two to one.[1] But she was not about to retire simply to make way for Sam.

As the lines of battle for the 1950 elections began to form, nothing appeared likely to upset the status quo. The incumbent U. S. Senator, Sheridan Downey, planned to run once more for the office he had initially won during the Culbert Olson sweep of 1938. But three other candidates entered the fray, presaging such a rhetorical and electoral donnybrook that Downey, two months before the primary, decided to withdraw, thereby retiring from politics without a fight. The figures who entered the race and scared away the veteran Downey were unusual, even for California, whose politicians are seldom dull.

The former Helen Gahagan was a successful stage and screen actress. In 1931 she had married actor Melvyn Douglas, and the two had been intricately involved in liberal Democratic political circles virtually ever since their marriage. Mr. Douglas had been one of the first screen actors ever chosen as a Democratic National Convention delegate, and solid Douglas support of the New Deal had earned them a position of stature in the southern California segment of the Democratic party. In 1942, Ms. Douglas ran successfully for Congress in the 14th district. Thus began a quaint California tradition that still lives—the sending of film stars into government.[2]

Ms. Douglas' congressional colleague from the 12th was a young Republican lawyer from Whittier, Dick Nixon, who was also on the rise. In fact, due to the activities of men like Alger Hiss and Whittaker Chambers, Nixon had become something of a television star in his own right. Nixon was looking upward and he saw the aging Downey as a likely new victim.

Ms. Douglas regarded Downey as a former liberal (he had been Sinclair's running mate for lieutenant governor on the EPIC ticket in 1934) whose once forward looking views had slowly eroded into obstructionist conservatism. Her entry into the race prompted that of a third contestant, E. Manchester Boddy, the erstwhile Technocrat and liberal who, like Downey, had gravitated to the conservative side of California politics.[3]

After Downey's sudden withdrawal, the stage was set for a bloody Senate campaign involving Nixon, Douglas, and Boddy. This gave Sam Yorty the opening he had wanted.

He quickly leaped into the race for Ms. Douglas' seat in Congress.

Cross-filing, then still in effect, enabled California politicians to seek the nomination of more than their own party, and each of the three Senate aspirants filed as Democrats as well as Republicans. Boddy was very harsh during the primary in his attacks upon the Douglas liberalism, but Nixon saved his ammunition for the general election campaign. Murray Chotiner, who ran Nixon's campaign, felt that Ms. Douglas would be the easier opponent of the two to defeat in November, and he did not want to see her lose the Democratic primary. Boddy's scathing attacks sufficiently damaged the image of the comely former actress, but he was unable to defeat her for the Democratic nod. On the Republican side Nixon won the nomination in a walk.

The tactics used by Nixon strategists to defeat Ms. Douglas were not new; he had utilized them before in his first fight for Congress (against Jerry Voorhis), but this time they were carried out on a far grander scale. His backers mailed out letters from Nixon to registered Democrats which began: "As one Democrat to another. . . ." They told glowingly of Nixon's nation-saving exploits in the Alger Hiss case. His researchers cunningly manipulated the liberal congresswoman's voting record to make it appear virtually identical with that of Vito Marcantonio, the leftist New York congressman.[4] Such "guilt by association" tactics paid dividends for the Nixon side when, during the campaign, North Korean military forces moved across the 38th Parallel, opening the Korean War. Dick Nixon won the election and Ms. Douglas was retired from Congress.

Almost lost in the uproar of the Senate race were several other lively and interesting political conflicts. The "nonpartisan" Republican governor of California, Earl Warren, had beaten back a hopeless challenge from James Roosevelt, and Jack Tenney had won reelection to his seat in the State Senate, defeating liberals Robert Kenny and Glenn Anderson. And in the 14th Congressional district, Samuel William Yorty had beaten a cast of also-rans and gained a ticket to Washington.

The Yorty record in Congress seemed to take the regular Democratic position as often as possible. If he ever opposed the national party line, it was because his party loyalty had been tempered by his allegiance to the interests of his home state. The various marine states, for example, had long been considered legally entitled to the fishing and mineral rights to their so-called "tidelands." (This term refers to the area of undersea land from the beach outward to a three mile limit, except in Texas and Louisiana where the limit was 10½ miles.)

When in 1947 the United States Supreme Court ruled that the federal government held dominion over the California tidelands, a controversy began which would last the better part of a decade, pitting California Republicans and Democrats alike against the national Democratic party, which favored federal control.[5] California congressmen during the period found the tidelands issue a tough parliamentary fight, but it was nevertheless handy because of its publicity value, especially around election time. Norris Poulson, Clair Engle, Cecil King, and Sam Yorty were among those congressmen whose names were often found in the headlines because of the tidelands controversy, but Sam Yorty was the partisan with the strongest and loudest voice.

Another great Yorty source of publicity stemmed from his opposition to the Central Arizona Project, a proposal to irrigate large arid areas of that state by damming the Colorado River at Bridge Canyon. Such a program would have seriously affected the already major water shortage at the California end of the river. Then, too, proponents of the Central Arizona Project explained away the financial cost of the dam and the irrigation system by pointing out that the greatest part of the bill would be paid by those municipalities that would purchase the electric power generated by the dam. This meant that the project would not only cut down on California's water supply, but also would simultaneously raise her electric power bill.[6] Although few California candidates were foolhardy enough to announce in favor of the Central Arizona Project, it was a powerful issue for incumbent California congressmen to parade before their constituents. Sam Yorty was on the House Interior and Insular Affairs Committee, and no California lawmaker was able to garner more favorable publicity over the matter than he did.[7]

Still one more uproarious situation paid off in reams of publicity for Yorty, even in the then conservative *Los Angeles Times*, which has been a longtime Yorty foe. (The *Times* has only endorsed Yorty for office once, in 1965.) This case, known as the "Fallbrook controversy," was precipitated by the Justice Department's clumsy attempt to usurp private water rights. The government began to take away the water rights of several small landowners near Fallbrook, California, which is immediately southeast of the giant U. S. Marine Corps complex at Camp Pendleton, in northern San Diego County.[8] Yorty and others maintained that private water rights were protected in the legal precedents of federal water law and that government usurpation was illegal.[9] The Fallbrook controversy became a cause célèbre among Californians, both in and out of Congress.

Typically, of all the public figures who loudly castigated the national government over its blunder in the Fallbrook case, no one could match the "Little Giant." True, Fall-

brook was not within his district, but Sam has never let the
boundaries of his constituencies restrain his interests—especially on popular issues.

While Sam was fighting for Californians' oil and water
rights, he was also introducing some liberal legislation. In
January, 1951, he introduced a bill to provide the privilege
of naturalization to Japanese aliens, whose unfortunate in-
eligibility he had played upon in 1939. He also presented
legislation to prevent racial discrimination in employment
and to improve the working conditions of migrant farm
workers. In a letter to the federal narcotics commissioner,
which he had printed in the *Congressional Record,* Yorty
suggested the execution of dope peddlers after their second
conviction, and the prohibition of American citizens less
than 20 years old from entering Mexico. The commissioner
replied that Yorty's proposal to make narcotics pushing a
capital crime would reduce convictions for that offense.

Probably Yorty's most strident congressional enemy was
Representative Tom Werdel, a conservative Republican
from Bakersfield, California. He had published in the *Congressional Record* some classified Defense Department documents about certain captured Nazi papers on universal
military training. (Werdel was evidently a forerunner of
Daniel Ellsberg.) Yorty had strongly criticized Werdel's
act as a security leak and castigated him for allowing the
classified documents to be made public. The latter felt his
patriotism was being impugned and responded by taking
the floor of Congress on May 7, 1951.

Werdel stated that before the members of Congress appraised Yorty's attack they should have some information
about Yorty's background. He then spoke for 15 minutes
about Yorty's reported involvement with radical groups
in the 1936–39 period. An article in the communist *Western
Worker* of May 24, 1937, the Bakersfield congressman noted,
mentioned that Yorty was a speaker at a meeting for the

benefit of Tom Mooney (a convicted bomber whose pardon was a left-wing cause throughout the 1930's) and that Yorty's speech followed the philosophical line of the *Western Worker*. Also presented were stories in the *Open Forum* and *Epic News* that announced Yorty would speak at an ultra left-wing school on February 4, 1937.

Werdel quoted the July 26, 1937, issue of the *Western Worker* which, he said, detailed a meeting of the left-wing Workers' Alliance at which Yorty allegedly spoke. After Yorty's speech, Werdel stated, the workers reportedly marched on the Los Angeles City Hall and the County Hall of Administration. Several other reported instances of Yorty's involvement with or sympathy toward communist-dominated causes were cited by Werdel, who challenged Yorty to refute what Werdel called "the evidence."[10]

Sam used his 10 minutes of rebuttal time not to deny Werdel's allegations but to point out that Yorty had personally initiated the first state investigation of communism. He later had his entire 1940 report to the California legislature entered into the *Congressional Record*.[11]

The year 1952 was one of considerable political turmoil. A spirited battle for the presidential nomination developed on both sides of the fence, and the nation elected its first Republican chief executive since Herbert Hoover. But for Sam Yorty, personally, it was a relatively calm year. Before the end of his first term in Washington, his congressional district had been reapportioned, but he still represented roughly the same territory and constituency. It was still a solid Democratic district; nothing had significantly changed but its number, which was now 26.

In his campaign for reelection, Sam was an easy victor. He cross-filed and won in the primary, defeating Ellis Patterson and several political unknowns. He was pleased at his early reelection, but as he awaited the next congressional session, he could not keep from his mind the political changes that were taking place—a Republican administration in Washington, new wrinkles in the California election laws, new political organizations, and the emergence of television into politics.

Yorty's opponent for the U. S. Senate in 1940, Hiram Johnson, had died five years later. Governor Warren had appointed William Knowland as Johnson's successor. Knowland was the son of a wealthy Oakland newspaper publisher who had given Warren his start in public life in 1925 by backing him for District Attorney of Alameda County.[12] Knowland was reelected in 1946, and again in 1952, when he had become the last major office-holder to win both major party nominations at the primary, by cross-filing.

At the start of 1952, Richard Nixon occupied California's other Senate seat, but when he ascended to the Eisenhower ticket and won the vice presidency, he had to be replaced in his former post. Governor Warren had a man for the position, and in he went. He was Warren's longtime protegé, a kindly and handsome young man from Orange County, Thomas Kuchel (pronounced Keekel).

Kuchel had graduated from the University of Southern California and also earned a law degree there. He had then been elected to the Assembly in 1936, serving two terms. In 1940 he had been the beneficiary of an intraparty squabble that prompted his rapid rise in party ranks.

At that time, Frank Merriam, the defeated Republican governor, was involved in a last-gasp attempt to maintain his position as the unofficial leader of the Republican party in the state. The Merriam forces wanted to pack the Republican State Central Committee with conservatives and give the California presidential delegation over to Robert Taft. The more moderate Republicans, led by Earl Warren (then Attorney General), favored Wendell Willkie, and they were looking for a committee chairman who could stand up to Merriam. The unlikely savior of the situation turned out to be Artie Samish, the liquor lobbyist, who suggested that Tom Kuchel would be a good choice.[13] Kuchel, who was well liked by both sides, could be trusted to oppose the Merriam faction. Kuchel gained the chairmanship and after the 1940 election he had moved over to the State Senate.[14]

In World War II, Kuchel had served in the Navy, rising to the rank of lieutenant commander. In early 1946, when a vacancy occurred in the state controllership, Governor Warren was quick to appoint his loyal protegé, Tom Kuchel. He was reelected twice to the controller's office, and in 1952 he had left Sacramento to take his place as California's junior senator. Upon joining the Senate, Kuchel began to emulate the example of his political godfather, Earl Warren, moving to the center of the ideological spectrum.

Besides these changes in the California delegation to the U. S. Senate, two other developments transpired in 1952 and 1953, which would greatly aid the Democratic party in California to emerge from the electoral shadows. The first was an attempt to change the cross-filing law and the second was the improvement in organizing California Democrats.

The cross-filing law had long been a major burden for Democratic candidates. Over the years scores of Republicans had swept into office, winning both major party nominations at the primary election. Democrats had been trying to do away with cross-filing for a long time. Among the many Democrats who condemned the cross-filing law, but wisely cross-filed anyway whenever they ran for office, was Sam Yorty, who said in 1952:

> I am strongly opposed to cross-filing because under this system the American people are denied the right to formulate policy and select a course of action their government should pursue. This right is the very foundation of

the American Ideal. We should abolish cross-filing and
restore the American two-party system because it provides
the people with the means of putting into effect the policy
they want as well as selecting the officials they rely upon to
put this policy into operation.[15]

Sam was a practicing authority on the subject of cross-filing.
He had used the procedure in 1938, 1940, 1942, 1949, and
1950. He would also cross-file in 1952, 1954, and 1956. He
had also voted against a liberal 1949 Assembly bill that
would have ended the practice.[16]

In 1952 the forces against cross-filing, championed by
wealthy Los Angeles oilman and Democratic party leader
John B. Elliott (the man behind Yorty's ill-advised 1945
mayoralty campaign), put an initiative on the ballot to
abolish cross-filing. Proponents of cross-filing counter-
punched by putting forth a proposition to retain cross-filing,
but sweetened it for Democratic voters by adding a clause
requiring party affiliation to appear next to each candidate's
name on the ballot. Both propositions passed, but the conservative one prevailed because it gained more votes. Still,
the net result was a partial victory for the Democrats.

After 1952 no Republican was able to appear on the Democratic ballot without the abbreviation "Rep." after his
name and thus fewer Democrats were fooled by Republican
"As one Democrat to another. . . ." appeals. In fact, in the
six years following passage of the party identification measure, the Republican strength in the 80-member Assembly
dropped from 54 to 33, and in the 40-member State Senate
from 29 to 12.[17]

The effort to organize a strong statewide unofficial Democratic network culminated in 1953 with the merger of two
separate organizations, the California Democratic Council,
and the "Dime a Day For Democracy" organization, headed
by former Governor Culbert Olson. Members of the "Dime
a Day" group were pledged to monthly dues of three dol-

lars, hence the name. Eleanor Chambers was one of the Dime a Day southern California regional directors. Between the two groups, Democrats could look forward to utilizing an efficient, coordinated, but unofficial mechanism to raise funds and handle local campaigns, as well as support candidates for the primary elections. As the 1954 elections approached, many Democrats felt they had reason to expect greater success for themselves and for the two-party system in California.

12

THE SECOND RUN
FOR THE U.S. SENATE

Sam Yorty had attempted to patch up his differences with the liberal wing of the Democratic party by joining a slate of delegates, led by Attorney General Edmund G. "Pat" Brown, that originally favored President Truman's renomination in 1952. Among the liberals with whom Yorty had appeared on the slate were Culbert Olson, Helen Douglas, Richard Richards, and Will Rogers, Jr., who had been the unsuccessful nominee against William Knowland for U. S. Senator in 1946.[1] By January, 1954, Yorty had decided that he definitely wanted to seek a U. S. Senate seat, but he would run only if he gained the endorsement of the unofficial party organizations.[2]

In early February, 1954, the California Democratic Council and the "Dime a Day for Democracy" organization, the two leading unofficial groups, held a joint convention in Fresno to choose a slate of candidates for the major statewide offices. Dore Schary, playwright and Metro-Goldwyn-Mayer Studios production head, was the keynote speaker of the convention. The purpose of the meeting was to decide upon and unite behind a strong slate of Democratic candidates and thus prevent the Republicans from winning any races in the primaries.

Attorney General Brown had been a rarity in 1950—a Democrat elected to statewide office in the primary via successfully cross-filing—and such strong vote-getting ability had not gone unnoticed. By late 1953 a number of prominent Democratic party leaders were urging Brown to run for the governorship.[3] He had declined, however, and by the opening day of the CDC-Dime a Day convention, three major candidates remained in contention for the gubernatorial endorsement: Ellis Patterson, Reverend Laurance Cross, and Richard P. Graves.

Patterson was the liberal former Assemblyman and former Lieutenant Governor who had later run unsuccessfully for Congress and Mayor of Los Angeles. Reverend Cross was a minister who had a strong liberal record as Mayor of Berkeley. Dick Graves was an erstwhile Republican (switching his registration to Democrat only 40 days before the convention) who had gained considerable publicity from his long tenure as executive director and chief lobbyist of the League of California Cities. The convention battle lines were drawn between the liberals (who favored Cross or Patterson) and the more conservative backers of Graves. Patterson withdrew from the contest, casting his support for Cross, but when the ballots were counted Richard Graves received the endorsement by a three-to-one margin.

Although party leaders had earlier approached Adlai Stevenson, pleading with him to move to California and run for Kuchel's U. S. Senate seat, he had decided against such a move, promising to campaign for the Democratic nominee.[4] Other prominent Californians also mentioned as possible candidates included General Omar Bradley and Robert Hutchins, past president of the University of Chicago.[5] Since Stevenson had declined, the battle for the convention endorsement was left to some of the Democratic party's lesser lights.

One candidate was Dewey Anderson, the executive director of the Public Affairs Institute in Washington, D. C., who had been state welfare head under Governor Olson in the late 1930's. Anderson was not willing to become a candidate unless he could count on grassroots support. In a letter to *Frontier* magazine, he outlined his position:

> Nothing short of a genuine draft from the grassroots would induce me to stand for the [U. S. Senate] nomination. Any campaign to nominate a "peoples' candidate" must come from the grassroots leaders themselves—spontaneously and genuinely. Sam Yorty or any other ambitious man may think this can be "promoted." This may be worked in an Assembly . . . district but . . . not . . . on a statewide basis. It is not my wont to discredit anyone. But I have known Yorty ever since he entered public life. I have watched him operate at close range. It is unfortunate that he seeks to become the Democratic nominee.[6]

Yorty had the strongest assurance of financial support when the convention began, but some of his floor leaders made quick enemies by labeling their opposition as "red" and "left-wing." [7]

Peter Odegard, chairman of the political science department at the University of California, Berkeley, had come to the convention as a delegate, but forces eager to keep Yorty from winning its approval urged Odegard to try for the U. S. Senate endorsement. Knowing that Yorty would not give in, Odegard refused, not wishing to split the party.[8] Mayor Cross, after his loss of the gubernatorial endorsement, wanted to try for the U. S. Senate, but Yorty supporters talked him out of any further effort.[9]

In his impassioned speech for Yorty, Los Angeles Democrat Richard Richards, himself a candidate for State Senate, maintained to the convention delegates that Sam Yorty was their best hope for a liberal Senator.[10] (It is sublimely ironic that Richards should have been the one to offer Yorty's name in nomination, for in later years the two were bitter enemies, and in fact in 1956 they were belligerent candidates for this same U. S. Senate seat.) Although Dewey Anderson himself did not attend the convention, his backers staged an impromptu "stop Yorty" campaign but without success.[11] Yorty won the endorsement by a vote of almost two to one.

In his acceptance speech Yorty called for unity among Democrats to end the Republicans' "misrule and bungling." He said that "to fulfill the American Dream and provide increasing security for all of our people, it seems clear that we must return direction of the government to the party that believes in the people. . . ." [12] He then pointed out that the Democrats were not far from control of the U. S. Senate, and "then [when this happens] we will be rid of these high riding committee chairmen like McCarthy." [13]

Most observers expected the contest for the U. S. Senate seat to be a model campaign, since Kuchel, like his mentor, Earl Warren, was a talented, charming practitioner of the "nice guy" image. He could be counted upon to remain somewhat aloof from the dirtier aspects of campaigning and to base his drive for reelection on his support of Eisenhower programs. It seemed that Yorty would be forced to temper his usually violent campaign rhetoric for fear of being made to appear as something of a guttersnipe next to the affable and smiling Kuchel.

Even though both Yorty and Kuchel were well known anti-communists, nothing would normally have kept Sam from trying to find some means of appearing more anti-communist than his opponent. But it turned out that neither man could make full use of the issue, because the 1954 campaign coincided with the violent confrontation between Senator Joseph McCarthy and the United States Army. The McCarthy-Army hearings were in the news literally every day, and as McCarthy became increasingly desperate, his popular appeal as reflected in several consecutive Gallup polls dwindled almost as rapidly as his credibility. As a result, neither Kuchel nor Yorty could afford to be publicly linked with McCarthyism, so anti-communism as an issue was softpedaled.

Yorty began his campaign on a friendly, harmonious note, stating that his rhetoric would be "on a level befitting the importance of the office and the gravity of the issues which confront us. . . . Nothing I have said here is intended as a reflection of the personal character or integrity of my Republican opponent . . . our differences are political, not personal. . . ." But this mellow disclaimer was dubious due to Yorty's innate aggressiveness and because it came right after he had described Kuchel as one who had "slipped into the net of the Old Guard while trying to swing adroitly from the coattails of former Governor Warren to the coattails of President Eisenhower." Yorty then served up a platter of pure political puffery:

> These are fateful years in which our children's future freedom depends upon the decisions we make today. Under such circumstances the holding of public office is both a great honor and a responsibility, the magnitude of which makes one feel humble in seeking God's guidance toward the pathways of justice and fairness. The reward I most desire is the continued confidence and goodwill of the many thousands of considerate and loyal friends who have elected me to represent them in the Congress.[14]

Despite his reference to Kuchel as a member of the "old guard," Sam seemed to be trying to keep the level of the campaign as respectable as he could. He referred to Kuchel as "Tommy," and for weeks he refrained from any outright attacks on Kuchel's record. Instead, he aimed his criticisms at President Eisenhower, implying that Ike had too much confidence in the dependability of the word of the Soviet leaders. "Anyone who depends on the Russians' peace intentions is jeopardizing the United States," [15] he said, adding that the Eisenhower defense programs had given the country a "one shot Air Force." [16] He entered into a curious arithmetical battle with the Republican administration, maintaining that the nation needed 143 air wings to be safe, whereas Ike wanted six fewer. His attack ended by terming Ike's defense policies as "phony and dangerous." [17] Sam also criticized the President on an economic note, claiming that the President's hard money policy had "pulled the economy up short." [18]

A photograph of Yorty in his World War II captain's uniform appeared in a campaign pamphlet circulated on his behalf and for the remainder of the unofficial Democratic slate. Also featured was a picture of Sam with his family, as well as one that portrayed him shaking hands with a Korean general, Paik Sun Yup. (In October, 1952, Yorty had made one of the junkets for which he would later become widely known, visiting Hong Kong, Formosa, Japan, and South Korea.) Next to the photographs was printed a list of Yorty campaign pledges: [19]

represent all the people of California.

expand employment, schools, highways, hospitals.

[provide for] sound national defense.

[implement a] clear foreign policy conducive to lasting peace.

strengthen democracy against intolerance and subversion.

safeguard our water supply, keep our ports busy, our industries running full speed.

protect the rights of veterans and senior citizens.

Practically the only information withheld from Yorty's list was the means by which he expected to accomplish his objectives.

Kuchel, in turn, argued that Eisenhower needed the support of a Republican-controlled Senate. He told his campaign workers at a rally on May 1, 1954, that he could win both party nominations if they would put their shoulders to the wheel. Kuchel was endorsed by Governor Knight in an unusual move; former Governor Warren had seldom made any endorsements before the primary election.

While Kuchel and Yorty wrestled quietly before the primary, James Roosevelt was fighting for Yorty's seat in Congress. Curiously enough, Roosevelt's chief stumbling block in his campaign was not one of his opponents, but the breakup of his marriage in a blaze of vitriolic name-calling, which the Republican press endeavored to keep on the front pages as much as possible. At the same time, the political career of Jack Tenney, the old Yorty cohort, came crashing down.

Since 1949, Tenney had become increasingly blatant in his sketchy blanket condemnations of suspected subversives. In that year a Tenney report had questioned the loyalty of a seemingly incredible number of prominent Hollywood personalities. Included were Frank Sinatra, Danny Kaye, Gregory Peck, Gene Kelly, Frederic March, Edward G. Robinson, Dorothy Parker, Artie Shaw, John Huston, Dalton Trumbo, Vincent Price, Katharine Hepburn, and Sam Jaffe.[20] He had further accused a Los Angeles Assemblyman, Edward Elliot, of being "on sabbatical leave from the Communist Party."[21] Tenney had closely aligned himself with right-wing agitator Gerald L. K. Smith, and had in 1952 run for vice-president on the ticket of the racist Christian Nationalist Party. He had also become stridently anti-Semitic and by 1954 had published three books on the subject of organized Jewry, *Zion's Trojan Horse, Zion's Fifth Column,* and *Zionist Network.*

Tenney's opponent for the Republican nomination for State Senate was Mildred Younger, wife of a prominent Los Angeles jurist, Evelle Younger, who was later District Attorney and state Attorney General. Ms. Younger had the backing of the entire Republican organization, and it was clear that Tenney was in hot water. Tenney maintained that he was being attacked by Jews, and he finally became so desperate that he inserted a political fifth ace into the deck. On the last day for filing, nominating papers were presented for a Hazel Younger in an obvious attempt to split the Mildred Younger vote. Although Tenney denied any knowledge of the plan, his chances for reelection fell completely flat when it became publicly known that a Tenney campaigner had filed the Hazel Younger papers. Further investigation revealed that the campaigner was a psychiatrist who had previously ordered Hazel Younger committed to the state mental facility at Camarillo.[22]

At first, in comparison to the vilifications flying back and forth in the Roosevelt and Tenney-Younger campaigns, Yorty and Kuchel had behaved like gentlemen. But as the primary election grew near, mud finally began to fill the air.

Sometime in May, Yorty supporters found out about a Kuchel campaign pamphlet issued by one of the Kuchel committees, Democrats For Kuchel. The piece was so unpalatable to Yorty that he felt forced to abandon the issue-oriented campaign he had so far followed. The booklet, entitled "An Open Letter to Registered Democrats," began by reciting all of Yorty's previous election defeats, and identifying him as "a candidate of the radical wing of the Democratic party—the Jimmy Roosevelt wing. . . ." But what Yorty found most objectionable was the letter's implication that he was a communist-approved candidate. The letter referred to Sam's radicalism of the 1930's, mentioning many of the Werdel assertions, including a 1949 statement from the *Peoples' World* portraying Yorty as "a true champion of the people." [23]

The letter had been signed by Henry I. Dockweiler, a member of a pioneer Los Angeles family of attorneys who had been staunch Democrats for years. Dockweiler had been the Democratic party state treasurer from 1946 to 1948 and had been a Truman delegate in the latter year. Sam Yorty's first unpleasant public connection with the Dockweilers had developed in 1941, when the late John Dock-

weiler, Henry's brother, was running for District Attorney
of Los Angeles County against Buron Fitts. Sam had endorsed Fitts, implying that Dockweiler had been fooled by
communists.[24] Now Sam, angered by the letter, launched
an attack on the motives of the Dockweiler endorsement of
Kuchel. Yorty said that he had earlier been buttonholed by
still another Dockweiler brother, Fred, on a Los Angeles
streetcorner. He said that Fred had promised him the family's support for the U. S. Senate race if Yorty could promise
to appoint one of them to a federal judgeship. Yorty said
that he had refused, and he implied that the Dockweilers
must have extracted a similar promise from Kuchel, since
they had now given their support to him.[25]

Democratic National Chairman Stephen A. Mitchell declared in Yorty's defense that the Republicans were using
"Communist smear techniques" though President Eisenhower had frowned upon such tactics. Mitchell continued,
"As for the contents of the letter, Rep. Yorty has shown
them to be a compound of statements out of context, guilt-
by-association tricks, and outright falsehoods." [26] Said Democratic Representative John McCormick (later Speaker of
the House), "This kind of attack made on Congressman
Yorty is clearly outside the political arena. There is no person in the United States who is a more vigorous opponent of
communism than the gentleman from California." [27]

Yorty became so incensed at the Dockweiler letter that
he took an action he would soon regret, and the resultant
furor diminished his already slim chance of unseating
Kuchel. Yorty had earlier entered one of his patriotic
speeches into the *Congressional Record.* He now put together a four-page pamphlet bearing excerpts from that
speech, entitled "Let's Build a Better America." At the end
he tacked on a condemnation of the motives and content of
the Dockweiler letter. He then rushed the pamphlet off to
the Government Printing Office and paid to have more than

4 million copies run off. Then Sam Yorty blundered. Instead of buying postage stamps, he allowed the pamphlets to be mailed out free of charge, bearing only his signature, under his "franking privilege" as a member of Congress.[28] Almost immediately he began to wish that the pamphlet had never been conceived.

On June 3, less than one week before the primary, the story of Yorty's franking abuse broke into the headlines. It was the first appearance of Yorty's name on the *Los Angeles Times'* front page since the senatorial campaign had begun. The mailing was termed a "world record" and the cost was first set at $61,620, based on the normal bulk rate of 1½¢ per piece. But soon the Post Office Department pointed out that the average cost of handling franked congressional mail was 2.9¢ and upped its cost estimate to $119,000. The latter figure represented a sum equal to about eight times Yorty's annual salary as a congressman. Officials then divulged that the Yorty pamphlets had filled 611 mail sacks and had taken up almost an entire railroad car en route from Washington, D. C. to California.[29]

William Knowland, the Republican senior senator, verbally attacked Yorty, describing the mailing as "a gross abuse of the congressional frank [which] in effect transfers the campaign cost to the American taxpayer." Replied Yorty: "I don't consider it a piece of campaign literature in my behalf."[30] Next, Yorty maintained that no legal limit existed on the volume of items mailed out under the franking privilege, as long as the mailing was "official business." And then he asserted that since his pamphlet contained excerpts from the *Congressional Record,* it indeed qualified as official business.

Republicans and conservative Democrats then assailed Yorty for two other reasons. The 26th Congressional district, they pointed out, had nowhere near 4 million residents, and therefore Yorty must have been aiming at potential voters in the imminent senatorial election. Besides, they added, his pamphlet merely began with the speech excerpts, whereas the remainder consisted of a series of recriminations about the Dockweiler letter which began: "A turncoat Democrat is planning a last minute smear-campaign against me."[31]

To this Yorty phrase, Republican National Chairman Leonard Hall replied: "When a man seeks public office the people are entitled to know his entire background. To date I have seen no denial by Mr. Yorty or his supporters of the specific data contained in the disputed document. . . . Whatever the curious facts about Mr. Yorty's past, this record breaking performance is a fact about Mr. Yorty's present."[32]

The *Los Angeles Times* published a scathing editorial with the headline, "Yorty Adds to Taxpayers' Burden." Then, as further "proof" of the political nature of the mailing, Yorty opponents derided the "shotgun" approach by which Yorty neglected to address the pamphlets to individual addressees, but rather utilized a general bulk mailing address whose modern day equivalent is "occupant." The *Times* also published an interview in which Yorty was cross-examined by a reporter as follows:[33]

REPORTER: You said this was not a piece of campaign literature sent out at the taxpayers' expense, but now you say that you enlarged the mailing, and referred to the Dockweiler letter in your pamphlet. Isn't that using your franking privilege to send out your own piece of campaign literature in response to one sent out by the opposition at their own expense?

YORTY: No, it's simply my effort to tell the people the truth. It is not a campaign mailing. It is not improper to use the franking privilege to tell the people the truth.

REPORTER: On that definition, then, couldn't any incumbent Member of Congress running for office use the franking privilege to send out all kinds of campaign literature on his behalf on the ground it was "telling the truth?"

YORTY: The people have the right to know the truth.

As a final, more humorous note, the *Times* later in the campaign reprinted an article from a midwestern paper that satirized the Yorty mailing and its cost to the taxpayer by computing an "average cost per word," and then applying this average to various highlights of Sam's pamphlet. For example, the sentence "Certainly we must preserve for our children the freedom and liberty which was won and preserved for us by former generations of Americans," was appraised at $2,371.50. Next to that expensive bit of truth, the following Yorty statement was a bargain at only $853.74, albeit the phrase had a somewhat familiar ring: "We have nothing to fear but fear itself."[34]

On the day after the Yorty mailing first made headlines, Sam bought space for a political advertisement in the *Los Angeles Times.* Under the heading "An Open Letter to Tommy," the ad carried a bitter missive accusing Kuchel of approving the Dockweiler letter and of backing a communist candidate against Yorty. Here are some excerpts from the advertisement:[35]

Dear Tommy:
You are painfully aware of the fact that I have the wholehearted support of all but a small extreme left wing of the Democratic party. Isn't this why you are in desperation resorting to gutter level "smear" tactics while refusing every invitation to meet me openly in face to face debate?
. . . You know as well as I do that of all the Democratic leaders in our state, I am the one most hated by the Communists. While you remained passive, I was leading the fight against the Communists. You are passive now except

for a few campaign speeches. I am still fighting them. They are still fighting me. Your disgusting attempt to link me with my bitterest enemies involves an outright lie of which you are well aware.

. . . The Communists are in reality helping you in this campaign. This is because they are much more intensely opposed to me. Long before the Democratic Convention they boasted that if I were endorsed by the Democrats, they would file another candidate. On the last filing day and during the final hour, Leo Gallagher filed against me on the Democratic ticket. He was formerly the official Communist Party candidate for Secretary of State. He is obviously trying to split the Democratic vote which can only help you. Perhaps you can disclose who is financing his campaign.

. . . I know the results of polls have made you disheartened and desperate, but isn't one's honor and self-respect worth enough to make honorable defeat preferable to dishonorable victory? You must search for the answer in your conscience.

Sincerely,
/s/ Sam

Yorty next accused Kuchel of circulating falsified photographs. He said that Kuchel had doctored a photograph of President Eisenhower and several Republican Senators, so that Ike appeared to be alone with Kuchel. Yorty maintained that the picture had been cropped to cause the inference that Kuchel was especially close to Ike.[36]

The superficial similarities between Yorty and Kuchel were remarkable. Both were 44 years of age, married, with one child. Both were southern California lawyers. Both had originally entered the California legislature in 1936, and both had served as military officers in World War II. Finally, from a political standpoint, both Yorty and Kuchel were then (and would continue to be) less than consistently loyal to the leadership of their respective parties. Yorty clashed with many Democrats over the years, and Kuchel during his career in the United States Senate maintained a high rating (for a Republican) from the liberal Americans for Democratic Action. In the 1960's both men would often refuse to back the candidates chosen by their parties.[37]

Despite their similar backgrounds, Yorty and Kuchel were far from similar personally. The *New York Times* characterized Kuchel as a calm, bespectacled, scholarly figure, and Yorty as a "sandy haired mixer who loves a political scrap."[38] Obviously Kuchel would have been politically unwise to have accepted Yorty's invitation to debate. Yorty would have talked rings around him.

As the primary election drew near, the *Los Angeles Times* editorially summed up the Republican side of the campaign:[39]

> What could be more important than electing a United States Senator from California who may be counted upon to support the President's program for national security and stability? What could be better calculated to impair our position abroad or to weaken it at home than to elect a Senator already committed to do all in his power to embarrass the President and to handicap him wherever and whenever posible? . . . When you break it down to a practical consideration of returning to the Senate the incumbent, Thomas Kuchel, with his record of stability, competence and sincerity, or of replacing him with an opponent whose claims to public consideration include a remarkable agility in changing political pace and direction—usually without notice.
>
> [Kuchel is a man of] demonstrated ability, integrity and courage [who has] won the esteem of his colleagues and earned the confidence of his constituents. The Times recommends to Republicans and Democrats alike that they vote for Senator Kuchel in the June primaries.

When the votes were counted after the primary election, Yorty had won the Democratic nomination by a large margin, precluding Kuchel from successfully cross-filing. However, in aggregate vote, Kuchel had a substantial advantage:[40]

Democratic Ballot:		
Yorty	829,977	52.4%
Kuchel (R)	455,530	28.7
Gallagher	168,970	10.9
Others (2)	130,151	8.0
Republican Ballot:		
Kuchel	1,118,312	88.5
Yorty (D)	100,746	8.0
Others (2)	43,510	3.5
Total Vote:		
Kuchel	1,573,842	55.2
Yorty	930,723	32.7
Others (5)	342,631	12.1

In other races James Roosevelt had managed to win the Democratic nomination in the 26th Congressional district despite being refused support by the Democratic National Committee. Jack Tenney had been soundly defeated in his attempt to keep his seat in the State Senate. And Dick Graves had won the Democratic nomination for Governor, surprising many Republicans, who had been virtually certain that Governor Knight would successfully cross-file. It is commonly agreed that the presence of party designation on the ballot for the first time in four decades was responsible for a definite rebirth of the two-party system. In California's 30 congressional races only 6 percent were decided in the 1954 primary via cross-filing. Two years earlier the figure had been 46 percent.[41]

Thomas Kuchel took most of the summer off, but Sam Yorty, realizing he had a large handicap to overcome, increased both the pace and the vitriol of his campaigning. There were parades, speeches, and gala fundraising dinners. At one of these events the scheduled guest speaker was young

John Kennedy of Massachusetts, but he was forced to cancel due to a recurrent attack of malaria.

Foreign affairs, one of the inevitable Yorty campaign subjects, made its entrance in early fall, when Communist China launched an air-sea attack on Quemoy, an island between Taiwan and the Chinese mainland. Yorty had consistently maintained a more hawkish position than Ike, and when Quemoy came under attack, he quickly accused the Eisenhower administration of indecision which, according to Yorty, contributed to the success of the communist invasions.[42]

Yorty continued his running arithmetical battle with Eisenhower's defense secretary by claiming that the administration was putting the United States into a position of aerial inferiority by cutting down to 120 air wings. Sam had years of experience that he maintained gave him the authority to speak out on defense matters. He had maintained during the Korean War that while "our boys are facing the enemy in battle, loose talking politicians at home should restrain themselves." Later, after the MacArthur-Truman incident, Yorty could "restrain himself" no longer. He said, "Ike's army seems to be burdened with too many individualistic generals so accustomed to flamboyant head-line hunting . . . that they cannot adjust themselves to the hard work and relative anonymity that is [their] necessary role."[43]

The Democratic National Committee was encouraged by polls that indicated the Yorty-Kuchel race to be extremely close. The committee sent its party stalwarts to California, including Adlai Stevenson, Senators Symington and Kefauver, and Congressman Sam Rayburn, to aid the Yorty campaign. President Eisenhower and Vice President Nixon campaigned personally for Kuchel; Nixon's extensive participation included a statewide tour.[44]

Yorty renewed his attacks on Ike's economic policies, re-

naming him "Eisenhoover." President Eisenhower, he implied, was leading the country into another depression.[45]
Still another aspect of economic policy that came under the
Yorty guns was the question of supporting farm prices.
Here Yorty was caught on both sides of the political fence.
In 1953, as the congressional representative of an urban district, he had been quoted as saying: "I do not believe the
people will stand for continuance of the present ridiculous
butter buying program." By 1954, however, Yorty felt a
need to extend his appeal to a broader constituency, which
now included farmers, and he needed to shore up farm
support by expressing favor for butter price stabilization.
The result was the perfect picture of the two-sided politician. Claude Botkin, agricultural chairman of the Democrats for Kuchel, described Yorty's farm stand as "shiftier
than the wind."[46]

In September Kuchel reentered the campaign, terming
Yorty the candidate of the "left wing" and an obstructionist
in Congress. Kuchel, who had been somewhat inconspicuous
since he had come to the Senate, was taking the campaign
offensive for the first time as the consensus was that Yorty
was gaining on him.[47]

As the campaign drew to a close, Yorty grew desperate,
and he decided to make a regrettable attack on Kuchel's
record in World War II. Kuchel had long been plagued by
poor eyesight, and the Navy had at first rejected him as an
officer. He had persuaded the Navy to waive the eyesight
requirements and had emerged after the war as a lieutenant
commander. At a press conference on September 22, Yorty
injected Kuchel's past into the campaign. He charged Kuchel with using "every manner of political influence to
avoid combat duty and to remain safely stationed in San
Francisco during the entire war."[48]

Kuchel was naturally aghast at this low blow and replied
that "only a despicable mind would call into question hon-

orable military service." He then added, "Any person who would stoop so low should be regarded as a scoundrel. I refuse now, as I refused in the past, to dignify Mr. Yorty's irresponsible conduct by associating with him in any fashion."[49]

Late in the campaign a Kuchel press release proclaimed a proposed meeting between the Senator and President Eisenhower, at which Kuchel would suggest the President ask Congress for tax concessions to allow industries to purchase expensive pollution control equipment. Yorty accused Kuchel of making a political grandstand play over the issue of smog. He claimed that Kuchel had no plan to alleviate air pollution, but Sam had no such plan, either. He wound up the campaign by pointing to Kuchel's refusal to debate. He also announced in favor of the impending Senate censure of Joe McCarthy and called attention to Kuchel's reluctance to take sides on that question.

By November, pundits had predicted a sound defeat for Richard Graves, who had been handicapped by poor publicity and a lack of important issues with which to combat the incumbent Governor. Knight himself had immensely aided his own chances by adopting a strong un-Republican labor stand in which, among other things, he vowed to veto any right-to-work legislation crossing his desk.[50]

In the general election, Graves lost to Knight by more than 500,000 votes. Sam Yorty made a somewhat better showing, but he, too, was defeated:[51]

Kuchel (Republican)	2,090,836	53.2%
Yorty (Democrat)	1,788,071	45.5
Cerney (Independent-Progressive)	50,506	1.3

In the race for Los Angeles County's sole seat in the State Senate, Richard Richards won convincingly over Republican Mildred Younger, substantially outpolling Sam Yorty in his home county. James Roosevelt also won his contest for Yorty's seat in Congress.

The aftermath of the election was bitter for Yorty. He maintained that Richard Graves was responsible for his defeat, since Graves had lost so overwhelmingly to Governor Knight.[52] Almost a month after the election, Yorty was urging Democrats to protest the seating of Senator Kuchel, claiming that Democratic voters had been tricked into voting for him. "There is no doubt," he said, "that enough Democrats were fooled by this deception to affect the election result."[53] His protest fell on deaf ears. Sam Yorty was a private citizen again, and it was not what he had planned for himself. Grimly he returned to Los Angeles and the practice of law.

13
WIRED, PACKED, RIGGED, AND STACKED

After first losing at the polls to Thomas Kuchel in 1954 and then failing in his bid to deny Kuchel his seat in the U. S. Senate, Sam Yorty practiced law for a year. But clearly the mundane life of a courtroom or boardroom attorney was not Sam's preferred calling. He wanted the spotlight and for him that meant political office. Although he had lost many times in the past, political defeats had never dimmed his passion to campaign. He now directed his attention to the U. S. Senate election of 1956.

Tom Kuchel had won only a short term in 1954 (the remainder of Nixon's term), and thus two years later he again had to defend his seat. The year 1956 would also be presidential election time, and Democrats were anticipating a much closer race than the contest of four years before. Eisenhower's health was questionable, as he had experienced both heart and intestinal trouble. Many observers, Republicans and Democrats alike, believed that he would not run for reelection, and support for Vice President Nixon was less than complete. A strong movement, led by Harold Stassen, got under way to drop Nixon from the Republican ticket.[1]

As Democrats cast about for a viable candidate to put up against Kuchel in 1956, Pat Brown emerged as the brightest prospect. He alone among statewide Democratic officeseek-

ers had survived the Republican tide of two years earlier
that had swamped Richard Graves and Sam Yorty. A poll of
the membership of the Democratic State Central Committee, published in October, 1955, by the *Los Angeles Mirror,*
reported that about two-thirds of the party leadership supported Brown's candidacy for U. S. Senate; no mention was
made of Sam Yorty.[2]

But Pat Brown decided, as he had in 1954, that he would
wait until Goodwin Knight sought reelection as Governor
in 1958. Brown announced that he would not seek Kuchel's
seat but would instead lead the California campaign of
presidential aspirant Adlai Stevenson.

About this time Sam Yorty made a highly important career decision. The Southern Nevada Gambling Commission
had offered him a position in which he would be responsible
for maintaining harmony between the commission and the
Las Vegas gambling casinos. He wanted to accept the post,
but he wanted one thing even more—Kuchel's seat in the
U. S. Senate. He declined the gambling commission's job
offer, saying that he wanted to remain in California politics.[3]

Sam felt reasonably certain that Eisenhower was too sick
to run for reelection, and he believed that Kuchel could not
hope to win if deprived of Ike's popularity at the head of
the ticket. Despite his victory in 1954, Kuchel still seemed to
be too unassertive to win contests on his own. Democrats
recalled how at the last election he had been bailed out by
the Eisenhower and Nixon campaign visits. Members of the
opposing party were becoming increasingly critical of Kuchel, describing him as "Senator McBlank . . . a zero . . .
a weak mouse in the trap of reaction."[4]

By late 1955, several Democrats besides Yorty were interested in running against Kuchel. Among them were influential, conservative State Senator Hugh Burns, former Navy
secretary Dan A. Kimball, and Los Angeles County's State

Senator Richard Richards. Yorty, however, was the only announced candidate until early in the next year.

Since Yorty had been the party standard bearer in the
1954 race against Kuchel, he felt that he was entitled to the
opportunity to combat Kuchel again. He claimed that he
would have won with a stronger gubernatorial candidate
than Richard Graves and that he had "led the ticket" despite
his defeat.[5]

A large majority of California Democrats felt otherwise.
Yorty's electoral failure in 1954, his questionable campaign
tactics, the ghost of his radicalism in the 1930's (which was
certain to resurface in any campaign), and his unpredictable
mixture of conservatism and liberalism combined to make
him an undesirable candidate for many Democrats. Then,
too, many felt that Yorty's performance in leading the ticket
was not nearly so great an accomplishment as he had proclaimed. The following table documents Yorty's "ticket-
leading" performance in 1954 by comparing his total general election vote with that of several other Democrats seeking statewide office:[6]

Yorty (U.S. Senate)	1,788,071
Roybal (Lieutenant Governor)	1,764,035
Collins (Controller)	1,741,025
Graves (Governor)	1,739,368

Not only was Yorty's margin over the others small, but in his
statement about being the frontrunner he had conveniently
ignored Attorney-General Brown's total of more than 3.5
million votes (Brown had successfully cross-filed).

The anti-Yorty sentiment was strongest among the party
regulars—those who labored in campaign headquarters and
out in the hustings to sell Democratic candidates to the people. These hardworking party stalwarts did not enjoy wast-
ing their efforts on behalf of losing candidates; Yorty had
already made two unsuccessful attempts—14 years apart—to

unseat a Republican U. S. Senator. And it was precisely this kind of regular, working Democrat who made up the membership of the hundreds of unofficial, volunteer Democratic clubs within the California Democratic Council.

The results of the 1954 primary had demonstrated the success of the CDC. Democratic clubs and extraparty organizations had appeared in the state over the years, but none had ever demonstrated the permanence or the electoral power of the CDC. Its practice of making preprimary endorsements was not universally admired (especially by candidates who did not receive its sanction), and some Democrats claimed that to make such endorsements was illegal. The latter argued that such a plan deprived the people of making their own choice in the primary. But defenders of the CDC practice felt this claim was nonsense, because the voters could always reject the CDC choice if they so desired by simply voting for some other candidate. The preprimary endorsement, they said, was vital to prevent the Republicans from splitting the Democratic primary vote. A thorough study later concluded that preprimary endorsements and other manifestations of political support were inevitable, and that the CDC at least democratized the process and brought it out into the open.[7]

In 1954, when the California Democratic Council had endorsed Yorty for U. S. Senator, it had done so with mixed emotions. A large part of the membership would have preferred another candidate, if a strong one had been available. The CDC had endorsed Yorty, in the view of most observers, because it had foreseen a difficult, if not impossible race and had felt a moderate to conservative Democrat would have the best chance.[8] Most of these same members held much higher hopes in 1956, and many planned to oppose Yorty if he ran. The convention was scheduled for February, 1956, in Fresno.

As soon as word got around that Yorty would have an uphill battle for CDC support, he became angry. More than two months before the opening of the convention he began to downgrade the importance of its endorsement. In doing so, he attacked the basic purpose of the convention. The idea, it will be remembered, was to combat Republican cross-filing by uniting the Democratic party behind a viable candidate at the primary election. Although Yorty had been glad to accept this idea (and the CDC endorsement) two years before, he now maintained that the CDC was usurping the rights of the state's nearly 3 million registered Democrats to choose their candidate at the primary. His position was at odds with his stance in 1954 when he had said that he would not run without the convention endorsement.[9] If the CDC membership had been ill disposed before he began this vituperation, Yorty's new attacks served to strengthen its opposition to his candidacy.

As Yorty grew increasingly convinced that he would not gain the California Democratic Council endorsement for the senatorship, he became more critical of the group. He called it a creation of "Eastern-type party bosses" who were headstrong and ambitious and who would be "roundly applauded by the extremists of both right and left, the reactionary Republicans and the equally reactionary Communists."[10]

On January 18, 1956, Yorty was joined as an announced candidate for the U. S. Senate by Richard Richards, who had placed Yorty's name in nomination at the CDC convention only two years before. Richards was a fast talking (he was once clocked at over 200 words per minute), Iowa-born Democrat who had migrated to California in 1926, a year earlier than Sam Yorty. He had earned a law degree at the University of Southern California and had been long active in Democratic party circles. Before defeating Mildred Younger for Los Angeles County's seat in the State Senate, he had served as chairman of the Los Angeles County Democratic Central Committee from 1950 to 1954.[11] He was bright, blond, and good looking, and more important, he was a winner. While Sam Yorty and Dick Graves had lost Los Angeles County decisively in 1954, Richards had piled up an equally decisive margin of victory over Ms. Younger.

No sooner had Richards announced his intent than Yorty spoke out in criticism of his decision, saying that Richards should not run for another office until his four-year term as State Senator had expired.[12] Of course, if Yorty ever applied this rule to his own career, his total number of losing campaigns would be about half as large as it is.

Richards had qualified his announcement of candidacy by saying, as Yorty had in 1954, that he would run only if he got the unofficial preprimary endorsement of the CDC. Most observers felt he would not need to withdraw because they believed that a majority of its delegates looked with favor upon him.

After several weeks of Yorty denouncements of the "usurping private clubs," the date of the Fresno convention drew near. Yorty had announced that he would not allow his name to be placed in nomination if the rules of the convention required unsuccessful candidates to withdraw from the primary race.[13] Although Yorty could not gain exemption from this rule, he decided to attend the convention anyway, saying that he had many friends who would be there.[14]

Yorty wrote to Adlai Stevenson, who would be attending the convention along with his opponent, Estes Kefauver, pleading with Stevenson to remain neutral on the senatorship endorsement. Not wishing to make any enemies, the presidential candidate agreed. Yorty publicized this Stevenson concession, and in the same breath he compared his political strength in California with Stevenson's. He said it seemed strange to him that some people could favor Stevenson for President and not favor Yorty for Senator, because the former had received 42 percent of the vote in 1952, which was less than Yorty's 45 percent in 1954. In an amusingly accurate self-appraisal, Yorty said of those Stevenson supporters, "Some people fit their arguments to their preconceived notions."[15]

Yorty next increased the intensity of his verbal attacks on Richards, downgrading his victory over Mildred Younger by calling her "a young woman making her first try for public office."[16] It was true that the 1954 State Senate campaign was her initial effort, but she had lost out to Richards only after waging a vigorously successful primary campaign against Jack Tenney. Moreover, the vote totals in Los Angeles County in the 1954 general election show Richards outdrew Yorty. Sam was even outdone in this county by that "young woman," Ms. Younger, although the combined Kuchel-Yorty vote exceeded the combined Richards-Younger vote:[17]

Richards	786,823
Younger	769,997
Kuchel	853,925
Yorty	755,151

Yorty then criticized Richards for his short tenure in public office, saying it was unlikely that California voters would approve Richards, a state legislator with "barely six months actual experience."[18] It should be pointed out that Richards' "actual" experience compared favorably with that of Yorty at the time of his first U. S. Senate try in 1940!

In a final blow, Yorty accused Richards of signing a request to a federal court to drop prosecutions against certain alleged communists. Richards replied that the petition had been filed as a "friend of the court" and dealt with a constitutional question having nothing to do with communism. He also offered Yorty a compromise. He said that although many Democrats considered Yorty unelectable, he would be willing, in the interest of party unity, to withdraw (if Yorty would also do so) in favor of a compromise candidate. Yorty answered, "If Richards wants party unity, all he has to do is withdraw from the race himself."[19] Sam added a final verbal stab at Richards for announcing he would not run if he failed to get the CDC endorsement. Yorty implied that this was not proper procedure, evidently forgetting his own similar announcement two years earlier.

On February 4, 1956, the convention of the California Democratic Council got under way in Fresno, and Sam Yorty was the first person nominated for U. S. Senator. He had asked that his name not be entered because of the rule requiring withdrawal from the primary election of those failing to get the endorsement, but he was nevertheless nominated by Richard Russo, a Sunnyvale real estate broker.[20] As Sam stepped up to the podium to reply, the conventioneers braced themselves for the usual Yorty barrage.

Yorty started his speech mildly enough by thanking his supporters for placing his name in nomination. He then took a breath and resumed in a different vein:

> This convention is wired, packed, rigged, and stacked. The professional politicians of the CDC have become so power drunk that they're determined to demonstrate they control the convention vote by taking a tally in the Senate race even though I have withdrawn my name.[21]

According to a ruling adopted by the convention, a candidate could withdraw his name only if he signed a written promise to withdraw from the primary race; Yorty had refused to comply.[22] His short speech caused a near riot of boos, catcalls, and cries for recognition and points of order. Yorty had made the delegates even more opposed to him than they had been before his speech.

When order was restored, Culbert Olson nominated Richards. In his speech, Richards, still conciliatory toward Yorty, said he continued to respect Sam. Richards then aimed his guns at Republicans instead of Democrats, attacking John Foster Dulles and Thomas Kuchel, describing the latter as a "nondescript, vacuumatic rubber stamp" for Knowland Republicans.[23]

The actual delegate voting was held on Sunday, February 5, and Yorty was not present. He had gone into the council's convention, according to some sources, as a two-to-one underdog.[24] But when the votes were counted it was evident that Yorty's disruptive antics had alienated even more support than he had expected. Richards won the California Democratic Council endorsement for the U. S. Senate, receiving 1,480 votes to Yorty's 127.[25]

After Yorty's explosive performance at the CDC convention, three months remained until the primary election. He refused to withdraw from the race and renamed the CDC "Captive Democrats Club."[26] Instead of campaigning against Republicans, he ran a one-issue battle, that issue being Richard Richards. Richards was bitterly characterized as inexperienced and unelectable[27] and was called an irresponsible legislator and attorney.[28] Sam said Californians must stop "Eastern-style bossism" in the state immediately, before its "ugly imprint mars and defaces our political institutions."[29] He termed Richards a "subservient tool of the would-be bosses."[30]

Yorty's next tactic had long been part of his political bag. He proclaimed his profound opposition to "the evil nature and activities of the Communist party" and bemoaned "the intensity of the current Communist campaign against [him]."[31] Yorty complained that the CDC's platform was filled with planks that communists approved.[32] He then became still more direct in his criticism, saying that Richards was communist sponsored, and adding that a Richards election would be a "victory for the Communists."[33]

A group of nine prominent Democrats, led by California's National Committeeman Paul Ziffren, responded to

Yorty's various broadsides by accusing him of "giving his own party the McCarthy treatment."[34] They pointed out that Yorty had not felt the CDC to be communist inspired in 1954 when he had wholeheartedly accepted its endorsement. At a press conference Yorty claimed that Richards' campaigners were falsely implying that John F. Kennedy's appearance at a fund-raising dinner for several congressional candidates was an endorsement of Richards. Yorty maintained that Kennedy had told him he did not even know Richards.[35] From this time on Yorty referred to Ziffren as "Boss Ziffren."[36] Yorty was relentless in his attacks on Richards' personality and character, at one point even trying to be humorous as he slung his mud:

> During twenty years of political battles I have never had an opponent as slippery as Richard Richards. He not only has a double name, he is a master of double talk. Many call him "Double Dick" for more than one reason![37]

Using his common technique, Yorty finally attacked Richards' war record, implying that Richards tried to avoid service in World War II by serving in the merchant marine. (Richards was a navy reservist during the war, serving aboard convoying merchant vessels, and receiving an honorable discharge in 1945.)[38]

Throughout this vitriolic Yorty performance, Richards maintained his composure, knowing that any reciprocation would only serve to accentuate intraparty differences and would benefit Kuchel. He therefore kept his own campaign guns trained on the Republicans, asserting "my only major opponent is Senator Kuchel."[39]

Organized labor had been reluctant to choose between Richards and Yorty, and the CIO Political Action Council had rated the voting records of both men above 90 percent, with Richards' performance ranked slightly higher.[40] Support by labor organizations, however, was estimated to be stronger for Richards, by a margin of about three-to-one.

Yorty would not take a negative answer from labor any more than he had done from the CDC. "I have always enjoyed the support of all legitimate labor organizations," he wrote in a letter to *Time* magazine.[41] This statement was not only untrue in 1954; it completely misrepresented labor's position in the 1930's when he had often failed to get endorsements from the American Federation of Labor.

As the primary election drew near, various polls showed that Yorty appeared to be fighting a losing battle. Richards campaigners characterized Yorty as a desperate man making a last political gasp, and as one who had "thought well enough of the [labor and CDC] endorsements to race from one end of the state to the other in an attempt to win them," but having failed was "now demonstrating a 'sour grapes' attitude."[42]

Yorty's final blow was a four-page "open letter" to Richards in which he branded the latter a practitioner of "political subterfuge" and an "extremist who has continuously identified himself with left-wing elements and movements . . . ."[43] By primary election day Richards seemed well ahead of Yorty, but some people thought Richards might lose the Democratic nomination to Kuchel. The results showed that Richards was stronger than Yorty had believed and showed the falsity of Yorty's incessant "bossism" claims that the "people didn't want" Richards:[44]

Democratic Ballot:

Richards	1,004,336	53.3%
Kuchel (R)	494,066	26.3
Yorty	383,813	20.4

Not only had Richard Richards beaten Sam Yorty by almost three-to-one, Republican Tom Kuchel had also defeated him in the Democratic primary by more than 100,000 votes.

Even though Richards, Kuchel, and Yorty garnered a considerable amount of newsprint during the primary campaign, they were overshadowed by another electoral battle. Adlai Stevenson and Estes Kefauver were both depending

upon the California primary to put them into the command-
ing position at the upcoming Democratic National Convention. Stevenson had been the frontrunner, but his momentum had been seriously deflated by a Kefauver victory in
the Wisconsin primary.

No real axis of support existed between Stevenson and
Richards on the one hand and Kefauver and Yorty on the
other, as might be supposed. The loyalties were more complex than that, with Yorty supporters split between the
presidential aspirants. At one point in the primary campaign, Clara Shirpser of Berkeley, a state coordinator for
the Kefauver campaign, made an effort to tie in Kefauver
with Yorty. This relationship was shortlived, however, for
the Tennessee Senator wanted no part of it.[45] He may have
seen Yorty operate in Congress or he may have wished to
avoid the bitterness inherent in a Yorty campaign. If Kefauver lost the nomination he would want to run as Stevenson's
vice-presidential nominee, and Yorty's alliance would offer
him little support.

Another strong Democrats for Kuchel organization
emerged, this time led by Manchester Boddy, who had supported Earl Warren for Governor in 1950. Boddy had sold
his newspaper, the *Los Angeles Daily News,* in 1952, and
retired to his camellia bushes (he was reputed to be the
state's largest camellia grower).[46] Boddy was joined in the
campaign effort by Henry Dockweiler, another consistent
Democrat for Republicans. Before setting out after Yorty
in 1954, Dockweiler had gravitated so far right as to have
endorsed Jack Tenney for State Senate in 1950.[47]

Stevenson won the California Democratic primary, Ike
recovered successfully, and Nixon remained on the ticket.
The Stevenson-Eisenhower election of 1956 was generally a
landslide for the incumbent, but in California the two contenders were fairly close. Richard Richards ran a smooth,
well-coordinated campaign against Tom Kuchel, and Yorty

did not endorse Richards. In fact, next to Yorty's acidic oratory, campaigners for Kuchel were mellow in their descriptions of Richards. Earl Adams, who was Kuchel's southern California campaign chairman, termed Richards as a "formidable, subtle, and clever" opponent.[48]

Yorty's earlier estimates of Richards as a poor vote-getter were convincingly disproven. Not only did Richards lead the Democratic ticket by outpolling Adlai Stevenson in Los Angeles County and throughout the state, but he also did slightly better on a statewide basis against Tom Kuchel than Yorty had done two years before.[49] Richards' performance was superior despite the immeasurable damage done to Richards by Yorty's earlier bloodletting.

Sam Yorty had been sent home to pasture once again. Not only was he a defeated candidate who had accepted his defeat ungraciously, his relations with the state's Democratic party leadership were never to be friendly again. None of these party chieftains would forgive him for allowing his bitterness over losing the California Democratic Council endorsement to result in his working against the party's interest by campaigning more harshly against a fellow Democrat than even Republicans generally did. Most leaders of both parties wrote Sam off as a serious future contender for statewide office.

14

THE QUIET
BEFORE THE STORM

The Sam Yorty track record now stood at five wins and six losses. Through both victories and defeats he had disenchanted many Democrats and Republicans, and his partisan political strength in California had declined until it had virtually evaporated. Sam's political tantrums had so antagonized normal sources of partisan support that the only course left open to him would be to bide his time and study Los Angeles' nonpartisan politics and in the meantime return to the practice of law. His last fling at municipal office had been in 1945, when he was a newly returned, uniformed soldier running for Mayor.[1] He had been a near-unknown and had finished sixth. He wanted his next attempt to be more successful, so he would now, in 1956, sit back and observe the city more closely, trying to develop a strategy that might catapult Sam Yorty back into the headlines and into public office.

At the end of World War II Los Angeles had entered the greatest period of growth in its history. The city grew so large that its municipal conflicts no longer revolved around issues like the number of vice prosecutions achieved or the number of conventions booked. The problems of big cities had begun to make themselves felt in Los Angeles, which previously had pictured herself as a sort of giant village, a far different entity from the gray, smoky behemoths of the East and Midwest. Guiding such a metropolis had become an ever tougher proposition for a mayor whose absolute power was limited by a city charter adopted two decades earlier.

Mayor Fletcher Bowron, swept into office by the recall of 1938 and subsequently reelected every four years, had settled into City Hall as a noble, pleasant, almost grandfatherly figure. Although nominally a Republican, and conservative in many matters, Mayor Bowron's liberalness on some issues rankled his Republican supporters. His unquestioned integrity, however, served to make him the odds-on favorite for reelection each time he ran. Always photographed either in a sincere, attentive, listening pose or with a wide, mirthful grin, the rotund Mayor had become something of a permanent fixture. Even after 10 years in office his backers thought of him as a reformer.

His last term, beginning in 1949, would be his most tempestuous and, ironically enough, he would be subject to a recall election. Lloyd Aldrich, the second-place finisher in the 1949 contest for Bowron's position (the election that Jack Tenney lost, precipitating the great Sacramento peanut-push), was a conservative city engineer who refused to allow the voters' electoral verdict to stall his momentum. Unlike most losing candidates, Aldrich continued to campaign after he had lost the election. His followers eventually obtained a large number of signatures on recall petitions, and a special election was set to coincide with the regular statewide election of November, 1950.

The basic difference between the recalls of 1938 and 1950 was that by now a mayor could not run as a candidate to replace himself if he were recalled. Unlike 1938, more than one candidate could therefore seek the position without diluting the anti-incumbent vote and harming the recall effort. Aldrich was joined as a candidate by several others, including Robert Kenny, the liberal Democrat who had lost to Earl Warren in 1946, and Dean McHenry, a professor of political science at the University of California, Los Angeles.

The most bizarre aspect of the 1950 recall campaign, which was largely overshadowed by the Warren-Roosevelt gubernatorial race and the Nixon-Douglas battle for the U. S. Senate, was a contest dreamed up by anti-Bowron campaigners. The entrants in the contest merely had to guess the number of votes by which Mayor Bowron would be recalled. The winner would receive a new Chevrolet sedan donated by a prominent automobile dealer. More than $1,000 in other prizes would be awarded to the runners-up. The unusual aspect of the contest was that no one who predicted a Bowron victory could submit a guess; if the Mayor was not recalled there was no contest! As a result of this twist, entrants in the contest could be expected to enhance their own chances for a new car by helping to recall the Mayor.[2]

Fletcher Bowron handily defeated the recall, but his tenure as Mayor was reaching its finale. In 1953 he was caught in the dilemma of needing to choose between his liberal attitude on an issue and the political expediency he despised. He chose to stand by his belief; the voters chose to elect a new chief executive.

In 1949 an extensive public housing program had been started in Los Angeles to provide 10,000 units of low-rent housing. Land clearance and construction had begun immediately, but the project was plagued by delays and mismanagement and only sporadic construction resulted. Three years later the project was still in its early stages when in June, 1952, Los Angeles voters passed, by a three-to-two margin, an advisory referendum proclaiming their opposition to the housing program.[3]

Mayor Bowron advocated the completion of the project, pointing out that the city already had invested more than

$13 million. (Although the project was federally funded, the city bore the cost of land clearance and lost taxes.) Opponents of the project banded together in organizations such as the Committee to Defeat Socialized Housing and exerted strong pressure on the Mayor and the City Council.

The Mayor refused to politicize the issue, steadfastly pushing the project along. He had had smooth relations with the City Council for several years, but the housing issue split the legislative body into two factions. In late 1952, the City Council, by a one-vote margin, swung over to the anti-housing side of the question, refusing to authorize further funds for the project. This action resulted in a contempt of court ruling from the State Supreme Court and a $700,000 lawsuit against the city, which was brought by the Los Angeles Housing Authority.

Despite the political implications of his strong liberal stand, and the proximity of the primary election for Mayor, Bowron refused to capitulate to the anti-housing forces, offering instead a compromise reduction of the project to 7,000 units. The united anti-housing forces, which included most of the downtown business community, would accept no compromise, and at the primary election Bowron was opposed by eight candidates, including Republican Congressman Norris Poulson. Poulson was strongly backed by the *Los Angeles Times,* thus making this the first time in more than 20 years that this newspaper had opposed the reelection of an incumbent chief executive of Los Angeles.

One week before the primary election, the housing situation was further clouded by an investigation conducted by a congressional subcommittee into the delays and cost-overruns involved.[4] This served to deteriorate Mayor Bowron's position further. Bowron and Poulson were the leading vote-getters at the primary election. All four major newspapers in the city strongly endorsed Poulson, and at the May runoff Fletcher Bowron was voted out of office:[5]

Poulson	290,239	53.3%
Bowron	254,114	46.7

Norris Poulson, 57 years old when inaugurated, was an Oregon-born farmhand who had become an accountant. He had married the daughter of the owner of the ranch he had worked as a boy, and the couple had migrated to Los Angeles in 1923. Poulson had served in the Assembly in the late 1930's and had subsequently been elected five times to Congress. He was a moderately conservative legislator who had established a reputation as a friendly man who liked to conduct political business in a sincere, quiet manner. Unlike most politicians, Poulson disdained both political infighting and campaigning.

Virtually handpicked by the metropolitan daily newspapers as Bowron's leading opponent, Poulson made it a practice throughout his mayoral career to try to keep the press informed about his decisions before they were publicly announced. He liked to think of himself as a talented jokester and a skillful molder of compromises. He was adept at maintaining cordial relations between his office and the City Council (especially when compared to his successor) and was proud of his part in the winning battle to bring the Brooklyn Dodgers baseball team to Los Angeles.

The integration of the Los Angeles Fire Department was an unsuccessful Poulson reform attempt. The department had remained segregated since its inception, with Black firemen assigned only to two ghetto area firehouses.[6] Poulson, though a conservative, felt that the situation was anachronistic and illegal. His losing campaign to end the practice resulted mainly in the resignation of the fire chief and the mental and physical harassment of Black firemen.[7] Despite Poulson's early attempts, the problem of unfair racial discrimination in the Fire Department has remained an issue. In 1972, the national government sued the City of Los Angeles for alleged discriminatory employment practices.[8]

Poulson faced only token opposition in 1957, mainly from automobile dealer Robert A. Yeakel, who was a "household word" in Los Angeles due to his extensive use of television commercials to sell cars. Poulson got a majority of the votes in the primary, thus winning another four-year term. The ballot contained a question more hotly contested than the mayoralty race, one of considerable significance in the future—rubbish. The city wanted to take over trash collection but was strongly opposed by private rubbish collection interests who used the scare term, "monopoly." Although the voters approved this ballot proposition to put Los Angeles into the refuse business, the issue soon again would come before the people.

Sam Yorty, from his tiny law office on South Bonnie Brae Street in Los Angeles,[9] had represented private sanitation firms in some litigation and was therefore familiar with the political possibilities of trash. Sam noted that it was a telling issue with many citizens, especially women. In January, 1961, he would start to plan a campaign against Norris Poulson; Sam would then decide to use the controversy over rubbish in an effort to regain public office.

The next statewide election following the Yorty-Richards fraticide featured the races for Governor and U. S. Senator in 1958, the year William Knowland decided to pull his grand political switch. He pressured Governor Goodwin Knight to run for the U. S. Senate so that he could go for Knight's post, thereby assuring the Republicans the loss of the Governor's mansion (for the first time in 20 years) and one of the GOP-held seats in the U. S. Senate. Knowland's performance also was so weak that many Republican candidates for lesser offices sought to disassociate their campaigns from Knowland's, fearing a reverse coattails effect.[10]

Although Sam Yorty's name had been mentioned by others for the gubernatorial race, he did not take the opportunity seriously, as 1958 was the year in which Pat Brown would finally relinquish his post as Attorney General

and seek the governorship. Sam wasted no time in beginning
a campaign of public criticism of Brown, painting him as an
insignificant bureaucrat, "Unless Brown intends to conduct
himself as a big leaguer," said Sam, "he had better stay in
the minor league."[11] Yorty badgered Brown during the
campaign, insisting incongruously that Brown should debate with Knowland on television, advice that Brown wisely
did not heed. He was far ahead of Knowland in most polls,
and he was also aware that public speaking was not his
strongest skill. In the general election, Knowland and
Knight both lost to their Democratic opponents, Brown and
Clair Engle, in the worst California Republican debacle in
20 years.

Sam Yorty again came out of political obscurity in 1960,
when California Democrats were busy arguing over whom
to support for President at the Democratic National Convention in Los Angeles. Many Democrats wished to see
Adlai Stevenson given a third chance at the presidency, and
still more were backing John Kennedy. Typically, Yorty
was in neither major camp, choosing instead to urge the
nomination of United States Senator Lyndon Johnson of
Texas. Sam said Johnson's "mature judgment, common
sense, and qualities of leadership will assure us of our best
chance to make steady progress toward greater economic
stability in the free world and a more dependable peace."[12]
When Yorty was excluded from the California delegation
to the Democratic convention, he became embittered and
when the convention chose Kennedy, Sam refused to support him and endorsed Richard Nixon. Sam outlined his
objections to Kennedy in a 27-page diatribe entitled "I
Can Not Take Kennedy."[13]

The scathing pamphlet struck out at Kennedy's youth,
wealth, and religion. Purporting that JFK was not "ready"
to be President, it accused the Kennedy family of risking the
destruction of the Democratic party by impatiently forcing

JFK's candidacy on the nation. The pamphlet charged Kennedy with using the power of his family's wealth to buy the election. It also accused Kennedy of taking "undue advantage of his religious affiliation."[14] The document went on to condemn the California Democratic Council and the leadership of organized labor. It ended with an attack on what Yorty termed "the awesome power [of] the federal government."[15]

Another 1960 event would similarly raise the eyebrows of politically-minded Angelenos. Mayor Poulson, expected to follow precedent by again seeking reelection as Mayor, was about to make a surprising announcement of special interest to Sam Yorty.

15

THE POLITICS OF RUBBISH

In May, 1960, Sam Yorty, who had been awaiting an opportunity to enter nonpartisan politics, was excited to read in his newspaper that Mayor Norris Poulson would not seek reelection in 1961. Poulson had confided to close friends that he felt the strain of another campaign and an additional four-year term would be more than his physical resources could endure. He made the announcement public on May 3, 1960, saying that his mind was made up, "My decision is absolutely final. I want the voters to have ample time to find new candidates."[1] The next day, after the City Hall switchboard had been assaulted by concerned callers, Poulson further clarified his intended retirement. "My decision is irrevocable. I am definitely going to return to private life."[2]

The Poulson announcement incited rampant speculation about the probable candidates to succeed him. The voluntary stepping down of an incumbent chief executive had not happened in Los Angeles since the 1920's. Among the many names mentioned were those of Airport Commissioner Don Belding, State Senator Richard Richards, Councilman Patrick "Pat" McGee, and Congressmen Glen Lipscomb and Joe Holt. No one mentioned Sam Yorty.

In September, Mayor Poulson reversed his field and announced that the persistent pressure of business and civic groups had convinced him, after all, to seek reelection. Prominent financial and professional interests had been unable to find a substitute candidate to their liking and had therefore pleaded with Poulson to reconsider his decision.[3] After some hesitation, the Mayor agreed to run, stipulating that he would not provide from his own pocket any financial support for the campaign.[4]

Poulson's announcement had the effect of reducing the field of challengers, because most prospects realized that his incumbency was too great an advantage to overcome. By December, 1960, the "probables" were reduced to Richards, McGee, and Holt. Richards was canvassing for support via a postal poll, wishing to have an accurate measurement of his potential vote. Holt was by this time a lame duck congressman, having been defeated in November by James Corman. Poulson was the first major candidate to take out his nominating papers at the city clerk's office. Six days after Poulson, Pat McGee took out his papers, showing the early pundits to be correct. Then, the same day, a third contender, not a major figure most agreed, joined the fracas: Samuel William Yorty.

Yorty had commissioned a poll by Hal Avery's Opinion Research firm and had been pleased at the closeness of the results, which indicated his name was still remembered in the city. The poll showed 32 percent of the respondents preferred Poulson, 25 percent were for Yorty, and the rest were either split between McGee and other candidates or were undecided.[5]

Although Yorty and Poulson were members of opposing parties, they had never been bitter political enemies. They had served on legislative committees together and had co-authored several bills in both the Assembly and Congress. Poulson had habitually referred to Yorty as "son," and Yorty had addressed Poulson, who was only 14 years his senior, as "grandpa."[6] At first, in the mayoralty campaign, Yorty made few direct attacks on the incumbent, merely stating his feeling that Los Angeles needed a change.

Poulson was clearly the favorite in the race. He enjoyed the editorial support of all four major metropolitan newspapers, and he could call upon a war chest estimated at more than a half-million dollars.[7] A prominent professional campaign management firm, headed by Herbert Baus and William Ross, directed his campaign. They were fresh from successfully managing Richard Nixon's presidential campaign in California. (A later Baus and Ross triumph was the 1964 California primary effort for Barry Goldwater.) Yorty, in contrast, had little financial support and even less professional campaign advice.

No one will ever know for certain what prompted Sam Yorty to seize upon rubbish as a major campaign issue with which to assault the seemingly impregnable Poulson. Some said that he chose rubbish largely because he wanted an issue about which he was well-informed; he had had an intense interest in rubbish operations both as an investor and as an attorney. Others maintained that he had been forced to turn to television because Poulson had monopolized major daily newspaper support, and that the cheapest television time was during daylight hours. Because the daytime audience was composed predominately of housewives, an issue of interest to women was needed. Boredom would certainly result for housewives bombarded by political diatribes about harbor commissions or charter reform, but trash collection was a subject that struck close to home.

The confused situation over refuse collection in Los Angeles played right into Sam Yorty's hands. Until 1961 the city had sold its organic garbage to a combine of hog raisers who then fed it to their hogs.[8] When this practice was discontinued, the city still collected rubbish in three separate trips. Garbage would be taken one day, combustible trash another, and on a third day the city would take tin cans. The housewife therefore needed to maintain three separate hoards of refuse. The city was a party to a contract with the Los Angeles By-Products Corporation, which paid $50,000 yearly for Los Angeles' tin cans and recycled and sold them to the can industry. Yorty campaigners figured that the payment rounded out to two cents per housewife per month, and (in an unwitting racial slur) proclaimed that Poulson was forcing Los Angeles housewives to perform "coolie labor for a salvage firm." [9]

Yorty had truly struck a sensitive nerve in a city that seemed to harbor something of a fetish about its trash. The Yorty-Poulson-McGee race came to be called the "tempest in a trash barrel" [10] and if Sam Yorty had carried a coat of arms, somewhere on it would surely have appeared a rubbish can. A spirited member of Yorty's newly cultivated housewife brigade summoned news photographers to her home and ceremoniously dumped empty dog food cans in with her combustible rubbish in defiance of the municipal program. [11]

The farcical nature of the rubbish issue is best illustrated by Sam's about-face in recent years. Though he depended upon the promise of combining metallic refuse with regular trash as a lever to open City Hall, he now prides himself as a leader in the recycling movement. One currently can see posters reading "Mayor Sam Wants You!" plastered throughout the city exhorting citizens to "Join the Saturday Reclamation Corps."

Initially Pat McGee had been considered the major challenger to Poulson, but insufficient funds hampered his campaign. As a councilman, he also suffered from identification with forces that had fought the ordinance allowing the Los Angeles Dodgers to build their new baseball stadium at Chavez Ravine, which had been designated earlier as a public housing site. Of the multitude of Dodger fans, surely

7,100 of them (Yorty's eventual margin over McGee) on entering the voting booths might have remembered McGee's
much publicized anti-Dodger stand in the City Council.

While Yorty had leaped at the chance to become a television and radio personality in the 1961 mayoralty campaign, Mayor Poulson had actually curtailed his regular appearances on Radio Station KFI. He explained that they
were public service programs and he wanted them to remain
that way. He promised his listeners that the broadcasts
would return after the election when politics would recede
from the spotlight.[12] Poulson had another reason for limiting his personal appearances, however. Riding in an open
car during a Christmas Eve parade, he had contracted a severe cold which had affected his vocal chords. The first
weeks of campaigning had served to worsen his condition
until it became obvious that he was suffering from a severe
case of laryngitis, if nothing worse. He could not appear on
television or radio without harming his image as a healthy,
articulate city father.

Few observers expected Poulson to have trouble winning
reelection at the primary, as he had done in 1957. The pro-
Poulson press showed him to be smilingly confident as the
city went to the polls on April 4, 1961. When the results
were in, the Poulson complacency was gone. He had failed
badly in seeking to poll the required majority to win the
office again in the primary, and his runoff opponent was
not the Republican Pat McGee, who would have been a
mildly threatening foe, but the unpredictable Sam Yorty:[13]

Poulson	181,653	39.8%
Yorty	123,816	27.3
McGee	116,774	25.5
Others (6)	34,414	7.4

Despite the fact that political observers feel incumbents
who are forced into runoffs in Los Angeles city and county
elections should be considered underdogs, in the Poulson-
Yorty contest most evidence pointed to Poulson as the fav-

orite. He had the greater financial support by far and the only professional campaign organization, and he could count on editorial backing and preferential news coverage from the four major metropolitan newspapers.

Even more indicative of Poulson's position of strength was the support he received from organized elements of the Democratic party. Los Angeles municipal elections are officially nonpartisan, that is, party identification on the ballot and party-type primary elections are legally forbidden. But partisan organizational support for candidates is not prohibited and is, in fact, growing. Strange though it seems, a coalition of Democratic activists supported a Republican candidate (Poulson) against a Democrat (Yorty) in a nonpartisan contest. California Democrats, divided between Stevenson and Kennedy in 1960, were in a sense brought together by Yorty's anti-Kennedy diatribe and, by the following year, members of both factions were working to reelect Norris Poulson. Poulson thus seemed to be in the enviable position of having unofficial support from both major parties.[14]

While Yorty obviously could count on some Democratic backing, unquestionably more activists of this party worked for Poulson than for Yorty.[15] The most visible sign of Democratic aid to Poulson was the publication of a series of anti-Yorty articles in a tabloid named the *Los Angeles Democrat*. The first issue, dated May 1, 1961, carried the headline, "Democrats Benefit by Progress With Poulson." The issue praised the incumbent for his efforts to bring the Democratic National Convention to Los Angeles in 1960 and, in an editorial called "Best Man for the Job," it presented "highlights of Mayor Poulson's outstanding achievements in office," and proclaimed "Norris Poulson has proved himself a man of principle.... For our best interests, as Democrats and Angelenos, we must reelect [the] Mayor." [16]

Anti-Yorty Democrats were motivated by more than resentment of Yorty's past antagonism toward Olson, Richards, Brown, and Kennedy, although the *Democrat* did make ample mention of Yorty's renegade past. The other factor stimulating party activists to support Poulson was the fear that Yorty, as Mayor of Los Angeles, would have a strong base of support from which to pursue the gubernatorial nomination in 1962, or at least have a handy platform from which to give his support to Richard Nixon.[17] The second edition of the *Los Angeles Democrat*, which appeared on May 25, treated Yorty, the maverick, more harshly. Under a front page headline reading "Yorty Traitor to Democrats," the issue carried a cartoon portraying Sam stabbing Kennedy in the back.[18]

Besides the refuse issue, the major Yorty verbal onslaught against Poulson was to compare him to "eastern-type bosses" involved with political "machines," men like Richard Daley of Chicago. Yorty's tactic of talking about the "downtown machine" scored affirmatively with many Los Angeles voters not so much because of the veracity of the accusation but for more subtle reasons. Few knowledgeable Angelenos denied that a common interest existed between the various business leaders who had their corporate headquarters downtown—real estate men, stock brokers, banking leaders, and newspaper publishers, for example—but the evidence is insufficient that such a cabal ever "controlled" City Hall. In fact, contrary evidence predominates. The so-called "downtown machine" strongly opposed Fletcher Bowron in 1938 and Yorty in 1961, but both times to no avail. As a student of Los Angeles civic history has concluded, "The *Times* and the business interests simply have not won often enough to let us say that they were the wheels of a machine which functioned behind the screen of nonpartisanship." [19]

One aspect of the Yorty "downtown machine" onslaught found fertile ground. Los Angeles is a city of far-flung residential and commercial satellite neighborhoods, many of which had come to feel neglected by City Hall. To the south, the San Pedro-Harbor area had long felt that the city government treated it like a poor relative. Many citizens of the burgeoning San Fernando Valley felt isolated and powerless, even though the city had spent millions of dollars to set up a City Hall annex in Van Nuys. While the "downtown machine" of Yorty's campaign literature was not a machine in the Chicago sense and apparently did not control City Hall, major downtown business interests did, in the view of many residents of outlying areas, exert a disproportionate influence on the city government. It is certainly significant that both of Poulson's leading opponents, Yorty and McGee, made strong pitches for the Valley and Harbor vote.

Pat McGee, whom Sam Yorty narrowly defeated to qualify for the runoff with Poulson, had represented the western portion of the San Fernando Valley since 1950, first in the Assembly, and then in the City Council. After losing in the primary, McGee hesitated, then lukewarmly endorsed Norris Poulson. Yorty immediately belittled the move, saying that McGee had turned his back on his former supporters and joined hands with the "downtown machine." He declared that two former McGee aides had joined the Yorty campaign, and added, "I bear no malice toward Pat, but I am sorry to see him sacrifice principles to make deals with his enemies. They will use him and throw him to the wolves. . . ." [20]

As an extension of his "downtown machine" tactic, Yorty complained that the metropolitan newspapers had turned themselves over to the "Poulson machine and the big lie." He said that they had ceased to report news, and instead were substituting "deliberate distortion and deceit." [21] In an amusing civic-minded plea Yorty suggested that mayors should be limited to two terms, in order to "insure healthy democratic processes and an orderly transition of city government each two terms, thwarting any ruthless machine politics and self-interest group that feeds on continued control of City Hall." [22] This is another in a list of Yorty maxims which, if ever applied to him, would have wreaked havoc with his political career!

The most obnoxious part of the "downtown machine" story was Yorty's dredging up of Mayor Poulson's cattle ranch holdings in Baker, Oregon. Yorty insisted that Poulson had far more extensive investments than could accrue to a public official who received compensation of $25,000 a year. Sam told his listeners that some of Poulson's prize bulls had been appraised at as much as his entire yearly salary as Mayor. Poulson replied that Yorty was describing the accumulations of his life savings as well as the investments of his wife, who came from a wealthy Baker ranch family. The Mayor then offered a humorously derisive comparison, claiming that his two Black Angus bulls had been purchased at a cost of $1,200: "So you see that the specifically designed television 'bull' that Yorty puts on the air is worth $25,000, but the actual Poulson bull on the farm in Oregon is worth only $600." Poulson belittled his Oregon holdings, offering to sell out to Yorty at a modest fee. This ploy may have backfired, though, as Yorty averred he would "make [his] investments in Los Angeles." [23]

Throughout the campaign Yorty incessantly invited the almost voiceless Poulson to join him in television debates. Sam pretended to sympathize with Poulson's condition, placing the blame on the Mayor's "downtown machine" backers. Although Poulson had attempted to allay voter concern about his health by undergoing an extensive, well-publicized physical examination by a team of leading doctors at the Good Samaritan Hospital, the maneuver was less than successful. The panel reported that the Mayor was in excellent health for a man of his age, but Poulson spoke with a hoarse croak and could not stifle persistent rumors that he was suffering from throat cancer.[24]

Yorty did all he could to keep the question of Poulson's health in the forefront. Said Sam: "I accuse the machine backing Poulson of sacrificing his health . . . and perhaps endangering his very life by its callous and total indifference to his physical condition. . . . My opponent appears to be incapable of conducting his office. . . ." [25] He went on, "Those who have seen the Mayor in person or on television or have heard him on radio are shocked by his effort to speak or respond to questions and by his obvious physical discomfiture. . . . His backers have strained his endurance to the peril point." [26] *Time* magazine reported that Poulson's appearance on television "left the impression that he was a sick and tired old man." [27]

Because of Poulson's support by the metropolitan newspapers, Yorty and Eleanor Chambers (who had come down from her hillside home in Cambria, near San Simeon, to run his campaign) had early decided that they would be forced into an unorthodox campaign. They chose to spend the majority of their sparse campaign funds on radio, television, and community newspapers. These small newspaper publications were eager to join the fray, having long been jealous of the "downtown four," and television interests were anxious to enter the world of politics, to show their power in a field that had long been dominated by the *Los Angeles Times* and the Hearst syndicate.

Yorty could not buy blanket coverage in large segments in the communications media as his campaign coffers had little cash, but circumstances put him in touch with George Putnam, a controversial figure in Los Angeles television, who was itching for an issue to expand his local fame. Putnam, who was more actor than newsman, saw most issues in simplistic, absolute shades of black and white. He regularly gave over a small time segment on his show as a forum for both candidates, but only Yorty appeared continuously.[28]

Putnam's news show was on KTTV, a station then owned by the *Los Angeles Times*, which was solidly in the Poulson camp. Because of his strong support and encouragement of Yorty, Putnam was put under extreme pressure. He was even sued by several Poulson backers whom he had connected with a Yorty-Putnam exposé of a certain questionable harbor oil lease. The lease was apparently something of a red herring in this election campaign, as after six years of litigation and exploratory drilling, it had, in the words of writer James Phelan, "not yielded enough oil to lubricate a door hinge." [29]

The scheduling of Yorty's first television experiences had brought forth a high-level decision concerning a campaign prop he had carried with him for over a quarter-century— his mustache. Over the years it had mysteriously grown darker and then lighter and had ranged from a bushy brush to a pencil-thin line. But in 1961, as he prepared to go on television, Yorty found that the mustache was a problem. Unless he dyed it black it would show up on camera as a faint grayish smudge. If he did dye it he might look like a vaudeville villain. The mustache had to go, and Sam shaved it off. While it had originally been grown to enhance Yorty's mature visage, now that it was gone he beamed gratefully as his friends told him how much younger he looked! [30]

The Yorty television personality took on a seemingly natural populist character. He spoke in his flat, metallic, midwestern nasal tone as a common man trying to "beat City Hall" and often used colloquial phrases that would appeal to many of his viewers. Friends and opponents alike agreed that he came off well on the tube, especially when compared with Mayor Poulson, who seldom appeared at all and was largely forced to conduct a shadow campaign through endless press releases and speeches by aides.

As he became increasingly pressured to respond to Yorty's "downtown machine" allegations, Poulson fought against himself in an effort to avoid taking the low political road. It must have been especially frustrating for the Mayor to be held back not only by his dislike for mudslinging but also by his speech difficulty. Finally he could no longer resist the need to fight Yorty's fire with a torch of his own. Voters were asked to recall some of Sam's more unusual proposals from the 1930's, such as a bill he originated to authorize the state government to open parimutuel bookmaking offices.[31] The 1955 job offer to Yorty (at $50,000 per year) from the Southern Nevada Gambling Commission was dragged out once again into public view.

Then Poulson's campaign aides told of Yorty's involvement with the New Frontier Hotel and Casino in Las Vegas. Sam had attempted, they said, "to get a gambling license" for the casino, even though "the Nevada State Tax Commission refused the license . . . because two of the stockholders were being sued by the State of California for conspiracy." The two had been accused in the mid-1950's of defrauding the State of California by selling it a downtown Los Angeles building at four times its value.[32] The implication of the Poulson treatment of these past Yorty gambling associations was that Sam was connected with the "underworld."

Irate, Sam fired back that his associations with the New Frontier were those of an attorney with his client, and he threatened to call for an investigation of the Mayor by the California State Bar Association for impugning the lawyer-client relationship.[33] The *Los Angeles Times,* which represented the Poulson viewpoint, replied, "Professional—or personal—association with gamblers, punctiliously legal as it may be, is not a recommendation for the mayorship." The *Times* then adopted what it considered to be an apt slogan: "Don't Gamble On Yorty!"[34]

Yorty, continuing his counterpunching, blithely told reporters that if he was ruled by the underworld, Poulson, then, was ruled by the "overworld," the "downtown machine."[35] He then slapped the Mayor with a $2.2 million slander suit, charging him with trying to create the impression that Yorty was backed by underworld gangsters. With incredible luck, from Yorty's standpoint, the taking of depositions for his lawsuit was scheduled to occur the Friday before the runoff. Poulson would have to produce his evidence, said Yorty, or the people would judge him. Poulson spokesmen announced that p'enty of evidence would be presented. The lawsuit was eventually expanded to $3.3 million, and Poulson's campaign managers, Herbert Baus and William Ross, were named as codefendants with him.[36]

Recriminations over the Yorty slander suit brought to the surface word of a rift that had developed within the Poulson camp, causing the once professional organization to slip into disarray. Baus and Ross had begun the campaign with sole responsibility and control. They had planned a quiet, clean campaign, the usual course for an incumbent who was at least moderately popular. Wanting the campaign to remain seemingly nonpartisan, they nevertheless had worked through John McFadden, an independent campaign management specialist, who very quietly went about enlisting Democratic support for the Mayor. Baus and Ross were well aware that Democratic registration was superior in the city, by a 60-to-40 margin, and they wanted Poulson to seem as nonpartisan as possible.

The unexpected closeness of the primary results, however, caused Poulson and some of his most intimate advisers, such as wealthy automobile dealer Martin Pollard, to insist on a dilution of Baus and Ross' authority by adding another campaign firm. In one of the weirdest twists of an already strange campaign, Pollard, a lifelong conservative Republican, urged the replacement of John McFadden by the firm of Snyder-Smith Advertising. This agency generally had been aligned with minority interest groups, labor unions, and such prominent California Democrats as Jess Unruh, and Carmen Warschaw, the Democratic "Dragon Lady" of the party's State Central Committee.[37]

Snyder-Smith, sensing that Poulson was the underdog, suggested that he answer Yorty's "machine" charges. Baus and Ross were adamant against such a course. The result of this internal tug of war is history; Snyder-Smith won and Norris Poulson lost. The remainder of the campaign was rife with disagreements in tactics between the two campaign factions, and on occasion they even worked directly at cross-purposes.[38] In a way, both the crudity of the assaults on Yorty in the *Los Angeles Democrat* and the "underworld" allegations leading to the Yorty slander suit may be traced to this dichotomy in the management of the Poulson campaign.

After Yorty announced his lawsuit, he continued to hurl issue after issue in Poulson's direction, drawing extensively from his quiver of political arrows. He continued to insist that the Mayor agree to debate with him, knowing all the while that Poulson could not have accepted even if he had possessed the forensic talents of a Clarence Darrow. When Poulson campaigners mentioned Sam's liberal Assembly record and some of his 1930's associations, Yorty complained that he was the intended victim of "a Communist smear campaign of alarming proportions."[39] "The machine," he said:

> is trying to smear me with a red brush just as they did Judge Fletcher Bowron eight years ago. They have spread these false rumors and almost libelous propaganda for so long they're now insensitive to truth or fact. They are expert character assassins.[40]

The Yorty platform included planks promising to bring an extra councilmanic district to the San Fernando Valley, more harmony to Mayor-City Council relations, and a viable rapid transit program, which are all areas of doubtful mayoral control. Mayors had never before claimed to have the authority to combat smog, but Sam turned a new page in Los Angeles politics by declaring that Mayor Poulson was doing nothing to fight air pollution:

The Mayor has his heart and soul in his $250,000 cattle
ranch in Baker, Oregon, and is not interested in the problems of this city. The Mayor must display the initiative and
be the leader and advocate in the fight against smog. Poulson has done nothing and every person who suffers from
smog knows it.[41]

Yorty also proclaimed an urgent need to cut the cost of city
government and offered to start the ball rolling by selling
off Poulson's Cadillac and buying a Rambler, if elected.
Yorty even brought out his own wartime involvement in
reorganizing Philippine civil government. Curiously absent from the Yorty attacks on Poulson were the heretofore
inevitable innuendoes about his opponents' war record.

Yorty's repeated assaults upon the Los Angeles practice
of rubbish separation, combined with his assertions of extensive personal knowledge of the sanitation industry,
prompted Poulson to draw the voters' attention to Yorty's
source of information. Yorty, according to a Poulson campaign spokesman, had a valid reason to be intensely interested in municipal rubbish collection, as he had been in
competition with the city himself as a private dump operator. Not only had Yorty been such an operator in the San
Pedro area, said the *Los Angeles Times,* but his dump there
had been "in constant violation of county rules and ordinances governing rubbish dump operation."[42] In a press release, Poulson informed readers that he was quoting from
official government documents, not political propaganda
sheets. He related that the county had filed six violations
and 24 negative reports concerning Yorty's alleged dump,
citing "infestation by rats, water pollution, [and] failure
to cover rubbish." "Yorty is a master at misrepresentation,"
Poulson observed, "but these are incontrovertible facts."[43]

Yorty's name had also been connected with another dump
operated in Angeles National Forest by the Broadway and
Main Corporation, of which Sam was reportedly a major

stockholder. Finally, Yorty was purported to have played an important role in negotiations attempting to form what would have become the largest privately-owned rubbish combine in the nation. Sam's coy reply may have been a clever retort, but it was in no sense an answer; "It's rubbish!" he said.[44] After all it was Sam who had originally drawn attention to his sanitation background, in order to lend authority to his remarks on the subject.

Although Sam had properly dismissed the Poulson "underworld" charges as examples of "guilt-by-association" tactics, he was not adverse to using such tactics himself. Poulson, he noted, had his own gambling connections. Sam claimed that a Poulson appointee to a city commission was a partner in a law firm that had handled cases involving poker clubs in Gardena, which is a Los Angeles suburb that offers legalized card-playing. This Yorty outburst had been prompted by the revelation that in 1958 Yorty had been hired as Assistant City Attorney in Cabazon, California, a tiny desert town that aspired to become a second Las Vegas. The Poulson appointee mentioned in Yorty's claim was Michael Kohn, a police commissioner, and Yorty promised to fire him, if elected.[45]

Yorty had made other attacks upon the police commission during the campaign, including the claim that Poulson had promised in 1953 to fire Police Chief William H. Parker. Poulson, Parker, and Emmett McGaughey (a police commissioner under both Bowron and Poulson) flatly denied the allegation.[46] Yorty further charged that Poulson's appointees were "shattering the morale of the Police Department," a claim Yorty had not used since the Fitts-Dockweiler District Attorney race 21 years earlier.[47] At the conclusion of a regular meeting, the police commission announced that Yorty would never get the chance to fire Kohn or any other member; they would all resign if he were elected. They concluded their meeting with the prediction that Los Angeles would suffer "a complete breakdown of law enforcement . . . if Yorty became Mayor."[48]

The Friday of the scheduled depositions in the slander suit arrived amid frantic efforts by Walter Ely, Poulson's attorney, to have them postponed until after the election. No decision was made at the hearing, which collapsed into a shouting match between Ely and Phill Silver, who represented Yorty. The conflicting charges flew back and forth, out of order, and the judge was forced to admonish all parties. The case was finally postponed until July 6, weeks after the May 31 runoff.[49] While promising to drop the suit if Poulson was defeated and apologized, Yorty raised the amount to $4.4 million, included Walter Ely as a codefendant, and reminded the voters of his promise to win the lawsuit and liberate Poulson's ranch and return it to the people.[50]

Yorty had openly sought minority votes, reminding Blacks that as a congressman he had appointed members of their race to service academies. Poulson, however, had fared well in every pre-election poll among Black voters.[51] But as the runoff election came very close, an incident occurred which would hurt Poulson in this area. On Memorial Day, a gathering of picnickers in Griffith Park had developed into a disturbance involving 75 policemen and 200 Blacks and, according to most accounts, the resulting mini-riot was largely due to police overreaction.[52] The sorry event played right into Yorty's outstretched hands. He reminded Police Chief Parker, who had termed the disturbance a "race riot," that "This is not the South," and said that Parker would have to undergo some "schooling" if he planned to remain as Police Chief after Yorty won.[53]

To add to the mounting Poulson debacle, the week before the election brought a sharp increase in the city's unemployment ranks due to automotive assembly line layoffs and a cancelled federal contract.[54] Yorty, who had at first

predicted a victory margin of 35,000 to 40,000 votes, said
that Poulson's police force had further tipped the scales and
the race would not even be close. He flatly predicted a landslide margin of 100,000 votes, ending his campaign with a
rash of television and radio appearances in which he told
the audience that Poulson had slandered him with the "big
lie" and refused to debate with him. He described Poulson
as a tired, sick old man who did not want to be Mayor, and
termed the campaign as "the people . . . against . . .
downtown."[55]

Poulson supporters were helpless in trying to combat
Yorty's repetitive debate challenges, and they hoped the
campaign could be saved by a large turnout of voters. The
Los Angeles Times, which had editorialized for weeks about
the danger inherent in the abdication by citizens of their
electoral responsibility, published a last-resort editorial
summarizing the case against Yorty's alleged gambling and
rubbish background. Poulson had been favored by a 60-40
margin in a poll completed only four days before the runoff,
but when the votes were counted, Sam Yorty had narrowly
won. Less than half of the city's 1.1 million registered voters
had bothered to turn out:[56]

Yorty	276,106	51.5%
Poulson	260,381	48.5

The *Los Angeles Times* resigned itself to Yorty's victory
in a post-election editorial entitled "There's Nothing Left
But Hope." The newspaper said Sam got Los Angeles at
a bargain price, referring to the low voter turnout. Said
the *Times,* the citizens "hadn't had a fire in City Hall for
some years, so they let their insurance lapse." Picturing
Yorty as an untrustworthy soul who merely sought a political podium and a partisan launching pad, the paper observed that he carried "the colors . . . of a political pri-
vateer."[57]

The multiplicity of negative factors surrounding the unhappy candidacy of Norris Poulson had combined to defeat him, but when they are measured up against the vote tally, it seems remarkable that Yorty's margin was so small. The most significant Poulson stumbling block was undoubtedly his original lack of enthusiasm for a third term, combined with his unfortunate and inopportune vocal disability. Pointing to a possible connection between the two factors, a highly ranked Poulson campaigner later remarked that he felt the voice loss was a psychosomatic reflection of the Mayor's desire to retire.[58] A motivational research survey conducted immediately after the election suggested that Yorty's television appearances had been a decisive factor in convincing undecided voters to abandon Poulson for Yorty. "Relatively few Los Angeles voters felt that 'real' political issues were at stake," explained the psychologist who conducted the survey. He reported that his respondents tended to picture Yorty as "direct, frank, and to-the-point," and Poulson as "hesitant, hedgy, and indirect."[59]

The greatest political lesson that can be drawn from the 1961 election was that the "downtown machine" strategem was an unqualified success. The disillusionment of the San Pedro area was reflected in the returns: the area went to Yorty. The San Fernando Valley, which Poulson backers had hoped would swing into their column after the McGee endorsement, gave support to the political truth that endorsements are easier to deliver than votes. Yorty carried all four City Council districts in the Valley.[60] These areas saw Yorty as their champion and felt that through him they could truly "beat City Hall." In his victory speech Yorty told his listeners that the victory was theirs and that they had waited a long time to be able to cheer.[61]

Factors were present besides Poulson's mute reluctance and the parochial protest. Some observers felt that the harshness of the Democratic tactics backfired against Poulson because they served to identify Yorty as a Democrat, an on-and-off one, to be sure, but a Democrat.[62] The disorganization of the incumbent's campaign staff took its toll. Then, too, the much publicized police brutality which occurred almost at the last possible moment could easily have accounted for the Yorty margin of less than 16,000 votes. Finally, the election represented one of the first triumphs of television publicity over the political coverage of the metropolitan dailies. One telecaster said of the outcome of the battle, "That was the day that we draped the *Times* building in black crepe."[63]

Whatever the causes of his victory, Sam had reason to be elated. It was probably the most notable win of his political career and put him where he wanted to be. From the "corner pocket" in City Hall he could plot his future moves into greatness, his drives for a U. S. senatorship, the Governor's mansion, and higher places still. Reflecting on his triumph over Norris Poulson, Sam said, "I must say I'm not surprised. I've looked up at that City Hall for years and thought, 'Someday I'll be Mayor.' "[64] Heaven only knows what other public buildings have caught the Little Giant's wistful gaze!

16

PARTY POLITICS AGAIN

The first statewide electoral contests after Sam Yorty's election as Mayor of Los Angeles occurred in 1962. It was a political season rife with controversy in the Golden State. Pat Brown was up for reelection as Governor, and his Republican opponent would be either Richard Nixon or conservative Joseph Shell. Nixon, who had lost the 1960 Presidential contest despite Sam Yorty's support, would make a supposed last-gasp attempt to rescue his political career. Although Nixon had carried the state in 1960, he was reluctant to run against the popular Brown. Ronald Reagan was still beyond the political horizon; he had just signed a $150,000-a-year contract to host the television program, *Death Valley Days.* Many people wondered whether Sam Yorty would take this first opportunity to use his base as Mayor to run against Brown.

No sooner had Yorty become Mayor than he began to fight with his governing partner, the City Council. The Mayor-Council relationship in Los Angeles had seldom been one of great harmony, but with the advent of the Little Giant on the municipal scene, civic warfare had approached the outright battle stage.

In the early 1950's, Eleanor Chambers, who at that time was Congressman Yorty's field representative in Los Angeles, spotted Rosalind "Roz" Weiner, a 22-year old local university graduate with a dew-fresh appearance. Ms. Chambers had long wanted to see a woman elected to the City Council and had herself once run unsuccessfully for that body. Armed with the help and advice of Ms. Chambers, with campaign work by many college student volunteers, and with little bars of soap suggesting she would "clean up" City Hall, Roz Weiner was elected in 1953.[1]

Nine years later, in 1962, Eleanor Chambers was Sam Yorty's Deputy Mayor and chief political oracle, and Roz Weiner Wyman was an anti-Yorty voice in City Hall. More important from a statewide political standpoint was the fact that Eugene Wyman, Roz's husband, was a prominent Beverly Hills attorney and a kingpin in Pat Brown's political entourage. Yorty felt that both Wymans had their eyes on political office and that they wanted to manipulate the Mayor's office for personal gain. What the Wymans really represented at that time was the liberal wing of the state Democratic party, which did not want any part of Sam Yorty as a statewide candidate.

Sam and Eleanor must have decided that 1962 was not the appropriate year to make a new move into state politics. Pat Brown was a formidable one-term incumbent, and Sam had less than a year under his belt as Mayor. The muscle of political action—cash—was in short supply for Yorty, who decided to stand back from both the Nixon-Brown race and the battle between Tom Kuchel and Dick Richards, his old enemies, for U. S. Senator. Nixon lost out to Pat Brown, made his famous "You won't have Nixon to kick around anymore" speech to the mass media people, and moved his base of operations to New York City.[2] Kuchel beat Richards again, and Yorty sat on the municipal sidelines, gathering strength for another penetration into California politics.

In 1964, many political observers expected Sam to run for Clair Engle's seat in the U. S. Senate. Yorty and Engle were not outright enemies, but Sam had said, "I won't say that I

will not be a candidate. I want Engle to worry a little."[3]
Engle subsequently became terminally ill with a malignant
brain tumor. He withdrew from the race although it was
too late for his name to be removed from the ballot. This
left the battle to former JFK press secretary Pierre Salinger,
state Controller Alan Cranston, and longtime pension cru-
sader George McLain. Sam had declined to run. When the
ballots were counted later, Yorty's endorsement of McLain
did the latter little good; McLain finished a distant third
as Salinger won the nomination.

Much preliminary jousting took place for the leadership
of the California delegation to the Democratic National
Convention in 1964. The early rumors suggested that Pat
Brown would campaign as a favorite son. He eventually declined, however, choosing instead to chair a nominally uncommitted slate known to be backing Lyndon Johnson.
Sam Yorty was also for Johnson, as he had been four years
before. But aside from his past differences with Brown, two
factors bothered Sam enough for him to consider mounting
a frontal attack against Brown with a presidential delegate
slate of his own. First, Sam suspected that Brown had national political ambitions—such as Vice President or Supreme Court Justice—in mind when the Governor decided
to chair the so-called uncommitted slate. Second, Yorty was
unyieldingly opposed to naming Eugene Wyman to the post
of chairman of the Democratic State Central Committee.
Brown nevertheless went ahead and named Wyman to the
position. This made Sam fearful that Brown would follow
through and support Wyman for Democratic national committeeman, if the Governor controlled the California delegation.

In March, 1964, Yorty made his move, filing a rival uncommitted slate for the June primary election. To avoid
the prevalent assumption that Brown's slate was the "official" Johnson slate, Sam said, "Neither delegation can be

considered official unless the President so states in writing."[4] Although both slates were clearly for LBJ, Yorty stated, "Democrats in California should have a choice."[5] "It's no secret that Brown wants to be Vice President," he later added.[6] He continued to harp against the Wyman appointment and characterized backers of the Brown slate as "a threat to the democratic way of life. . . ."[7]

The Yorty campaign was weakened on April 2, 1964, when a White House spokesman stated that Pat Brown was LBJ's political representative in California. Several former Yorty staff members also hit Sam with a lawsuit in which they accused him of using city materials, employees, and telephones in his campaign against the Brown slate.[8] Then a political reporter for the *Los Angeles Times* revealed that Brown had earlier offered to bury the hatchet by naming Yorty to the "official" slate, despite Sam's past political activities that had offended the party regulars. According to this reporter, Sam had refused to join the slate, maintaining that such action would constitute an implicit endorsement of Wyman.[9]

Despite these difficulties, only six days before the primary election, Yorty campaigners released the results of a poll conducted in two southern California counties that showed Sam ahead of the Governor. They refused to name the organization responsible for the poll, but termed it a well-established and professionally run operation. Yorty pointed to the high proportion of the sample polled that was undecided, saying that the outcome of the race would rest with these people. He then criticized the Brown activities as making "for a bad Tammany Hall type of political machine and . . . a sordid kind of power politics."[10] Brown fired back, "If I've tried to establish a political machine, I've been very unsuccessful."[11]

In a late onslaught against Governor Brown, Yorty called a press conference during a campaign visit to Sacramento.

He accused the Governor of manipulating the Democratic party, picking and choosing among the potential candidates for various offices. He said that Brown was guilty of favoring interests which wanted to keep a purportedly dangerous drug on the market. (The drug in question was a pain-killer with the trade name of Percodan.)[12] Yorty said that the election was a choice between a slate of the people of California and one made up by party bosses, led by a man who wanted to be Vice President. He also recalled for his listeners Brown's difficulty in controlling the California delegation to the 1960 Democratic National Convention. Despite the heavy odds against him, Yorty maintained throughout the campaign that the people had a choice; at no time did he refer to his effort as a protest campaign.

By primary election day the Pat Brown slate was believed to be well in front and the main question centered on Brown's margin of victory. Yorty made a last minute radio-television blitz in which, among other things, he reminded voters that Eugene Wyman's law firm had represented handlers of Percodan and that Brown had appointed Oscar Weiner, Roz's father, to the State Pharmacy Board. These guilt-by-association tactics were a final desperate gasp.

The results of the election were a crushing blow to Yorty's ambition and demonstrated his inability to erase the feeling of dislike among many Democrats generated by his actions against Richards, Kennedy, and Brown over an eight-year period. The primary's outcome denied Sam Yorty a trip to the Democratic National Convention at Atlantic City. Pat Brown's slate was a two-to-one victor over that of Yorty, and Sam lost in every county in the state:[13]

Brown Slate (uncommitted)	1,693,813	68%
Yorty Slate (uncommitted)	798,431	32

Official returns also showed that Yorty had even lost badly on his home ground. Brown garnered 62 percent of the vote in Los Angeles County.

Following his defeat, Sam shifted his terminology and for the first time referred to his race as a protest candidacy. "I am very grateful to the large percentage of Democrats who joined me in a protest against the Wyman-Brown control of the Democratic party in California," he said.[14] It is true that although the Yorty percentage was not huge, it did represent a sizable erosion of Pat Brown's political power.

Sam had failed in his first attempt in eight years to penetrate statewide politics. He was able, as always, to recoup after the defeat and look forward to the next political fight. He knew his forte was municipal politics. On that battlefield a new conflict was just around the corner; in 1965 he would be able to campaign once more for City Hall.

17

A ROOSEVELT
IN A LANDSLIDE

Among the accomplishments Sam Yorty attributed to his first term as Mayor was the fulfillment of his most strident campaign promise. After three years of conflict, combined rubbish pickups had finally begun in July, 1964. As a result of his stubbornness, however, Sam had been caught in a running battle with the equally obstinate City Council, thus lessening the possibilities of achieving other civic progress.

The most remarkable juggling act Yorty performed in that first term involved the entity he had called the "downtown machine" in 1961. A number of members of the political clique that had opposed him so strenuously in the Poulson race had subsequently rallied to Sam's side. In the short period of four years he had converted people who once viewed him as a municipal calamity into out-and-out Yorty admirers. Even the *Los Angeles Times,* which had opposed him for almost 30 years, remarked about his coming of age, "It is a proven fact of political life that most men undergo a sea-change . . . once they gain public office. . . . Mayor Samuel W. Yorty . . . has matured in office to a degree that surprises many who opposed him. . . ."[1] Many business leaders and other conservatives who had fought Yorty in 1961 were quietly raising money for his reelection four years later.

Several candidates appeared anxious to assault Yorty's incumbency, but Patrick McGee and James Roosevelt were the major threats. McGee remembered how close he had come to edging Yorty out of the Poulson runoff in 1961. Although McGee was obviously courting Republican voters, some observers felt McGee in 1965 was a stalking horse for James "Jimmy" Roosevelt.[2]

Jimmy, the eldest son of Eleanor and Franklin, had followed a twisting political course. His first public political post was as press secretary for his father, when he succeeded Louis Howe in 1936. Later in the 1930's he migrated to California to try his fortune in motion picture production and soon advanced to high executive positions in that field. Roosevelt parlayed his splashy World War II record into a post as chairman of the Veterans' Committee in the fruitless gubernatorial campaign of Robert Kenny in 1946. Jimmy was subsequently elected state chairman of the Democratic party, and from this position he tried unsuccessfully to influence the national party leaders to pick Dwight Eisenhower as the 1948 Democratic candidate for President. That course alienated many Truman supporters from the James Roosevelt cause. In 1950 the invincible Earl Warren soundly trounced Roosevelt in his bid for the governorship. When Sam Yorty abdicated his seat in Congress in 1954 to run unsuccessfully for the U. S. Senate, Roosevelt won the Yorty seat.

In Congress, Jimmy Roosevelt had a moderately liberal record which included attacking the seniority system and working for legislation to improve urban conditions. He had been easily reelected four times, but the seniority system had become increasingly stifling to his desires to rise politically. By 1964 he was searching for other pastures.

The political allies of Pat Brown, still smarting from Sam Yorty's upstart 1964 campaign of opposition to Brown's delegate slate, were shopping for a viable candidate with whom to evict Sam from City Hall. Thus feeling assured of solid support, Jimmy Roosevelt decided to file his candidacy for Mayor of Los Angeles.[3]

So began what is possibly the most complex involvement of divergent state political interests in the modern history of Los Angeles politics. California Democrats had long been split between conservatives like Yorty and moderate liberals like Pat Brown. But in the mid-1960's a second split had opened in the anti-Yorty camp. Jesse (now Jess) Unruh, the powerful speaker of the Assembly, had broken with Brown and the California Democratic Council in 1964, when this organization supported Alan Cranston in the primary election for U. S. Senate. Unruh had long been at odds with the Governor over legislative matters, and he supported Pierre Salinger. Salinger's victory had damaged the prestige of Brown and the CDC and had further divorced Unruh and his considerable following from the main line of liberal California Democrats.

Coincidentally, before the CDC had endorsed Cranston, its former president, it had briefly considered picking Jimmy Roosevelt for the Senate race. In 1965, when the Brown-Wyman-CDC forces were preparing to stand behind Roosevelt in his fight with Yorty, Jess Unruh was faced with a difficult decision. On the one hand, he had no liking for Yorty; he had openly endorsed Norris Poulson in 1961. Since then, Yorty had been highly critical of him, saying at one point, "The Wymans and Jesse Unruh are attempting . . . to gain control of the state. But I'm determined they'll never gain control of the City of Los Angeles."[4] Still, Unruh felt he could not stand by and allow the Brown-CDC faction to gain a foothold in Los Angeles. He also feared that Roosevelt, if elected Mayor, would be a strong political opponent in future statewide elections. Jess Unruh thus found himself in an unlikely alliance with the Little Giant.

The most visible sign of Unruh involvement in the Yorty campaign was the presence of Unruh aide Don McGrew,

who helped Eleanor Chambers run the fight against Jimmy
Roosevelt.[5] In addition, even though Roosevelt prided
himself on his sympathy to minority interests while in Congress, he was the victim of considerable erosion of support
from the Black community in the mayoralty contest. For
instance, Councilman Billy Mills and Assemblyman
Mervyn Dymally, who were Unruh allies, supported Yorty.
They maintained that Roosevelt was doing well in Washington and Yorty in Los Angeles, and therefore both of
them should stay where they were.

Sam Yorty was uncomfortable in playing the position of
favorite in a major election, as it was not his usual stance.
He had always enjoyed portraying himself as the "little
man" against various cliques, conspiracies, machines, and
other strong, sinister forces. In the race against Jimmy
Roosevelt, therefore, Sam insisted that he was being victimized. Referring to Brown, Wyman, and the California
Democratic Council, he railed at vested interests in the
"state Democratic machine" who were allegedly out to retire him from public office. Then pointing to Roosevelt's
long residence in Washington while in Congress and to the
famous surname, Sam claimed that a national Democratic
conspiracy was out to undermine him as Mayor. These tactics were calculated to draw independent and Republican
support to the Yorty column.

Oddly enough, Roosevelt was almost defeated months
before the election. A Beverly Hills attorney, who had lost
to Roosevelt in the 1964 congressional race, filed suit to
keep federal officials (such as Congressman Roosevelt) from
running during such tenure for municipal office. After considerable legal maneuvering and an errant opinion by attorney Sam Yorty, who predicted it would be upheld, the
suit was dismissed.[6]

Yorty began the campaign by alluding to Roosevelt's
strong financial backing. Sam made no direct accusations,

but he publicly fretted that some wealthy people were in a position to "buy" elections. Campaigners for Roosevelt stated that Yorty was also prepared to spend substantial amounts of money on the campaign.

Yorty ran his early campaign on the few real issues that were available to him—his appointments of some minority members to various city commissions, his claims of credit for the supposed end of racial difficulties in the Fire Department, and the combining of rubbish into one collection. Sam also complained that outside interests were trying to gain control of City Hall. This contrasted with a theme of his 1961 campaign; then the "interests" he criticized had been on the inside!

Pat McGee, sensing that Yorty was effectively garnering the bulk of Republican support, ended speculation about his being anyone's stalking horse by vigorously directing his campaign at Roosevelt. "Many Republicans," said McGee, "are so frightened by the prospect of Jimmy Roosevelt as Mayor that they would turn to Sam Yorty as the lesser of two evils. Sam Yorty is no prize package, but he is better than Roosevelt."[7]

The major thrust of the Roosevelt campaign revolved around proposed city improvements and opposed Yorty suggestions for city building. Jimmy attacked Yorty for pushing for a convention center, suggesting instead that the Mayor devote some of his power and prestige to the establishment of a park in the Santa Monica mountains. He asked what Yorty had achieved in rapid transit and air pollution and suggested that the Mayor had ignored the need for a salt water desalinization plant and a community center at Wrigley Field, an abandoned baseball park.

Roosevelt campaigners later seized upon Yorty's city-paid membership in the private Jonathan Club, which was an exclusive social organization with headquarters downtown and large beach facilities in Santa Monica. According to several civil rights organizations, the club at the time practiced *de facto* segregation against Blacks and Jews. Roosevelt assailed Yorty, first for his membership in an allegedly segregated club and then for allowing city taxpayers to subsidize his leisure activities.

Yorty irately responded to Roosevelt, saying that he held a membership in the club but knew nothing about any purported racial or ethnic bias. He explained that the membership was for his own personal convenience and that of official city guests. At a news conference he defended his record on minority relations, stating, "This city's accomplishments in the field of race relations take on added significance in the light of disturbances in other parts of the country."[8]

During the latter part of the campaign, Sam adopted a long familiar Yorty campaign ploy. "Never before in the history of the city have [we] seen left-wingers and mercenaries working together hand in hand, to take over the government of the city," he announced. Sam repeatedly complained that Roosevelt was backed by a "left-wing crowd,"[9] and also warned that the Los Angeles Police Department would come under partisan control if Roosevelt were elected.

Jimmy Roosevelt relied heavily on his family name to lure liberal and minority voters. He also depended upon a high-spending campaign featuring extensive doses of television speeches, thus trying to capitalize on a successful Yorty tactic of 1961. Yorty's television coverage against Poulson had been largely free, however, due chiefly to the George Putnam show, whereas Roosevelt's appearances were clearly paid political broadcasts. Roosevelt reportedly outspent Yorty in the campaign by a three-to-two margin.

The most damaging aspect of the Roosevelt candidacy may have been the stigma of being an outsider. Actually Jimmy moved to California in 1938. But the "East Coast"

connotations of the Roosevelt name, combined with his
long incumbency as a Congressman in Washington, helped
to seal Roosevelt's political doom. In the largest turnout
in at least 40 years for a municipal primary election in Los
Angeles, Sam Yorty was reelected by a landslide over Roosevelt, and Pat McGee finished a dismal third. No runoff was
held because Yorty had received more than one-half of the
total vote:[10]

Yorty	395,208	57.9%
Roosevelt	249,099	36.5
McGee	32,944	4.8
Others (5)	5,015	0.8

The voters provided Yorty with a political bonus. Roz
Wyman, with whom Yorty had clashed continuously, in
and out of City Hall, was unseated in a reelection bid.

Sam Yorty had once again waved his wand over the city
of Los Angeles. He had somehow levitated a substantial portion of the voters into an electoral expression of satisfaction.
In a few short months after the election the magic show
would be over.

18
WATTS

In the early 1930's various local politicians and private leaders had spoken of Los Angeles as a "white spot" among the corrupt major cities in America. Soon afterward, the town had been rocked by some of the wildest civic scandals in many years. In 1965 civic figures were once again making high-sounding claims. They, like their predecessors, would soon have second thoughts about their optimism.

Sitting behind his desk in the "corner pocket" of City Hall, Sam Yorty once boasted proudly about the achievements he claimed in the field of minority involvement in municipal affairs. "I brought Negroes into city government," he said. "Four of the five members of the Civil Service Commission are from minority groups. We also have Negroes on the housing and library commissions—in the fire and police departments—and in almost every office in City Hall."[1] He had earlier beamed, "I think we have the best race relations in our city of any large city in the United States."[2] But Sam had not been to Watts.[3]

About ten minutes by freeway from City Hall lay Watts, partly in and partly outside the city—a near-perfect mixture of the problems of urban decay. In 1965, the quality of its housing was deteriorating. Less than one-third of its residents held high school diplomas, and about one-eighth of its population was illiterate. About one-third of its children lived in broken homes.[4]

Although the schools were not legally segregated, the high school serving the Watts area was 99 percent Black. Racial discrimination aside, poor medical facilities and sparse transportation effectively walled off many residents from good health and economic well-being. Watts was a ghetto of wide avenues and dusty lawns—even in its segregated areas, Los Angeles was a spread-out town.

In the two decades following World War II, a large proportion of the residents of Watts had migrated from the Deep South, where the policemen they had known fitted well into the Bull Connor and Jim Clark stereotype. Watts provided the Los Angeles Police Department with more than its share of business. Complaints of officially condoned police brutality were commonplace. Even more often complaints were heard about inadequate police protection.[5]

In 1962, when a team of investigators from the United States Commission on Civil Rights visited Los Angeles and Watts, Sam Yorty had pounced on them, warning against their serving as "a sounding board for dissident elements."[6] As Blacks continued to throng into the city at a rate of more than 1,000 a month, the brutality complaints increased. Mayor Sam vigorously denied the claims, asserting that "Communists" had been screaming "police brutality" throughout the country for years.[7]

In 1950, when William H. Parker had become chief of police, the average tenure of a decade of his predecessors had been 18 months. By 1965, Parker had lasted considerably longer. Known as a "cop's cop," he was proud of the way he had cleaned up and professionalized the department, which had long been troubled by scandal. The chief had always frowned upon politics and was extremely sensitive to any outside encroachment or criticism. He had taken ill early in 1965 and had offered to resign, but Yorty felt him to be indispensable and so he stayed. This attitude was a marked contrast to Sam's 1961 statement that Parker needed "schooling" if he wanted to remain as chief.[8]

Parker's major flaws were a decided preference for law and order over social reform and a poor sense of public relations. "We are not interested in why a certain group tends toward crime," he had once declared, "we are interested in maintaining order."[9] In 1961 he had possibly cost Norris Poulson the mayoralty by referring to a Griffith Park disturbance as a "race riot." The chief had also been widely quoted in several clumsy remarks that sounded like blatant racism to many ears. Regarding Blacks, he had seemed somewhat blind to their difficulties, saying, "This is the only city where their treatment is good."[10]

The complaints of Watts changed from words to actions on the evening of August 11, 1965. A relatively minor traffic violation escalated into a full-scale riot and Watts became a household word across the nation. Most Angelenos were slow to comprehend the scope and meaning of the fires of Watts—but not Chief Parker. "[The riots were] no surprise to me," he said.[11] Parker's most remembered quote at the height of the violence went, "One person throws a rock and then, like monkeys in a zoo, others started throwing rocks."[12] The story of the burning and looting, the death of 34 people, the injury of 1,032, and the arrest of 3,952 is recounted in detail in several volumes, official and unofficial;[13] it will not be retold here. But some of its political implications are of interest.

Chief Parker first suggested bringing in the California National Guard on Thursday, August 12. But Yorty delayed until the following morning before making the request to Sacramento. Pat Brown was vacationing in Greece, and Lieutenant Governor Glenn Anderson hesitated to comply with Yorty's request. Brown, contacted in Athens, authorized the guard deployment, ordered an 8 p.m. curfew, and hurried home, cutting short his Grecian holiday. "From there it is awfully hard to direct a war," he said.[14]

Like Governor Brown, Sam Yorty had been unavailable when the ordeal had begun. He had flown to San Diego on the 11th to attend a gala reception and then had been driven to Tijuana, Mexico, to visit a fair. On the Friday that Governor Brown had called out the National Guard, the mobile Mayor was again out of town; he had flown north to keep a speaking engagement in San Francisco.[15]

When the streets of Watts were once again calm, a war of words began. Yorty said outside agitators caused the riots and used techniques employed elsewhere by communists. He blamed civil rights workers for stirring up Black resentment and defended his refusal to allow Martin Luther King to visit the riot area, maintaining that King might have further enraged the rioters. Parker also blamed civil rights leaders, saying, "You can't keep telling [these people] the Liberty Bell isn't ringing for them and not expect them to believe it. . . . You cannot keep telling them they are being abused and mistreated without expecting them to react."[16]

Yorty also cast some of the blame on Washington. He severely attacked Sargent Shriver, then head of the Office of Economic Opportunity, citing "deliberate and well-publicized cutting off of poverty funds to this city."[17] Shriver was quick to fire back, castigating the "mentality and attitude" of Yorty and Parker and revealing that before the riots Yorty had turned down an offer of extra government funds.[18] According to Shriver, despite Los Angeles' refusal to comply with OEO guidelines for citizen participation in the administration of the poverty funds (more than 500 cities had already complied), $17 million had already been forthcoming.[19]

Soon after the riots, Governor Brown appointed the Commission on the Los Angeles Riots, headed by John A. McCone, a former Central Intelligence Agency director. At a cost of $300,000 the commission in December, 1965, released a 101-page report of conclusions and recommendations about the riots' underlying forces. The commission termed the events of August, 1965, in Watts, a "formless, quite senseless, all but hopeless violent protest." [20] It said "while the Negro districts of Los Angeles are not urban gems, they are not slums. . . . The opportunity to succeed is probably unequaled in any other major American city." [21]

Critics called the McCone commission's report a white-wash of the causes that led to the uprising. But Sam Yorty felt that the report was too critical of Los Angeles official-dom. He railed against the appointment of one study commissioner, the Reverend James Edward Jones, picturing him as an ultraliberal.[22] Others criticized the report for being too general, superficial, politically motivated, and for not offering any new observations. A reviewer said that the most serious shortcoming of the McCone Commission lay in its "violation of the responsibility to seek truth and its frequent hiding behind opinion and hearsay." [23]

Many laid the blame for Watts at least partially at the feet of Sam Yorty and William Parker. "Sam Yorty is a great believer in Overwhelming Force as a solution to racial difficulties. This approach has not gained much favor in Watts," said one reporter.[24] *Time* magazine was more direct. It said Yorty expressed merely a "paternalistic interest in the city's Negro population and made little effort to understand its problems or anticipate its difficulties." [25]

Throughout the claims and counterclaims, Yorty stood steadfastly behind his police chief, especially when Black leaders requested authorization to establish some form of community supervision to watch for alleged police brutality in the future. Sam told of receiving 12,000 letters of approval of his defense of Parker and the department. In July, 1966, Chief Parker collapsed and died of a heart attack while attending a testimonial dinner in his honor. Sam Yorty was still defending the chief at his funeral, when he eulogized: "God may not be dead, but his finest representative on earth has just passed away." [26] At a Sacramento luncheon, Yorty also had praise for the young men of the National Guard, saying, "What a difference between these fine young men and the people they were sent to control." [27]

The major beneficiary of the Watts riots, in a political sense, was the Little Giant of City Hall. Yorty's staunch law and order position was exactly what many voters wanted to see. His political fortunes rose markedly during and after the riot period. Coincidentally, just before the riot broke out Sam was making eyes at the Governor's mansion. "I don't know of any Democrat," he said, "who would possibly challenge [Brown] next June . . . except myself." [28] Yorty had emerged from the ashes of Watts with a new image—an enforcer of laws and anything but a coddler of criminals. Simplistic though it was, he hoped that the new look would be enough to launch him to a successful landing in Sacramento.

19

BROWNOUT IN CALIFORNIA

Edmund G. "Pat" Brown had passed the zenith of his career by the beginning of 1966. Starting his long political rise as a Republican when he campaigned in the San Francisco Bay area for Herbert Hoover, he later joined the Democratic party. During World War II Brown was elected District Attorney of the City and County of San Francisco. After the war he fashioned himself after Republican Earl Warren—catering to both major parties—and was elected state Attorney General in 1950. Pat built up a formidable base of support that eventually culminated in his election to the governorship in 1958.

For a politician, Pat Brown was an unpretentious, compassionate, and almost humble man. One of his favorite photographs depicted him, as Governor, spilling coffee on himself. He was proud of the myriad state-funded benefits offered by California, once remarking, "In Washington they call it the Great Society. We just call it California." [1] Brown liked to listen to all sides of important and complex questions, a habit which sometimes caused him to seem indecisive. But he had made great strides fighting for the expansion of the state water project and the University of California and had also proposed the state's first fair employment practices act. He had never been an outstanding public speaker, however, and his portly form suggested to some the embodiment of a ward politician—a visage that would register strongly with the voters in 1966.

Although Brown had sent both William Knowland and Richard Nixon to their first California defeats and had earned a reputation as a hard campaigner, he was treading on shaky ground as he leaned toward running for a third term. Incumbency is a political asset that almost always dissipates markedly during the second term of a California chief executive. Only the unbeatable Earl Warren had ever held the Governor's mansion more than eight years in this state. The weight of political feuds and scandals, combined with the bulk of an unwieldy bureaucracy, tends to make administrations grow top heavy in their later years. In 1966, several people were anxious to tip over Pat Brown.

On the Republican side a clear split had opened between moderate and conservative elements. The leading man for the conservatives had spent some years broadcasting football games over the radio in Des Moines.[2] He had journeyed to Hollywood in 1937, acted in numerous grade-B movies, and become a tough president of the Screen Actors' Guild. He later had emerged as a public relations figurehead for the General Electric Corporation. As Ronald Reagan, citizen politician, he had figured peripherally in the Eisenhower campaigns of 1952 and 1956, though he did not register as a Republican until 1962.[3] In that year he had served as honorary campaign chairman for conservative Loyd Wright in an unsuccessful attempt to unseat U. S. Senator Tom Kuchel. Two years later he had been state co-chairman of Citizens for Goldwater-Miller. In 1966 he left his position as host of *Death Valley Days* to grasp for the reins of what would soon be the largest state in the nation.

The first choice of the moderate wing of the Republican party for Governor in 1966 was Tom Kuchel, who refused to run; he was satisfied with his growing seniority in the U. S. Senate and he had not forgotten the Knowland fiasco of 1958. The second choice of this faction was Assemblyman

Robert Monagan of Tracy, but he was deemed to be unknown by too many people in the populous southern half of the state.[4] So the moderates settled on San Francisco Mayor George Christopher. He was a wealthy dairy owner who as a candidate for the lieutenant governorship had led the defeated Republican ticket in 1962, even outdrawing Richard Nixon.

On the Democratic side, most observers did not expect a serious challenger to confront Governor Brown. The interests of the Democratic party depended on the weak paste that held party factions together, and a hard-fought primary campaign traditionally had disastrous effects at the general election. A primary battle could be counted upon to decimate the campaign treasury as well as worsen friction between factional leaders. Primary fights had another damaging effect—they often forced candidates to present in great detail their stands on certain emotional issues, thus setting themselves up as beckoning targets for general election opponents.

Sam Yorty had never evinced much party-mindedness in the past and 1966 would prove no exception. In February he announced a "growing sentiment in the Democratic party to demand new leadership" and called for an end to "influence peddling, false promises, favoritism, and power politics."[5] He castigated Pat Brown as a pawn of "left-leaning CDC-ers and cynical mercenaries."[6] He assaulted Brown for allegedly mishandling fiscal affairs and for appointing unsatisfactory judges to the State Supreme Court ("The background of some of the judges would prove shocking to the people if they were aware of the facts," said Sam).[7] He accused the Governor of doing nothing about air pollution, rapid transit, school finance, and dangerous drugs. Sam covered most of the bases in terms of Brown's alleged faults, but many listeners wondered if any Yorty alternatives existed.

Brown was under pressure from the liberal wing of the

Democratic party as well as from Yorty and the Republicans. Ultraliberal publisher Simon Casady had used his podium as president of the California Democratic Council to speak out strongly against the war in Vietnam. Governor Brown, a staunch supporter of President Johnson, had worked to remove Casady from his post, thus disenchanting many party liberals from his third-term designs.

Brown also suffered from unimaginative campaign management by Don Bradley, who had successfully guided LBJ's 1964 California race. Bradley believed that Yorty was not a solid threat to Brown and therefore counseled the Governor to pay little attention to the Los Angeles Mayor and concentrate on the two leading Republicans.[8] Here again, Brown was misled. His advisors believed that Ronald Reagan would be the weaker opponent in November, so they had Brown direct his fire at George Christopher. Furthermore, the campaign became cluttered by a regrettable smear. Dairyman Christopher had been convicted in 1940 of violating milk price-stabilization laws; he had been fined $5,000 and given a suspended prison sentence. Aides to the Governor reportedly leaked the information to newsmen and Drew Pearson devoted two columns to the smear.[9] Later, campaign materials were circulated which bore Christopher's mug shot under the headline, "WANTED."[10] The tumult created by the injection of Christopher's past into the 1966 campaign is believed to have hurt Pat Brown at least as much as the San Francisco Mayor.

Despite the mishandling of the Brown campaign, polls showed that Yorty was far behind the Governor. As a desperate move, Sam predictably reached back and brought out his old standby, the communist issue. Pat Brown, said Mayor Sam, "has the support of the Communist party against me in the primary because I'm anti-communist."[11] This claim seems almost humorous in light of the fact that Brown was unable to count on strong support from his former backers of liberal persuasion. But it did finally jerk the Governor out of his stance of ignoring Yorty. "This little man has flipped his lid," said Brown. "Yorty thinks everyone is against him . . . [the] psychiatric term for this . . . [is] paranoia—and I think this is the best way to describe the Mayor of Los Angeles."[12]

Another factor that worked against Brown was the Black unrest that had broken into rioting in Watts in 1965. When smaller disturbances occurred in March and May, 1966, Yorty reminded voters of the Governor's Grecian vacation at the time of Watts.[13] Somehow many voters apparently felt Brown should answer for the riots, not Yorty. Pat Brown was in a difficult position. He had been plagued by the Free Speech Movement and its accompanying unrest at Berkeley since 1964, and Los Angeles' Black ghetto had exploded three times in less than a year. He was under attack from both the political left and the political right. During the last two weeks of the primary campaign, Brown was forced to cut back on campaign expenditures to have sufficient funds to spend against Reagan or Christopher in the general election.[14]

As the votes were piling up on June 7, few people besides Sam Yorty believed Brown to be in jeopardy. As early returns showed a Brown trend, Sam remained optimistic, remarking that most votes were coming from the San Francisco Bay area, which he termed more "provincial" than the rest of the state.[15] When the results were official, Brown had won the nomination, but his five opponents, led by Mayor Sam, had dealt his candidacy a devastating blow:[16]

Brown	1,355,262	52.8%
Yorty	981,088	38.1
Others (4)	234,046	9.1

On the Republican side, Ronald Reagan had swamped George Christopher, gaining more total votes than Brown. Interestingly, Reagan also received 27,422 write-in votes from Democrats, a small indication of the Democratic support he would get in November.

Jess Unruh and Sam Yorty were conspicuously absent from Brown's general election campaign. Yorty had not backed Brown completely for a decade, and Unruh's differences with Don Bradley prevented him from campaigning openly for the Governor.[17] Brown tried to draw attention to Reagan's lack of experience in government. "I'm running against an actor," he said. "I'm not an actor; I just can't act. And he can't govern."[18] Combatting Reagan's reference to himself as a citizen politician, Brown told his listeners to imagine themselves hearing an announcement over the intercom on an airliner: "This is your citizen pilot. I've never flown a plane before, but don't worry. I've always had a deep interest in aviation."[19]

By the day of the general election, Brown was hopelessly behind. Attracting hundreds of thousands of Democratic voters, Reagan won the governorship by a landslide. Sam Yorty wasted no time in scurrying over to the Reagan victory celebration at the Ambassador Hotel in Los Angeles to congratulate the new citizen governor-elect, and later sat glowingly at Reagan's side at a victory breakfast.[20] Sam had once again been a shadowy factor in a Republican victory in California. State Democrats hoped he would return to Los Angeles politics.

Mayor Sam seemed to maintain his interest in state and national affairs, however. As late as 1967 he was still grumbling about the governorship. "If President Johnson had heeded my request that he appoint Pat Brown to something, I would be Governor of California today, not Ronald Reagan," said the Little Giant.[21] This was merely one of a series of Yorty-centered pronouncements and rumors that flitted about in the years between the Brown race in 1966 and the mayoralty contest three years later. "Somebody in Washington" had talked to him about heading a California delegation pledged to LBJ in 1968, Sam said.[22] More surprising still was a widespread rumor allegedly originating from Eleanor Chambers' office: Sam Yorty would replace Hubert Humphrey as Johnson's running mate.[23] The post was thought by many people to be perfect for Sam—no real duties or power, lots of speeches, and best of all, virtually unlimited worldwide travel. But, alas, it was only a rumor. Sam had been rumored as a vice-presidential choice as long ago as 1952, when some party luminaries had wanted a youngish running mate for Stevenson to match Ike's boyish Californian. But the youth vote was not so sought after in those days, and Sam stayed in Congress.

The closest Yorty actually came to running for office in 1968 was in the race to unseat U. S. Senator Tom Kuchel. The Senate seemed to be right for Sam, who had begun to speak out increasingly about international relations and less often about Los Angeles' problems. Few students of California politics believed Yorty could resist another battle with Kuchel. And, as things turned out, this race would have been Sam's best chance to make a successful splash in national politics. On the Democratic side, the main contender with Yorty was Alan Cranston, liberal former state Controller and ex-president of the California Democratic Council. Cranston had been defeated in statewide elections two straight times (U. S. Senate in 1964 and Controller two years later). Yorty had more than a fighting chance against Cranston.

The moderate Kuchel was practically a shoe-in if he could get past the Republican primary—he had been raking in conservative Democratic votes for years. But it turned out that Kuchel was derailed at the primary by ultra-conservative Max Rafferty. Rafferty, who was State Superintendent of Public Instruction, leaned so far to the right on the political spectrum that Cranston was able to waltz to Washington in spite of Nixon's presidential victory. Yorty has probably regretted his decision to stay out of the U. S. Senate race, initially because of the ease of Cranston's victory, and later because of Cranston's liberal stands on various issues.

Ironically, Yorty seems to have discarded his liking for the U. S. Senate (he had already sought election to it three times) because it no longer seemed prestigious enough for him. "I'd just be one of 100 Senators, and a junior one at that," he explained. "Right now I'm making decisions. I'm Mayor of the nation's third largest city. . . . I'm where the action is."[24] But he always maintained he could have won, on one occasion saying, "I'm the only one with a good chance, even people on the national scene feel that way."[25] In March, 1968, when he officially announced that he was out of the running for the senatorship, Sam said:

> I want to speak out for America. I want to tell the truth about the peril of this country. And I think as Mayor of the City of Los Angeles I can do it better than I can do it as a candidate for the United States Senate.[26]

So the closest Sam got at that time to the national political scene was by proxy— one of his clichés made it to the 1968 Chicago Democratic National Convention. In attacking the Humphrey forces on the convention floor, California delegate Carmen Warschaw borrowed some old Yorty lingo, drolly announcing to the entire assemblage, "This convention is wired, stacked, rigged and packed."[27]

Yorty rested from the political wars, conserving his energy and support for 1969. The next campaign would be a fight for his political life. The mayoralty race of 1969 would be the subject of as much nationwide scrutiny as any municipal campaign in California history. It would almost be the undoing of the Little Giant.

20
THE ISSUE OF RACE

By the time of the filing deadline for the 1969 Los Angeles municipal election, 13 candidates had leaped at the opportunity to unseat Mayor Sam, who seemed to be vulnerable. He was running for an unusual (but not unprecedented) third term, and his second four years in office had been marred by civil strife and rocked by scandals. The race for Mayor in 1969 appeared to be much more of a fight than the Yorty landslide four years earlier.

Three major threats to Yorty's job emerged from the list of challengers: Alphonso Bell, Baxter Ward, and Thomas Bradley. Eileen Anderson, a miniskirted gadfly whose platform consisted solely of a novel approach to air pollution control, was a fourth candidate. If elected, Ms. Andreson would dig a large round hole in the San Gabriel Mountains east of the city, insert a giant exhaust fan, and proceed to suck out all the smog from the Los Angeles basin. The hole has never been dug, and Ms. Andreson finished sixth in the primary election.

Congressman Alphonso Bell represented the 28th congressional district, which stretched for miles along the Pacific coast of Los Angeles County. The scion of a wealthy oil family and possessor of a large personal fortune, he was known in Congress as a moderate, sometimes liberal Republican.

Baxter Ward was a strange, almost eccentric political

figure—occasionally liberal, more often conservative—who possessed a certain populist charisma. A news broadcaster by trade, Ward seemed to ad lib portions of many of his broadcasts, once in a while replacing a news segment with a film of a fashion show. The dominant characteristics of Baxter Ward as a politician were his vocal demands for lower taxes, his muckraking, and his insistence upon abso-lute purity in government; so that he would have to make no promises, he refused to accept campaign contributions in any amount.

Tom Bradley was the candidate with the strongest or-ganization in the primary race. Born in Texas, he had mi-grated to California in the 1920's, settling in Los Angeles. In 1940 he had joined the Los Angeles Police Department and had served as a police officer for 21 years. At night he had studied law, graduating from Southwestern University in 1956. Seven years later, with Sam Yorty's endorsement, Bradley had run for City Council, and had won handily in a largely Black district.[1] He was one of three Black men elected to the Council in that year, the first of their race to attain that distinction after over a century of Los Angeles' existence as an American city.

During the primary campaign, Mayor Yorty seemed un-aware that he was in deep political jeopardy. He evidently expected the many challengers to burn each other out and therefore campaigned very little, depending on dozens of billboards that proclaimed him as "America's Greatest Mayor."[2] But a survey of voters taken in February, 1969, two months before the primary, clearly showed that Mayor Sam had managed to alienate a large number of his con-stituents. Almost one-third of the respondents to this sur-vey indicated that they would not vote for Yorty "under any circumstances." In the same sample, only about 4 percent expressed similar feelings about Tom Bradley.[3]

During the primary campaign, Bradley made sure that

voters knew he was a Democrat and stressed the issues of poor leadership and corruption under Yorty. Not a Black militant by any stretch of the imagination, Bradley was a cool, well organized speaker who held moderate views. "I believe the way you change the system is from the inside. Separatism won't work," he said.[4] Bradley openly courted Black votes, citing a purported change of heart on Yorty's part. "Yorty used to be known as a man who would not tolerate any kind of racial slur," Bradley had once observed. "He'd walk out of a party if they started telling anti-Negro jokes. But then came the Watts riots. . . ."[5]

Baxter Ward spent only about $8,000 in the primary race, and his chances were greatly diminished by his incapability to compete with the publicity being churned out by others. Ward was also hurt when Yorty campaigners publicized the fact that Ward's wife was the daughter of a deceased underworld mobster.[6]

In contrast to Ward, Alphonso Bell outspent all candidates in the primary, putting out over a half-million dollars and utilizing an extensive schedule of television spot advertisements. But he was unable to counteract the disadvantage of having been away in Washington for a number of years; his absence indicated to some a relative unfamiliarity with municipal problems. Furthermore, much of Bell's congressional district was outside the city of Los Angeles. His main strategy—to attract Republican votes—failed because of Yorty's ability to attract Republicans. Ward also siphoned off many San Fernando Valley Republicans from Bell.

Bell finished fourth in the primary election, but the big story was Tom Bradley's shattering conquest of Mayor Yorty. Bradley did not come close to the necessary 50 percent to win the election outright, but he outdrew Yorty by more than 100,000 votes. And almost three-fourths of the electorate voted against the Little Giant:[7]

Bradley	298,336	41.8%
Yorty	186,174	26.1
Ward	118,259	16.6
Bell	100,896	14.2
Others (10)	9,689	1.3

Yorty had run a bland primary campaign, but the lopsided result jolted him out of his complacency. On the night of the primary election, as the Bradley lead was piling up, Sam hinted that things were about to heat up, saying, "I haven't let loose on him yet."[8] Later he accused Bradley of running a racist campaign, implying that it was somehow racist for a Black candidate to be popular in highly Black precincts. Still more incongruous, Yorty insisted that Bradley, after more than 30 years with the city government, including 21 years as a police officer, was "anti-police."[9] Sam also bitterly chastised Bradley for openly courting Democratic votes, reminding, "I happen to be a Democrat, too. I have been for years!"[10]

What had been a loosely organized, directionless Yorty campaign changed into a finely tuned, well-oiled machine shortly after the primary. Reflecting Yorty's tacit support for Ronald Reagan three years before, Sam received the services of two of the Governor's closest financial angels, Henry Salvatori and Preston Hotchkis. After the primary the leadership of Eleanor Chambers was greatly augmented with the advice and direction of Salvatori, Hotchkis, and Haig Kehaiyan. Yorty may have believed himself to have been a "Democrat for years," but Salvatori, Hotchkis, and Kehaiyan were all prominent conservative Republicans.[11]

Haig Kehaiyan was fresh from successfully managing the 1968 congressional campaign of Barry Goldwater, Jr., and consequently was an expert campaigner in the San Fernando Valley, which contained much of Goldwater's district. On Yorty's behalf, Kehaiyan organized a crack corps of canvassers, made up largely of men and women working

in their own neighborhoods, where they were well known.[12]
It was of the utmost importance for Yorty to have a strong
effort in the valley, for he needed to offset obvious Bradley
strength in other areas of the city.

A major component of the Yorty campaign against Bradley centered on the police department. Ever since the Watts
riots, Tom Bradley had strongly believed in the need for
community review boards to investigate claims of police
brutality. Tom Reddin, Los Angeles' politically moderate
police chief, protective of the autonomy and professionalism
of his department, was adamantly opposed to review boards.
Yorty seized this issue, continued to portray Bradley, the
ex-cop, as "anti-police," and openly suggested that a victory
by Bradley might result in mass resignations from the police
department.[13] Yorty asked voters to envision the city in
mortal chaos, suggesting that they ask individual policemen
whom they preferred as Mayor.

At the peak of the campaigning, Chief Reddin resigned
from the force to accept a six-figure salary as anchorman for
KTLA television news. Although Reddin insisted that he
had resigned so that he could speak out more strongly about
urban problems, Yorty had a different interpretation for
the move. Sam used Reddin's resignation as police chief to
underline the "anti-police" issue, smugly claiming that it
"does dramatize the fact that there are over 1,300 men in
the police department who can retire today, if they want
to."[14] He also declined to propose a replacement for Reddin, saying that Bradley's "extremist-militant" backers
would only remove a Yorty choice if Bradley won.[15]

Almost as ludicrous as Yorty's "anti-police" charges was
Sam's attempt to portray Tom Bradley as a Black militant.
Yorty appeared night after night on television to attack
Bradley's backers. More than once, Yorty said, "This ex-
tremist group put up a Black man for the purpose of polar-
izing the community." When asked to specify which "ex-

tremist group" he meant, Sam replied, "This whole bunch
—the SDS [Students for a Democratic Society], the Black
militants, the gang behind Bradley."[16]

Yorty newspaper advertisements brazenly catered to the
subconscious fears of some white voters. "Will Your Family
Be Safe?" asked one ad.[17] "Will Your City Be Safe With
This Man?" railed another.[18] Billboards warned omin-
ously, "We need Yorty now—more than ever!"[19] A photograph of Tom Bradley was prominently displayed in most
Yorty campaign materials and advertisements; Sam wanted
to make sure that whites were made universally aware of
Bradley's blackness.

There were at least two examples of even more under-
handed fear tactics employed by anti-Bradley campaigners.
White neighborhoods were mysteriously littered with
pamphlets bearing Bradley's likeness, urging, "Make Los
Angeles a Black city!"[20] In addition, pasted on walls, curbs,
and street signs were spurious bumper stickers connecting
Bradley with militant Black groups.[21] "Bradley Power,"
screamed the stickers, and they displayed an upraised Black
fist, a well known Black Power symbol.

These tactics disenchanted some potential Yorty voters
who were knowledgeable enough to realize that Bradley was
not a militant—voters who knew that radical Blacks considered Bradley, charitably speaking, to be far too moderate. At one point in the campaign, Republican Alphonso
Bell could no longer stomach the open invitations Yorty
workers were making to the baser fears of white voters.
Terming Yorty a "ruthless character assassin," Bell accused
him of running "the dirtiest, most vicious election campaign
in the modern history of the city."[22] Bell then pleaded with
his backers to vote for Tom Bradley.

Roughly 10 percent of the Los Angeles electorate is Jewish, and Sam Yorty did not neglect this segment of the city.
In the 1965 mayoralty election, typical Jewish precincts

had supported Jimmy Roosevelt by tremendous majorities —often more than 80 percent. Yorty and his advisors realized that these votes were vital to any stop-Bradley effort. They seized on Bradley's blackness as a tool to attract Jewish votes to Yorty. Pamphlets were distributed in lower-middle class Jewish neighborhoods decrying Black anti-semitism in the East which had been dramatized by the Ocean Hill-Brownsville school dispute in New York City.[23] The obvious purpose of this technique was to link Tom Bradley with Eastern Negro anti-semitism. A small group of conservative rabbis endorsed Yorty, indirectly lending some legitimization to the anti-semitism implications.

Bradley, whose campaign manager, Maury Weiner, was Jewish, made a strong speech condemning anti-semitism, and a large number of moderate and liberal rabbis endorsed the Black councilman. Max Mont, one of Yorty's Jewish appointees, resigned his city post in protest, citing "false charges of anti-semitism emanating from the Yorty campaign."[24] But Yorty continued his tactics, also courting Jewish votes by reminding Jews that he had made Los Angeles a "sister city" with Eilat, Israel.

Yorty campaign strategists made a strong appeal for Chicano votes against Bradley. Although superficial observations may suggest that Blacks and Chicanos have much in common politically, for a variety of reasons this common interest is not always reflected at the polls. Yorty's "anti-police" characterization of Bradley scored heavily in Mexican-American districts of the city. Mexico City was also a Los Angeles "sister city," reminded Sam, and he proudly displayed the Mexican flag on Cinco de Mayo. Cesar Chavez's strong endorsement of Bradley and Bradley's promise to fight for Chicano representation on the City Council failed to reduce the ethnic campaigning of "Amigo Sam."[25]

Despite the intensity of the various Yorty attacks, the Bradley campaign should have done far better than it did.

But a major stumbling block affecting the smoothness of the Bradley bandwagon stemmed from the great diversity of the Black councilman's backers. There were ideological disputes between political liberals and moderates, as well as disagreements between Bradley's idealistic and pragmatic supporters. Remnants of the Robert Kennedy and Eugene McCarthy campaigns of 1968 had difficulty working hand in hand. Some advisors wanted Bradley to become more aggressive, to speak out more, to attack Yorty on his own terms. Others insisted that he remain calm, ignoring Yorty's jibes, refusing to debate with the Mayor.

The perils of pollsmanship, much a part of the national political arena, influenced Los Angeles municipal politics for the first time in 1969. And the polls worked against Tom Bradley in two ways. First, they cast him as the favorite. The Muchmore and Field polls claimed all along that Bradley held a substantial lead over the Little Giant. These continuous reassurances may have created a certain complacency among Bradley backers. Near the end of the race, a KNXT poll declared that Bradley's margin was 43 percent to 38 percent, with the rest of the respondents undecided. This not only created a sense of momentum for the Yorty forces (when compared with Bradley's much greater margin at the primary), but also many analysts feel that the abnormally high turnout, which worked in Yorty's favor, could be directly traced to this last-minute KNXT poll showing that Bradley was still ahead, but that Yorty could come from behind.[26]

A painful thorn in Tom Bradley's side as he tried to evict Sam Yorty from the "corner pocket" of City Hall involved a Bradley campaign worker. Don Rothenberg, a coordinator under Bradley's manager Maury Weiner, had once been a member of the Communist party.[27] He had quit the party, however, in 1956. Yorty campaigners unearthed evidence of Rothenberg's former membership, and it immediately became citywide news. Bradley at first expressed surprise at the revelation and ultimately refused to fire his aide, stating "He has paid for his mistake."[28] This was widely regarded as a rational and humanitarian move, but it allowed Yorty to use his favorite campaign rhetoric—communist baiting. In effect, Bradley would have been hurt regardless of his decision about Rothenberg. If he dismissed the former communist, he was admitting his mistake. If he kept Rothenberg on, he was open to the Yorty "communist backing" charges.

But by far the most profound misdirection of the Bradley effort revolved around Bradley's choice of issues. As the campaign wore on, Tom Bradley talked incessantly about lack of leadership in city government, corruption in Yorty commissions, the "uglification of Los Angeles," and pollution. According to an impartial survey conducted during the campaign, these were not the important issues as seen by the voters in Los Angeles. The overriding concerns, said the survey, involved crime in the streets and school-related problems, such as busing and vandalism.[29] The Yorty campaign was stressing the "right" issues, even though Yorty had been Mayor for eight years and could easily be held responsible for some of the voter dissatisfaction. But Bradley failed to counterattack Yorty's law-and-order exhortations.

In what was interpreted as a major upset, Sam Yorty came from the runnerup position in the primary, and riding to advantage a wave of fear, prejudice, and reaction, defeated his challenger in the runoff contest. In Jewish areas, which had gone strongly for Hubert Humphrey in 1968, Yorty and Bradley ran neck and neck, with Bradley doing best among wealthy Jews, and Yorty gaining ground in poorer Jewish areas.[30] In Mexican-American sections of the city, where Humphrey had easily outdrawn Richard Nixon, Yorty garnered well over 50 percent of the vote. The final totals showed that while Tom Bradley had not greatly increased his percentage since the primary, the Little Giant, through his multisided aggressive campaign, had more than doubled his primary vote:[31]

Yorty	449,572	53.3%
Bradley	394,364	46.7

Liberals in Los Angeles clucked at length about the seeming success of Yorty's encouragement of fear. The real source of Yorty's strength, however, lay not in his own campaign verbiage, but in Bradley's decision not to stress law-and-order, which could have been one of his strong points. And the background of current events at the time of the Bradley-Yorty race was also a factor. In Gary, Indiana, recently elected Black Mayor Richard Hatcher was plagued by recurrent outbreaks of racial violence. In Ithaca, New York, Black students brandishing rifles and Pancho Villa-type bandoliers occupied buildings at Cornell University. In Oregon, dynamiters struck at a bank and a church. As close as Berkeley, mobs of demonstrators battled against police and clouds of tear gas. In nearby San Fernando, hundreds of minority high school students fought with police. And in Los Angeles, war protesters burned draft records and UCLA students demonstrated on campus and in the streets.

Surrounded by this milieu of violent protest and uprising, and reminded of the turmoil each night on television news programs, many Los Angeles voters were susceptible to law-and-order rhetoric. Next to the bombing of a bank, Sam Yorty's prolific vacations and the charges of iniquities by some of his commissioners seemed pale in comparison. Yorty alone did not defeat Bradley. Militancy elsewhere and reactions to it locally were also important.

In the aftermath of his defeat, Tom Bradley reflected on the many lessons of the 1969 contest. Indeed he had done exceptionally well with white voters, which contrasted with the experience of Black candidates in Cleveland and Detroit in the same year.[32] Bradley received more than a quarter-million white votes, more than one-third of the total, despite the disjointedness and misfortune of his campaign strategy and tactics. In his analysis, he said:

> Relatively speaking, it was a great accomplishment. . . . We've created an attitude. People will accept a Black man running for high office now as a regular thing. . . . We've been disappointed in the Black community before, on many occasions. . . . It's just going to mean we're going to have to work even harder. . . .[33]

Sam Yorty was almost conciliatory after his third-term victory, saying that Bradley was not a bad man, merely a naive one, who had been badly fooled by communists and other extremists. Robert Welch of the John Birch Society announced that Bradley's defeat was the most important setback for the communists in 50 years.[34] A third observer was not so happy. Although the Little Giant had cast him as virtually a deathbed candidate eight years earlier, Norris Poulson was still going strong. "The voters," said the former Mayor, "have approved corruption in government and racism in the election. The city now has an awful black eye."[35]

21
TRY, TRY AGAIN

In January, 1970, the peripatetic Mayor of Los Angeles visited Washington, D. C., to confer with federal officials about urban affairs. He was also there to discuss the progress of the Vietnam war with Army Chief of Staff William C. Westmoreland. At a breakfast with reporters Mayor Sam revealed to the world many of his opinions on far-reaching subjects such as war, peace, and the Yorty political plans.

Sam termed "possible but very remote" the chances of his running for Attorney General of California and also debunked rumors that he would enter the Democratic primary for a United States senatorship. "I don't want to come back [to Washington] and yak around. The idea of all that yakking around does not appeal to me," said the Little Giant.[1] To many listeners, the image of Yorty as a person who did not like to speak was more than a little humorous. Yorty then went on to describe George Murphy, his potential opponent for the senatorship, as a "popular guy." Sam continued, "Everybody likes Murf, you know. . . . He gets lots of applause at meetings."[2]

Yorty was then asked about the chances of his running for the presidency in 1972 (one of the few posts he had never sought). Although he referred to himself as a "200 million-to-one shot," Sam admitted that "There have been times I wish I had been President."[3] At any rate, the Little Giant had plenty of time to ponder his future plans. In a few months he would reveal that his next outing would be a reprise of his 1966 quest for the governorship.

Political observers in California seriously doubted whether Sam ever believed he could win the contest for Governor in 1970. Incumbent Ronald Reagan was seen as virtually unbeatable, and Jess Unruh had waited for the appropriate time before making his first statewide move and thus had the inside track in the race to test Reagan. Also, a poll taken in February, 1970, showed that Yorty was in third place, behind Unruh and Pat Brown, among possible Democratic candidates for Governor.[4] Reagan himself was expected to have no opposition for the Republican nomination.

Two further problems hindered a possible Yorty candidacy in 1970. First, Yorty and Unruh had been allies in the past. Jess had indirectly supported Sam in the 1965 mayoralty race. Both men had considerable experience battling with the "main line" Democratic organization in California, and as late as 1968 Yorty had spoken favorably about the Assembly speaker.[5] Although Unruh had supported Tom Bradley for Mayor in 1969, he and Yorty were not yet outright political enemies. Furthermore, to defeat Unruh in the primary, Yorty would need to outdraw him among "regular" Democrats. This was seen as unlikely, because Yorty's past antagonisms had burned far more bridges to party leaders than Unruh's disagreements.

The second barrier to Yorty's success in 1970 could be attributed to a change in the makeup of the Mayor's political backing. Martin Pollard, one of the most influential men in the campaigns of Republican Norris Poulson, by 1970 had become an important financial contributor to Yorty. Also, Henry Salvatori, who with conservative automobile dealer Holmes Tuttle stood out in the original cast of Ronald Reagan's campaign, had emerged in 1969 as the director of Sam's mayoralty struggle. In short, a considerable portion of Democrat Yorty's support came from conservative Republicans. It seemed doubtful that these forces would seriously encourage Yorty to run against their star, Ronald Reagan.

Yorty began to eliminate the suspense when he scheduled a $100-a-plate testimonial dineer at the Hollywood Palladium in March, 1970. The tickets to the affair contained a message that was aimed at placating Yorty's Republican backers who did not wish to see their contributions work against Reagan. "Funds netted from the dinner," read the tickets, "will be earmarked for purposes other than campaigns . . . [such as] voter education, entertainment of distinguished visitors, travel expenses, among others."[6]

Five days later, on March 17, Sam Yorty officially announced his candidacy for the governorship. Ronald Reagan expressed his surprise, "[Yorty] was so recently re-elected [as Mayor] that I thought he would fulfill his contract with the people of Los Angeles."[7] But the former actor said that he was not worried about Yorty—he was a problem for the Democrats, not the Republicans. Reagan later added that he intended to campaign "about the issues" and hoped his opponents would do the same.

Yorty's strongest verbal attacks during the primary campaign were aimed at Reagan rather than Unruh. Characterizing Reagan as a political "amateur," Yorty maintained, "A competent Governor should not be dependent upon advisors and speech writers for decisions and statements of great importance to our people."[8] He termed his Republican opponent an "apprentice Governor" who was too emotional and also decried what he called Reagan's "lack of administrative ability."[9]

Another major facet of the Yorty campaign revolved around economics. Sam contended that Reagan had been swept into office by a great wave of voter demands for efficiency in state fiscal affairs and that Reagan had promised tax relief. Instead, said the Little Giant, Reagan had delivered "the largest state tax increase in our history."[10] He also accused the Governor of holding back his approval of state income tax withholding until he was sure it would be politically popular, thus costing the state millions in lost revenue. Realizing that high property taxes were vying closely with crime as major sources of citizen dissatisfaction in California, Sam struck out at Reagan's performance on school finance. He pointed out that the state sales tax had been sold years before to the voters with the promise that the state would pay 50 percent of the cost of school operation. Saying that Reagan had let the voters down, he accused the Governor of holding back funds so that the state now contributed far less than its proper share of the educational burden. Reagan, said Sam, did not understand urban problems.

Yorty did not let up in his onslaughts against Reagan, portraying the Governor as a man who was "all head and no heart."[11] Yorty said that Reagan cared too much about "dollars" and not enough about human needs. He also accused the Republican standard bearer of playing politics with the State Supreme Court. Chief Justice Roger Traynor had retired at the beginning of 1970, and his replacement had not yet been named. Sam claimed that Reagan and his backers had been "dangling the prospective appointment around in the right places" where more financial support might be forthcoming.[12]

But Mayor Sam did not reserve all of his barbs for the incumbent. Jess Unruh was "ruthless," had a "bad image," and could never unite the various divergent factions of the Democratic party, according to the Los Angeles Mayor.[13] Only Yorty, said Sam, could bring the party moderates back into the fold in sufficient numbers to defeat Reagan. When asked how he thought he could unite all of the divergent Democrats, Sam replied, "Even Jesus Christ could not unite all the Democrats in California."[14] In reference to Unruh's portly form during much of the time he had headed the state Assembly, Yorty brought back Unruh's old nickname, "Big Daddy." Later, implying that his extensive travels in foreign countries would make him a better Governor, Yorty criticized Unruh as a man who "knows nothing about foreign policy."[15]

A recurrent theme of the Yorty assaults against Jess Unruh related to the latter's support by the California Democratic Council. Yorty had never forgotten his snubbing by the group in 1956, and he took every opportunity to castigate the organization as left-wing. He said that Unruh was "tarred by the group's liberalism" and predicted that the CDC endorsement would hang around Unruh's neck like an albatross.[16] Sam went all out to combat Unruh for being "too liberal," but when he criticized Reagan he almost never referred to the Governor as "conservative." It could be that Yorty did not want to overdo his portrayal of himself as a Reagan antagonist.

During the primary campaign, Stephen Reinhardt, California Democratic national committeeman, put out an eight-page pamphlet which borrowed stylistically from Sam's 1960 offering about John Kennedy. Entitled "I Cannot Take Yorty," the pamphlet recalled that Yorty consistently charged that his opponents were duped by communists or had left-wing backing. It said that Sam was a wrecker and a destroyer of the Democratic party who worked more for Republicans than for Democrats.

Yorty became irate when he read the "I Cannot Take Yorty" booklet. Reinhardt, he said, was a "stooge for Jess Unruh" and should resign his party post. Sam accused the committeeman of "deliberate lies and distortion" and claimed that Reinhardt "insulted the intelligence of the voters. In a moment of near comic anger, Yorty called attention to Reinhardt's "bloated egotism."[17] Later, when Councilman Marvin Braude suggested that Sam was delaying the announcement of a record city budget for political reasons, the Mayor called Braude a "stooge for Jess Unruh."[18]

As the campaign tapered down to the finish, Yorty grew louder in his condemnation of both opponents. In response to a civil disturbance at Isla Vista, which adjoins the campus of the University of California, Santa Barbara, Yorty criticized Reagan for delaying five hours before calling in the state national guard to restore order. Sam said that he would have called in the guard after "two minutes."[19] He continued to portray Jess Unruh as an ultraliberal, terming him "consistently inconsistent."[20] But Sam was unable to poll the resounding support in 1970 that he had attracted four years before against Pat Brown. Unruh won the Democratic gubernatorial nomination decisively, sending the Little Giant down to his fifth straight losing bid for statewide office:[21]

Unruh	1,602,690	64.0%
Yorty	659,494	26.3
Others (8)	240,674	9.7

Reagan went on to defeat Jess Unruh in the general election, although his margin of victory was markedly smaller than it had been against Brown. Once more Yorty failed to endorse the Democratic nominee. The Yorty total in the 1966 primary had approximated the eventual margin of the Democratic gubernatorial defeat in November. His total in 1970 considerably exceeded the margin in the general election of that year. In each case a strong endorsement by Yorty probably would have narrowed the gap but would not have tipped the scales. A defeated candidate seldom can carry all his supporters over to a former opponent, particularly when they differ considerably in political philosophy.

Turned down once again by the voters of the state, Yorty was temporarily resigned to continuing as Mayor of Los Angeles and to picking up with his tourism. He may not have tired of the "corner pocket," the location of his offices in City Hall, but he had definitely grown weary of knocking at the Governor's mansion. His next campaign would be directed at the White House.

22
IN THE CORNER POCKET, SOMETIMES

Sam Yorty once wryly observed that the power of the Los Angeles Mayor is not commensurate with his responsibility. "Anyone who has ever read beyond the second paragraph of the city charter would be out of his mind to run for Mayor," he said.[1] His statement contains an element of truth, and the charter limitations on his power may well be part of the reason why Mayor Sam has often been moved to leave town on lengthy trips. The Little Giant has earned a reputation for tourism unmatched in its scope and consistency by any other local public official in America. He has been called "Travelling Sam" and the city over which he sometimes presides has been termed the "only city with a foreign policy."[2] Here are some of the foreign trips (usually said to be combined business-pleasure journeys) on which Sam's magic municipal carpet has carried him:

1963	Europe, Mexico
1964	Middle East
1965	Far East, Europe, Mexico
1966	Far East
1967	Europe, Middle East
1969	Mexico
1971	Around the World
1972	Europe, Central Asia

Not included above are his extensive campaign trips for many out-of-city offices since becoming Mayor. In the 1969–

70 fiscal year, the City Council president served as acting Mayor 125 days, including the Saturdays and Sundays when Yorty was out of town. The comparable figure the following year was 86 days.[3]

According to a former Yorty press aide, Sam often becomes irate at any attempts to add up his days absent, once asking if the days he left and the days he returned are included in the totals.[4] He maintains that his foreign trips are necessary to improve Los Angeles' relations with the rest of the world. They help improve the level of world trade enjoyed by the city as well as build up business for the Los Angeles harbor and international airport, claims Sam. In Yorty's arsenal of defense of his globe-trotting record is the Sister City program, the Mayor's pride and joy, which Sam believes to promote better understanding among the citizens of the world. Los Angeles may suffer from charter obsolescence, strangled traffic, and often unbreathable air, but as long as Mayor Sam presides, this city will never be short on civic siblings. The current list of Sister Cities includes Mexico City, Mexico; Tehran, Iran; Bombay, India; Berlin, Germany; Lusaka, Zambia; Bordeaux, France; Eilat, Israel; Pusan, South Korea; Salvador, Brazil; and Nagoya, Japan. Sam often brings home souvenirs of his travels and has been referred to as America's most decorated Mayor. Describing a medal from the Iranian government, he once said proudly, "I guess I'm probably the first Mayor to get a decoration from Iran that's this high!" [5]

Another familiar criticism of Sam Yorty is his inability to maintain harmonious relations with members of the City Council. The running war between Sam and the city's legislative body has involved dozens of specific impasses, from vetoed pay raises and protracted budget disputes to refuse handling and noise control ordinances. The city's chief executive has moved councilmen to speak of him in less than gentle terms. "He wants to be a little Hitler . . . a dictator of the city" is the way the Council president spoke of Sam in 1969.[6] Yorty has also been verbally harsh about Council members, once suggesting that certain councilmen "had their hands on the throat of the city."[7] But by far the longest running conflict between Sam Yorty and the 15-member City Council has revolved around the need for a new charter.

Los Angeles is saddled with a charter that went into effect in 1925 and has since been amended more than 200 times until it consumes about 300 printed pages. It provides for disjointed, quarrelsome administration of the nation's third largest city. In short, the charter is critically inadequate. Los Angeles is a giant of the 1970's trying to live under an antiquated governmental organization. As a result, the city has been forced to blunder along, hamstrung by a document that has been called a "legal spider web," "a monstrosity," and "the worst that any city possesses."[8]

Several major tenets of charter reform have been commonly proposed. One has been to increase and make more direct the authority of the Mayor over city administrative activities so that he can be justifiably held accountable for his charter responsibilities as chief executive. A second has been to take away from most boards and commissions their authority to be department heads by limiting them to advisory and appellate functions or eliminating them completely. A third has been to make departmental general managers, appointed and removed by the Mayor, the heads of departments where the powers of boards and commissions have been reduced. (The second and third recommendations were realized to a limited degree by a charter amendment in 1965.) A fourth proposal has been to relieve the City Council of much of its administrative detail, reduce the number of Council meetings from five a week to one or two a week, and possibly have some councilmen elected at large instead of choosing all of them from districts.[9]

Public administration experts widely support these tenets. Every attempt to implement them in Los Angeles, however, has produced a power struggle between the Mayor, who wants more authority, and the district-oriented, detail-laden City Council, which desires to relinquish few, if any, responsibilities.

The Los Angeles City Charter Commission, appointed by Mayor Yorty, released a 224-page report, including a full draft of a new city charter, in 1969, after three years of study. The draft greatly decreased the overlap between the executive and legislative branches, gave the Mayor the right to remove department heads without Council approval, and called for the establishment of an ombudsman and neighborhood councils.[10] The document encountered strong opposition from councilmen and commissioners, and the Council decided to draft, with the City Attorney's assistance, its own proposed charter.

The Council's product, although an improvement over the existing charter, emasculated most innovative features of the Commission's work, did not give the Mayor the authority to direct administrative affairs, and required his attempts to remove department heads to receive Council sanction. Yorty took a neutral position on this proposed charter, which made it possible for the Department of Water and Power, threatened with the loss of some of its financial autonomy, to wage a well-financed propaganda campaign in opposition. In November, 1970, the proposition was defeated, with the affirmative vote adding up to 46.3 percent.[11]

The Council's charter and administrative code committee, sparked by the persistence of Councilman Edmund Edelman, returned to the task of charter revision, and the Council voted to place the committee's slightly revised document on the May, 1971 ballot. Provisions were eliminated to which the Department of Water and Power (and the Board of Public Works) objected, and the Mayor's authority to administer most city departments and offices was strengthened despite the Council's retention of the right to approve or disapprove dismissals by the Mayor. Sam Yorty endorsed the proposed charter at a news conference and later joined 19 other persons in signing the supporting sample ballot argument. From this point on, however, his efforts in support of the proposal were skimpy indeed. The failure of the charter proposal to give him more complete administrative power may have piqued Sam, thus prompting little exertion by him on its behalf. Also, by the time of this local election, he had already begun organizing his presidential campaign and was giving it most of his attention. Nevertheless, it seems strange that Sam, who had made charter reform one of his principal objectives for most of a decade, would settle for nothing rather than most of a loaf. The charter proposal picked up only one additional percentage point of support. Its "yes" total stretched to 47.4 percent, but this was still substantially short of a majority.[12]

On an occasion in 1966 Sam was moved to comment on the lack of direct power he had in city government when he was under attack in Washington by Senators Robert Kennedy and Abraham Ribicoff. During hearings before a Senate subcommittee, Yorty fended off almost all of the questions fired at him concerning Los Angeles civic problems by denying that he had formal authority to deal with them. Such denials caused Ribicoff to remark that Los Angeles evidently did not "stand for a damn thing."[13] Later in the hearings Yorty was so repulsed by a Kennedy remark about lack of leadership in the city that he replied, "I do not need a lecture from you on how to run my city."[14] Yorty then tried to change the hearing to a discussion of the problems of Harlem. Subsequently Sam called Senator Kennedy a "headstrong, arrogant young man" and said that the hearings were merely a vehicle to "destroy all the friends of President Johnson."[15]

People who displease Mayor Sam often find themselves

in court. He sued the former Mayor, Norris Poulson, and some Poulson aides, for about $4 million in 1961, but he was unable to collect.[16] He also sued the *Los Angeles Times,* its publisher Otis Chandler, and its political cartoonist Paul Conrad for libel, asking for $2 million in damages. Conrad had drawn a picture of Sam about to be assisted into a strait-jacket after announcing his appointment as secretary of defense. The case was thrown out of court.[17] The Mayor has also threatened other lawsuits, once informing the City Council that even it was not immune. Backing up his threat, Yorty sued the Council, trying to gain additional funding for his office, but once again the courts ruled against the indefatigable Little Giant.[18]

As Mayor, Yorty has never forgotten that he is also the chief executive of Hollywood. The lure of a show-business life has never failed to reach Sam Yorty. From his early youth, when he played the banjo and led his own band, to his radio appearances in the 1930's, Sam has often displayed a longing for the spotlight, for a dramatic side of normally undramatic things. This love for attention has shown up in many of his campaigns for public office, in which he appears to enjoy controversy and adversity.

Since his election as Mayor, Sam Yorty has had his own radio show, "Ask Your Mayor." [19] He has also run his own commercially-sponsored television program. "The Sam Yorty Show." On this program, which ran for several months, Yorty interviewed guests ranging from Pierre Salinger to Mamie Van Doren and ex-King Peter of Yugoslavia.[20] He also has been the subject of a 13-minute color motion picture produced for the United States Information Agency.[21] During Sam's appearance as a banjo player on the Johnny Carson "Tonight" show he was such an enthusiastic performer that Carson reportedly had difficulty bringing out the following act.

More recently, Sam Yorty has reentered the field of radio,

serving in two different years as a pinch-hitting disc jockey on a morning radio program. This stint of playing the old songs, personally reading some commercials, and bragging about Los Angeles has drawn considerable comment from the Mayor's friends and foes. A competing disc jockey had the most biting observation about Sam's show. The height of his comedy is assured, offered the competitor, "if he reads the record of his administration."[22] Tom Bradley, Yorty's mayoralty opponent of 1969, merely said of the disc jockey escapade, "That's just too much."[23]

The scent of scandal and corruption has not been absent in the Yorty mayoralty years. Late in his second term in office, five of Yorty's commissioners were indicted for various alleged misdeeds. Four were subsequently convicted, although two of the convictions were later reversed.[24] The fifth commissioner met with a fate found in many television detective show scripts. He was found floating in the Los Angeles harbor, dead of "natural causes."[25]

Yorty has been accused of manipulating commission appointments to make it possible to keep his commissioners in his personal debt. Sometimes, say Yorty critics, the Mayor has allowed a commissioner to keep serving without formal reappointment even though his original five-year term had expired.[26] Yorty is also alleged occasionally to require commissioners to sign undated letters of resignation, which he then purportedly holds, allowing for a timely "resignation" if the appointee displeases him.[27] Yorty denies these charges, however. At one point in his tenure, Yorty suggested that commissioners should serve only a single term, but like his other suggestion about limiting the Mayor to eight years in office, this proposal has been forgotten.

In some instances Yorty appointees have failed to win approval from the City Council (which generally tries to cooperate with the Mayor on appointments). Yorty once proposed retired Admiral Horace Bird for a vacancy on the

City Planning Commission. Concerned citizens began to wonder aloud about how a career in the Navy had prepared the admiral as an authority on city planning, and the proposed appointment fizzled.[28] On another occasion, the Mayor tried unsuccessfully to award a campaign supporter, an ex-policeman, with an appointment to the Board of Public Works.[29]

It is hoped that the case of Angel Goodman, who was appointed to the Mayor's Community Relations Commission early in 1972, does not exemplify the amount of investigation devoted to Yorty's prospective commission appointees. Proudly showing off the signed certificate of appointment received by Ms. Goodman, his "niece," the man who sponsored her for the commission sadly informed the city that she was under age. He then revealed that she was also a toy French poodle. But she had "excellent community relations," insisted the sponsor. Mayor Sam was not non-plussed. She was probably a good dog, he said, refusing to remove her from the commission, but observing that the city now would have to be more careful about animal regulations.[30]

The Sam Yorty side of any mayoral evaluation is replete with glowing reports. In a 48-page picture-filled booklet, published in 1969 and entitled "The Yorty Years," the Little Giant enumerated what he considers to be a multitude of accomplishments. Listed are the elimination of urban unrest, the abolition of discrimination, citizen involvement in government, heavy emphasis on human relations, and urban renewal projects. Also included are the civic center mall, the convention center, and other building projects.[31] Some of these are really aspirations rather than attainments, and some that have been attained were at the time they were proposed (and still are) highly controversial. For instance, the location and appearance of the convention center and whether its operation will require deficit financing for many years have all been strongly argued. Moreover,

the record of the city's departments, which are staffed largely by professional civil servants, should not be attributed to
Yorty, although he lays claim to their attainments. These
departments are mainly self-generating, although sometimes somewhat sluggish.

In the final analysis Yorty's record as Mayor leaves a
strong feeling that something important is missing. Yorty
seems transfixed by the unveiling of statues, the laying of
cornerstones for new construction, the issuance of an endless stream of press releases, the posing for pictures with a
steady procession of people, and the listing of minority appointments. He also seems to be much more interested in
state, national and international affairs than in Los Angeles'
needs. He has taken nearly every opportunity to reach for
other heights, politically, yet insists that he really wants to
be Mayor of Los Angeles.

As many individuals and organizations have pointed out,
the Mayor of Los Angeles may be stifled by the restrictions
of the city charter, but he clearly has the option to serve as
an opinion molder and to provide imaginative leadership
toward resolution of the many complex problems of the city
of Los Angeles and the metropolitan area and region of
which it is an important part. Joseph Alioto, the Mayor of
San Francisco, has said, "There is a certain prestige given to
the Mayor's office which, combined with personality, can
get a job done [despite charter limits]."[32] If a Mayor chooses
instead to cater to petty grievances and obvious political
considerations, a city can only suffer as a result. And which
course has Sam Yorty taken? The answer is well displayed
in his abortive, quixotic fantasy of 1972—the quest for the
White House.

23
YORTY FOR PRESIDENT

The story of Sam Yorty's part in the 1972 presidential race is a confusing mixture of conflicting ideologies, objectives, and strategies. Sam lost big in the contest for the right to confront Richard Nixon, and his defeat will be considered from each of these several viewpoints.

Despite years of speeches by the Little Giant on nearly every imaginable subject from rubbish to warheads, the clearest statement of a Sam Yorty ideology emerged when he tried to win the highest political office in the land. In New Hampshire and Nebraska, no mention had to be made of the long maligned California Democratic Council nor any of the Yorty arch-enemies on the Los Angeles City Council. Sam was able to devote all of his breath to the issues he loved best. The reader hoping for some concrete, meaningful idea of Yorty's solutions for American problems will be disappointed, however. The dominant image of Sam as a national politician was that of a man with many slogans, but few solutions. But when all the various ideological and motivational threads are untwined, a clearer picture of Yorty as a person and as a politician may be revealed.

The first plank of the Yorty platform, one mentioned often during the campaign, dealt with national defense. America must rearm herself, said Sam, and must avoid the stance of a "second-rate power" at all costs. The communist countries were "malevolent," he said, and the only way to deal with them was by means of weapons buildup. Making concessions and trade agreements with Russia and China was dangerous.[1]

Yorty's position on the Vietnam war is most interesting because his main point during the presidential campaign was his professed consistency on that issue. Sam contended he had maintained his position on the war while all the other candidates were changing theirs according to the direction of the political winds. The only way the war would end, said Sam, was if the North Vietnamese "went home." Our objective was an honorable peace, and only when this was achieved and prisoners of war were safe, could American involvement end. Yorty said that he had never believed in "no-win" wars and had always felt that if action was to be taken it should be direct, swift, and uncompromising.[2] But had Sam always held this position?

As a congressman in the 1950's, during the Korean war, an illuminating Yorty debate was precipitated by the controversy between General Douglas MacArthur and President Truman that resulted in the firing of MacArthur. After the intervention of the Chinese communists into that war, the general pressed for bombing Manchuria, blockading the Chinese mainland coast, and using Chinese nationalist troops based on Formosa. Here the general was calling for swift, direct, and uncompromising action, and Truman was, in effect, heading toward a "no-win" war. Sam expressed his respect for the general, and built up his own image in the bargain, saying "When the Philippine Islands were liberated I stood as close to MacArthur as I am to this rostrum."[3] But then Yorty sided with Truman. Representative Charles Halleck of Indiana, taking the present-day Yorty position, attacked Sam on the floor of the House, asking, "If we are not going to fight to win in Korea, then why fight there at all?" Yorty replied: "We cannot, in my humble judgment, get out of Korea by setting off a world wide war. . . ."[4] Yorty clearly understood the need for compromise better in 1951 than he did about 20 years later.

Another plank in the Yorty presidential platform concerned the economy. Yorty pledged to fight inflation, reduce taxes, and cut government spending to a minimum. However, he called for increased expenditures for defense, more governmental support for the aerospace industry (such as a rebirth of the supersonic transport program), federal job guarantees, and provision of federal funds to "beef up" police departments.[5] In reality, this economic plank was composed of pledges to reduce government spending while increasing it at the same time.

Still another Yorty plank related to domestic unrest and violence, which he rightfully believed to be a major problem. Yorty called for stepped up infiltration of "subversive organizations" by government agents.[6] He said that the cry of "McCarthyism" (the Joseph McCarthy variety) must be ignored if the nation was not to be destroyed from within. Sam also called for a vote of confidence for then FBI chief J. Edgar Hoover. Yorty's view of domestic unrest was strikingly reminiscent of the late Los Angeles Police Chief William Parker's comment on police motivation, "We are not interested in why a certain group tends toward crime," said Parker," we are interested in maintaining order."[7]

A letter from Sam to Phillip Zeidman, executive director of the Democratic Platform Committee at the Miami convention, further illustrates Yorty's platform inconsistency. Sam outlined what he felt would be an "ideal Democratic platform." After stressing that this platform should not contain "vote-getting promises for special groups," Sam ignored his own advice, listing several such promises, including opposition to forced busing, secure borders and defense support for Israel, an end to unemployment, and solving the nations' health needs.[8]

As can be seen, Yorty interpreted the issues simplistically.
He claimed to see the nation's problems as separate and distinct, rather than interrelated. But the major issues on
which he chose to concentrate were in reality closely involved with each other. Spending necessary to prop up the
Saigon regime militarily and logistically could only detract
from funding available to bolster national defense. Sam was
equally incomprehensible on domestic policy. After castigating Nixon, McGovern, and Muskie in quick succession
for advocating "spending more and taking less,"[9] he advocated similar expenditures. Had Sam Yorty found mirac-
ulous new ways of providing government benefits at no cost
to the taxpayer?

In short, most politicians habitually present conflicting
campaign statements because voters have high expectations
and low tax tolerance. Most candidates profess highly involved schemes with which they hide or explain away the
conflicts. This is an area in which George McGovern ran
into trouble in 1972; his first welfare proposal, for example,
was actually too complicated for his own good. But Sam
Yorty was at the other extreme. In pushing simple, slogan-
istic campaign verbiage, Sam was offering New Hampshire
and Nebraska voters transparent catch phrases instead of
programs. It turned out to be a bad year for simplicity and
for Sam.

Ideology aside, the Yorty objective in entering the campaign appeared to change with each mortal blow to his like-
lihood of becoming President. At first, possibly he expected
to win the election. Before New Hampshire, Sam Yorty was
nearly invisible in national polls, but so was George Mc-
Govern. Yorty's first objective was to prove himself a viable
candidate, and then to allow his personal magnetism and
the popular appeal of his stance on various campaign issues
to sweep him to victory. The similarity between certain aspects of the McGovern and Yorty campaigns for the nomi-

nation is striking. Both began as token candidates with tiny followings. Both began in New Hampshire, hoping to build backing and momentum and wrest the nomination from Edmund Muskie, the front runner. The difference between the McGovern and Yorty campaigns to be the Democratic nominee is that one worked magnificently and the other was a complete flop.

When Sam lost New Hampshire, he must have abandoned the idea of actually winning the Democratic nomination. He shot his whole quiver at New Hampshire, and it got him nowhere. John Lindsay, another Mayor who foundered early in the 1972 campaign, recognized his defeat and withdrew from the race. But Sam was used to losing—he had lost in seeking elective public office almost as many times as he had won. It was simply against the Yorty grain to give up willingly after merely one defeat. So after New Hampshire Sam did not withdraw; he only retrained his sights. No longer seeking the presidential nomination for himself, he was attempting to redirect the Democratic party to a conservative position.

Yorty's objective in the Nebraska primary was to "wake up the nation" and at least gain some influence at the Miami Beach convention by picking up some delegates. After the debacle in Nebraska, Sam again changed his aim. In California, he wanted to help send a state delegation to Miami Beach that would "stand up for" California and avoid sabotaging the Democratic party with unneeded reforms and "left-wing" candidacies. After the New Hampshire and Nebraska primaries, far less mention was made of "Sam Yorty For President."

The Yorty presidential odyssey began in February, 1971. Sam wrote a 22-page letter to Edmund Muskie that was highly critical of the Maine Senator's position on American withdrawal from Vietnam. Sam did not stop after mailing the letter to Muskie, because the purpose of the missive was not to inform Muskie where Yorty stood on the war. The

purpose was to make the Yorty position known to many
people and to see if there was possible support for a Sam
Yorty presidential campaign. So the Little Giant distributed the letter to about 15,000 daily and weekly newspapers,
newsletters, and television and radio stations. Also sent
copies were President Nixon and his White House staff, the
Nixon cabinet, Vice President Agnew and his staff, all congressmen, senators, governors, members of the California
legislature, mayors of important cities, national labor union
leaders, the American Legion and the Veterans of Foreign
Wars, Republican and Democratic national committeemen,
former Yorty campaign contributors, many Los Angeles political figures, and the Pope. The envelopes carried, in bril-
liant color, the message, "Yorty is Coming!"[10]

Yorty was not really certain he was "coming" until he
held a $100-a-plate dinner in late April, at a Los Angeles
hotel, closely followed by a gathering in Manchester, New
Hampshire, which was reported to be one of the largest political events ever held in that state.[11] In May, Sam made
another visit to Manchester and to Nashua, the Granite
State's second largest city. Nashua's Mayor Dennis Sullivan
referred smillingly to Sam as "the next President."[12] In
June, Yorty visited Florida to test its political waters, but he
found that the conservatives leaned toward Senator Henry
Jackson and Governor George Wallace. Still, Sam refused
to admit that things looked bad for him in Florida. "Jackson
is . . . getting to the top. But there is something going on at
the bottom, I felt it," he said.[13] He also tried to woo Wallace
supporters by opposing the busing of school children for
the achievement of integration, saying "[Our Los Angeles
kids] don't want to get out of Watts. They like Watts."[14]
But a Florida politician said that Sam ranked "fairly well
down the line as far as popularity goes," adding that he remembered Yorty from his appearances on the "Tonight"
show and "Truth or Consequences."

The Yorty for President organization really began to roll

in October, 1971, when Sam Bretzfield, who was handling the overall campaign from Los Angeles, signed Robert Philbrick as campaign manager for New Hampshire. Philbrick was a dynamic young businessman from Milford, New Hampshire, who had worked diligently in Democratic circles in his home state and had been an alternate Humphrey delegate in 1968. He characterized New Hampshire Democrats as conservatives and said that Yorty would "probably" gain the endorsement of the state's largest newspaper, the *Manchester Union Leader.* The endorsement prediction was speedily confirmed.

William Loeb, arch-conservative publisher of the *Union Leader,* the Granite State's only statewide daily paper, referred to himself as a "Teddy Roosevelt Republican" and had a reputation for blatant personal attacks on political figures. An admirer of Senator Joseph McCarthy, Loeb had characterized President Eisenhower as "Dopey Dwight," Margaret Chase Smith as "Moscow Maggie," and Edward Kennedy as "Just Plain Stupid."[15] Loeb had termed Eugene McCarthy a "skunk" for winning 42 percent of the vote in the 1968 Democratic primary.[16] But Loeb liked Sam Yorty, and in mid-October, the publisher ran a front-page editorial endorsing Yorty "without reservation" as the best Democratic candidate for the presidency.[17] On the Republican side, Loeb preferred Congressman John Ashbrook of Ohio, an ultraconservative who was attacking Nixon. Though Loeb was a Republican, he was said to have more influence among Democrats because of the high concentration of members of that party in Manchester and its surrounding counties.

In October, Yorty made two campaign trips, attending a gala Democratic gathering in Coronado, California, and also making still another eastern trip, accompanied by Bretzfield. On his return, Sam told reporters at the airport, "We are moving so fast in New Hampshire, we can't keep these people waiting!" [18] On November 12, Sam at last officially announced his candidacy for President of the United States, and a week later he was again in New England to start his campaign in earnest. Also in November, Yorty aide Joe Quinn sent letters to 88,000 Californians, asking for volunteers for the Yorty state delegation to the 1972 Democratic national convention. And the head of the advertising agency handling Sam's New Hampshire campaign released the results of a poll that claimed Yorty was in the lead, ahead of Muskie and McGovern. [19]

Between November, 1971, and March of the next year the Little Giant made several additional campaign trips to New Hampshire, sometimes campaigning on weekends, other times spending a week at a time in the hustings. His mode of conveyance was a self-contained camper vehicle, 33-feet long, which Sam named the "Yortymobile." It had a loud public address system that played marches like "The Caissons Go Rolling Along" and was equipped with a platform at the rear that was reminiscent of old fashioned campaign trains. The Yortymobile could even emit old time train whistles. At various stops along the campaign trail, Sam would deliver his speeches from the rear platform in the style of a politician of the earlier 1900's.

In terms of strategy, Sam and his advisers tried to take a stance that would set him apart from the other New Hampshire contenders—Vance Hartke, Muskie, McGovern, even Richard Nixon. Remembering that the state's Democratic voters had chosen a conservative nominee for Governor in 1970, Sam felt that a strong conservative element existed. At one point it appeared that Henry Jackson would challenge and dilute Sam's appeal to this bloc, but to Yorty's relief Jackson decided against entering the New Hampshire primary. Sam staked his claim to the conservative, hawkish Democrats and risked his presidential hopes on their support, which he felt might be strong.

The Yorty campaign gave considerable attention to the large numbers of Catholics and Americans of French ancestry in the state. As a result of extensive coverage by Loeb's *Union Leader,* Yorty appeared in the news almost every day. Pictures were published of Sam visiting with James Francis Cardinal McIntyre, who had recently resigned as Archbishop of Los Angeles.[20] Repeated references were made to the fact that Sam's mother was an Irish-born Catholic. Sam and his wife, Betts, were pictured with uniformed students as the two of them spoke at parochial schools, and they were also photographed with smiling nuns.[21] Sam spoke out in favor of school prayer and urged federal aid for parochial schools.

Yorty campaigners further stressed Sam's many visits to France. Pictures were run in the *Union Leader* that showed Sam being awarded a medal, Knight of the Legion of Honor, by French Prime Minister Jacques Chaban-Delmas.[22] And inevitably, mention was made of Los Angeles' Sister City, Bordeaux, France. The *Union Leader* also featured a front-page photograph of Sam's presentation of the key to the city of Los Angeles to French Consul-General Jean Francis Roux.[23]

As the primary election in New Hampshire approached, Sam continued his full-scale assults on the President and his Democratic would-be challengers. Harping continuously at what he called Nixon's "Disneyland" economic policies, he said that Nixon had pulled one of the most complete reverses in American history by promising in 1968 to reduce the national budget deficit; according to Sam, Nixon had instead increased the deficit during his administraton to "almost $100 billion."[24] Sam compared this figure with Harry Truman's 8-year deficit of less than $2 billion. Yorty also criticized Nixon's friendly overtures to Russia and China, especially singling out the President's trip to Peking. Sam argued that any meeting between representatives of

China and the United States should have taken place on neutral ground.[25]

Yorty strongly attacked three of his Democratic opponents—Muskie, McGovern, and Hartke—referring to them as the "Fulbright triplets,"[26] an allusion to Senator J. William Fulbright's anti-administration foreign policy views. He criticized the trio for the defeat of the supersonic transport program (SST), their erosion of "patriotic principles" from the Democratic party, and their "weak" position on the Vietnam war. He said that these candidates were inconsistent and ambitious and that their votes against the SST program had cost many electronics job opportunities in the Granite State. According to the Little Giant, the three senators advocated defeat in Southeast Asia as well as deficit spending at home. Yorty even spoke harshly of fellow hawk Henry Jackson, who had not entered the New Hampshire primary. Sam pointed out that Jackson could not be a "real" hawk because he had voted for the Cooper–Church amendment, which sought to restrict Nixon in dealing with the communist threat in Vietnam.[27]

With about three weeks left in the New Hampshire primary campaign, William Loeb appeared in an interview on NBC News. He appeared confident of Yorty's chances of winning in his state, saying that Sam's relations with New Hampshire Democrats were "very good," and characterizing Yorty's campaign tactics as "person to person" electioneering. NBC newsmen speculated that the *Union Leader* endorsement by itself could be expected to bring any candidate about 15 to 20 percent of the vote, and Loeb did not disagree with their statement.[28]

While devoting gratuitous coverage to the Yorty campaign, Loeb saved his strongest attacks for Muskie, for whom he seemed to have a special dislike. When Muskie was alleged to have made disparaging remarks about French Americans, Loeb saw to it that the topic came up repeatedly

in his pages. He ran an "exposé" of alleged Muskie dealings
with a Maine sugar milling company which, according to
Loeb, made the Senator's ecology image seem hypocritical.
When *Womens Wear Daily,* followed by *Newsweek,* published articles suggesting that Muskie's wife Jane was fond
of salty language and alcohol, Loeb gave front-page treatment to the story, including a full reprint of the *Newsweek*
article. Muskie responded with an emotional outburst
against Loeb. Sam Yorty then said that such emotionalism
was uncalled for, telling his listeners that the *Los Angeles
Times* publisher, Otis Chandler, constantly attacked him,
but "I'm not going down and scream" at him in response.[29]
(Actually, Sam is more inclined toward lawsuits!)

Two days before the New Hampshire primary it was apparent that Yorty needed a miracle to come up with a respectable showing in the Granite State. A *Boston Globe*
poll showed that Yorty's popularity had actually declined
since he had begun to campaign extensively, and he would
be fortunate to garner as much as 10 percent of the Democratic vote.[30] However, the Little Giant insisted he was
confident, citing a poll taken by his own organization that
claimed Sam would receive about 36 percent.[31] When the
election was over, the *Boston Globe* poll proved more accurate. Sam had finished a distant third behind two members of his so-called "Fulbright faction," as Muskie outdrew
McGovern by a smaller than expected margin:[32]

Muskie	41,235	46.4%
McGovern	33,007	37.1
Yorty	5,401	6.1
Mills	3,563	4.0
Others (10)	5,648	6.4

After the election, Loeb attributed Yorty's poor showing
to a "peace trend" in New Hampshire, while Sam's campaign manager Robert Philbrick claimed that the people in
the state simply did not get his candidate's message. Yorty

himself maintained that he was victimized by the last minute write-in candidacy of national House Ways and Means
Committee chairman Wilbur Mills. He further claimed
that lobbyists and others seeking favors from Mills had
sought to buy the New Hampshire primary for the Arkansas
congressman. Sam estimated that the Mills campaign had
cost "$30 to $50 per vote."[33] Yorty's logic here is at best
muddy, because even given all of Mills' votes, Sam still
would have lost to the "Fulbright faction" by more than
eight-to-one.

Yorty's dismal performance in New Hampshire raised a
serious question about the importance of the extensive favorable coverage and editorial endorsement of the *Union
Leader* as a factor in that state's elections. Although the
newspaper had a statewide circulation of more than 60,000,
it could not stimulate significant support for Sam. In the
eyes of many observers, Loeb's newspaper support did not
aid Yorty but, strangely enough, worked for George Mc-
Govern. Loeb had called Muskie "Flip-Flop" and a "known
hypocrite," and had described the Maine Senator as having
a temper as obvious as "a worm crawling out of a bad ap-
ple."[34] Analysts felt that Loeb's unending personal attacks
on Muskie swung many votes from him to McGovern, despite the *Union Leader*'s bitter castigation of both men for
their ideological views. The *Union Leader*'s Republican
endorsee, John Ashbrook, also fared poorly, finishing third
behind Nixon and peace candidate Paul McCloskey.

Sam did not give up the presidential ship after it ran
aground in New Hampshire. He was on the ballot against
his will in Florida and had gone to court to try to have
his name removed. Sam felt that conservative votes were
wrapped up in that state by George Wallace and Henry
Jackson, and he did not wish to be humiliated by a minus-
cule showing. Like several other states, Florida lists all declared presidential candidates on its ballot, removing them

only if they agree to sign an affidavit declaring that they are not candidates. Yorty would not sign this declaration, but said in his suit that Florida was attempting to damage his political reputation. The *Los Angeles Times* was unable to resist a humorous retort at this Yorty claim. The *Times* said that if Yorty wished to sue to protect his reputation, he would be well advised to file suit in small claims court.[35]

After enduring the cold winds of the Granite State, the Yortymobile next invaded Sam's birthplace, Nebraska. Here in the heartland of America Sam hoped to prove that the bulk of the Democratic party lay at the center, not the left of the political road. Referring to himself as a Truman Democrat, Sam called for Nebraska voters to reaffirm moderate, restrained, sensible views, pointing out that only a moderate candidate (such as Sam) could hope to defeat Nixon in November. Sam continued his onslaughts on the Nixon economic policies, throwing a new farm twist into his condemnations of the President. Nixon was flooding the country with "printing-press money," according to Sam.[36] "The huge deficit being inflicted on the nation by the Nixon administration is a direct cause of one of the farmers' major problems—inflation," said the Little Giant.[37] Another new tactic was a heavy emphasis by Sam on the question of busing, which was undoubtedly prompted by the presence of George Wallace on the Nebraska ballot. Yorty continued his attacks on McGovern and Muskie and added a few swipes at Hubert Humphrey, who had also entered the Nebraska primary.

Yorty and his campaigners heavily stressed that Sam was a native Nebraskan and told extensively of his early days selling newspapers in the snow. A Yorty advertisement said that Sam was "a member of a solid American family that lived for many years amid the farms and close to the good earth of the great state of Nebraska" and assured readers that Sam had "the Nebraskan common sense and a corn-

husker's pride in America."[38] Yorty made amazing claims
about his part in building Los Angeles. Sam "has made Los
Angeles a model for responsible professionalism in local government operations," praised one of his advertisements.[39] On some occasions Yorty even claimed credit for
building one of the nation's finest police departments.[40]
Los Angeles city departments generally and its police operations in particular are well regarded, but this status had
been attained a substantial number of years before Yorty
became Mayor.

As in New Hampshire, Yorty's confidence was not borne
out in the polls as election time drew near in the Corn-
husker State. The Nebraska Poll, published in the *Omaha
World-Herald* on April 30, 1972, showed the Little Giant
faring dismally, with the projection being that he would
receive little more than 1 percent of the vote.[41] And even
though Yorty was said to have spent more time on the campaign trail in Nebraska than any other candidate on the
Democratic ballot,[42] its voters did not take kindly to their
prodigal son. Sam did even worse in Nebraska than he had
in New Hampshire:[43]

McGovern	79,309	41.2%
Humphrey	65,968	34.3
Wallace	23,912	12.5
Muskie	6,886	3.6
Jackson	5,276	2.8
Yorty	3,469	1.8
Others (6)	7,327	3.8

After the Nebraska disappointment, Yorty for the first
time admitted that his chances to become President were
practically nonexistent. He stopped referring to himself as
a "candidate for President," and now maintained that he
would fight to "lead a moderate delegation" from California. In essence, he had changed from a definite candidate to
a favorite son.

A look at Yorty's own observations on his campaign stra-

tegy and objectives may be the best way to determine his
motivation. During the Nebraska campaign, Sam had said
that if he had to "do it all over again" he would skip the
New Hampshire primary and concentrate on Nebraska and
California.[44] Evidently Sam still hoped before the presidential primary in his home state that he would be able to
arouse meaningful support among conservative California
Democrats. Even so, from the results of the 1970 primary
for the governorship in California, when Democrats gave
Sam only one-fourth of the vote in his loss to Jess Unruh, his
outlook in the 1972 primary looked bleak. When supporters
of George Wallace made it clear that they would mount a
well-financed, serious write-in campaign for the Alabama
Governor, Sam's chances took another deteriorating turn.
But he still maintained, until the last week of the campaign,
that he was going to turn things around in California. He
ignored several published polls that claimed he would receive approximately 1 percent of the primary vote. The
California Poll had shown Yorty's support as high as 4 percent in early February; after five months of further publicity, according to its findings, Sam had lost much of his earlier
appeal.[45]

Sam travelled up and down California in search of support and also made a pitch for what he called a "protest
vote." He began to compare himself to George Wallace,
suggesting that the two men appealed to the same kind of
person. (This was a comparison that had been made at various times in the past by critics of Sam's 1969 mayoralty
campaign.) "I expect and would like to receive the same
kind of protest vote which Wallace has been getting in other
states," said Yorty. "Both Wallace and I have a 'message' for
the voters, but I believe my 'message' is much better and
clearer," he added.[46] Although most political observers did
not disagree with Yorty's view of himself and Wallace as
ideologically similar, they felt that Wallace would have a

much better opportunity to collect on his "message." They believed this even though Wallace was hampered by his physical inability to campaign and by the difficulty of making a write-in campaign successful in California. In a final effort to gain the support of Wallaceites, Yorty announced he would accept the Alabama Governor as his running mate if Sam received the Democratic presidential nomination.[47] Despite his earlier statements about his candidacy being an appeal to a "protest" vote, Sam once again insisted that he was in the race "to win." He said he wanted to win and lead a delegation to Miami Beach that was "pledged to the best interests of California. . . ."[48]

As the California campaign drew to a close, the television networks scheduled a series of debates between the major contenders, Humphrey and McGovern. After the first of these debates was held, Congresswoman Shirley Chisholm of New York brought suit against the television networks, claiming that she was entitled to take part in any debate involving presidential candidates. The court ruled in favor of Ms. Chisholm, and the television networks were ordered to give her free air time to compensate for her exclusion from the initial debate. They were also instructed to include her, along with other candidates, in any further debate programs. A second debate between McGovern and Humphrey was held during the legal maneuvering, but the networks extended invitations to a third program to McGovern, Humphrey, Chisholm, a representative of Governor Wallace, and Sam Yorty.

Sam was seated on the stage, off to the side of the rest of the candidates. He seemed nervous and irked at the network and at the newsmen who formed the panel of questioners. Sam spent most of his speaking time complaining about not being considered a "real" candidate for the White House. He evoked considerable laughter among the viewers when, due to his nervousness, he slipped and said that he had been

"Mayor of Los Angeles for 11 days" (instead of 11 years) and was currently "Mayor of the third largest city in Los Angeles."[49] Sam insisted that he was still a candidate in the presidential race. His performance, he said, would surprise the analysts who had belittled his candidacy.

Most experts did not share Sam's view. The primary race in California, they felt, was clearly between Humphrey and McGovern, with some conservatives in support of Wallace. On the day before the primary election, at the last minute, Sam did surprise the experts. Although he had said Hubert Humphrey was a political opportunist who "bends with the wind"[50] and had not supported him in the 1968 presidential campaign, Sam now announced that Hubert was his kind of Democrat. Although Yorty amazingly insisted that he was not withdrawing from the quest for the presidential nomination, Sam said that he was "asking [his] supporters to support Senator Humphrey."[51] Displaying uncharacteristic party concern, Sam said McGovern was leading the Democratic party to "suicidal radicalization." When asked what good his 1 percent to 2 percent of the vote, as reflected by the polls, would do for Humphrey, Yorty testily informed reporters that "no one knows what percentage of the vote I would have."[52] When the votes were counted, however, Sam had about the percentage predicted by the polls:[53]

McGovern	1,550,652	43.5%
Humphrey	1,375,064	38.5
Wallace (write-in)	268,551	7.5
Chisholm	157,435	4.4
Muskie	72,701	2.0
Yorty	50,745	1.4
Others (3)	89,350	2.7

After the election the Little Giant was irate at reporters and analysts who did not feel Sam had contributed much support to Humphrey's total vote. Although most experts feel that votes are extremely difficult to hand back and

forth between candidates, Sam insisted that he had helped
Humphrey come within shouting distance of McGovern.
Yorty said that the media were "trying to squirm around to
avoid" giving him his proper credit.[54] He also maintained
that McGovern's victory would cause the "communists to
hang on" in Vietnam.[55]

Yorty seemed resigned to defeat in his presidential bid,
but new hope was later raised when a court decision attacked the legality of California's winner-take-all system of
awarding convention delegates. The court ruled that the
California delegation should be based on the distribution of
votes in the primary, thus giving each candidate some representation. Sam gaily put together a four-member delegation and was off to Miami Beach. His participation was not
allowed, however, because the convention eventually voted
to seat the entire McGovern delegation instead of the various groups created by the court decision.

Sam spent the days of the Democratic national convention running a disc jockey show for radio station KMPC of
Los Angeles, juggling records, interviews, and commercials.
He interviewed several important figures visiting the convention, including George Wallace, the man he had said he
would award the vice-presidential nomination if Yorty had
been successful in his presidential bid. (This was their first
personal meeting.) Joining Yorty in Miami was Jess Unruh,
an old friend but also an old enemy, who was representing a
competing Los Angeles radio station in a journalistic capacity. Sam was not well covered by the media as he ran his
radio show in Miami Beach, but he did manage to get his
picture in the news once, when he put his arm around Liz
Renay, an exotic dancer and former girl friend of ex-convict
Mickey Cohen.[56]

Although Yorty campaigned only in New Hampshire,
Nebraska, and California, he had also been entered in several other state presidential primaries. In these races, as

expected, Sam's cause was even more pitiful than elsewhere. In Florida he received 0.2 percent of the vote; in Maryland, 2.4 percent; in Massachusetts, 0.1 percent; in Wisconsin 0.2 percent; and in Rhode Island, the ultimate slight—Sam garnered a whopping 0.01 percent, receiving only 6 votes in the entire state.[57]

Why did Sam Yorty lose the presidency? Because of his image as an unpredictable maverick? Because mayors find it difficult to become President? Because he had no strong popular base upon which to build? The preceding examination of Sam's abortive try for the White House provides some explanation for his inability, after spending nearly one-half million dollars in three states,[58] to pick up many votes.

A Californian who has watched Sam manipulate issues, statements, events, and even prejudices (as in the Bradley campaign in 1969) is steeled to a view of the Little Giant as a typical politician, who is often hopelessly ambitious. But this is not how Sam is received in other states because California politics are not common knowledge elsewhere. Voters such as those in Nebraska and New Hampshire, who do not "know" the Yorty record as a campaigner, vilifyer, and constant candidate, may see him in an entirely different manner than do Californians. For this reason it is unfair to explain away Yorty's poor primary showings to his candidacy being a joke or a figment of ambition.

Yorty's weak performance in his presidential bid may instead be attributed to an electorate that simply and fatally disagreed with him about Vietnam and national defense. There seemingly were not as many hawks among registered Democrats in New Hampshire and Nebraska as Sam believed. His ill-fated attempts to emphasize busing in Nebraska may be a hint that Yorty himself saw that the hawk stance was getting him nowhere. If the New Hampshire results are measured along hawk-dove lines—Yorty–Mills as hawks and

McGovern–Muskie–Hartke as doves—the doves received about 86 percent of the vote, the hawks a relatively poor 10 percent. In Nebraska, the hawks (Yorty, Jackson, and Wallace) did somewhat better, but still lost to the doves by 17 percent to 79 percent. Sam Yorty did not lose the presidency solely because of his image; he also lost all chance of nomination because 1972 was the year of George McGovern, at least among a majority of the Democrats. And not to be overlooked are Yorty's verbal assaults on President Nixon during the campaign, which may have isolated him from those Democrats who did support Nixon and Yorty positions on the war.

In the final analysis, the Yorty for President campaign may be termed both a sincere effort and a joke. Sam believed that it was a hard-hitting, no-nonsense campaign to influence public opinion and put him on Pennsylvania Avenue. Most other people looked upon his entry as a joke. Veteran California political writer Lou Cannon insisted that Sam entered the race mainly to see his name in the news,[59] and the *Los Angeles Times* criticized Sam for "making a national joke" out of Los Angeles.[60] But the best analysis may have come from *Times* reader Ann Robson, who wrote that Yorty was silly to have said "You can't have a meaningful [television] debate without me in it." Said Ms. Robson, "Why not? We have had a Mayor's office without him in it" for years.[61]

24
FROM HERE TO ETERNITY

For four decades Sam Yorty has been a professional politician and a constant candidate. He has run often, and sometimes he has won, but his record of eight victories and even more defeats—nine— is mediocre. Compare the number of his political losses with those of some contemporaries with whom he has shared the political spotlight. Richard Nixon, Earl Warren, Pat Brown, Fletcher Bowron, and Norris Poulson each lost only once or twice. Many electoral rejections of Yorty may be attributed to his unyielding miscalculation for many years that the Democratic party has been going to move to the political right and thus make him its candidate. But the party has not moved in this direction nor does it currently show any signs of doing so. The Yorty ideology for partisan office-seeking has been molded to fit a certain type of California voter who simply has never achieved the dominant position anticipated by the Little Giant.

Yorty has fared slightly better in officially nonpartisan elections in Los Angeles than in state and national partisan contests, although most Angelenos are unaware of his first two local defeats—for City Council in 1939 and for Mayor six years later. On the local nonpartisan front, only his three consecutive mayoral victories are generally remembered. As a result of these recent victories (among which have been interspersed various partisan defeats), a number of people feel that Yorty has great political strength and near invincibility as a mayoral candidate.

Other explanations for the three wins for Mayor may be offered, however. For example, in the first two mayoralty contests of the 1960's his opposition was weak. Due to a physical disability, Norris Poulson had become virtually mute, and James Roosevelt, after many years in Washington, waged a poorly organized campaign that frequently revealed an inadequate knowledge of city affairs. Yorty was therefore able to portray Poulson as a kindly but weak old man and Roosevelt as an insurgent easterner—something of a carpetbagger. These, of course, were not the only issues that carried Sam to victory over Poulson and Roosevelt, but they are examples of Yorty's receiving unwitting aid from his opponents. And the Yorty–Bradley fracas of 1969 displayed the effects of poor campaign management on electoral results, but this struggle was in a category by itself—with strong racial overtones.

To dismiss Yorty's success in recent Los Angeles elections to mismanagement and ineptness by his foes would not furnish a full answer to why he has won three straight times. In his 40 years of political skirmishing Yorty has developed a certain visceral sense, an intuitiveness about political moods. He eyes his constituents with care, and he acts on the waves they send out to him. Every Yorty appearance is a campaign event; his campaigning for office never stops. He apparently makes no move or utterance without first gauging its political ramifications. When Yorty senses a feeling among the voters he responds by attacking the cause of that feeling. When he speaks to people, he usually speaks to their emotions, not to their reason. In 1961, when he was on the outside, Sam appealed to the hopes of the people, for better, more responsive government, for an end to control by the "downtown machine." But ever since then, from the inside,

he has generally appealed to the fears of the electorate—fear
of radicals in 1965 in his contest against Roosevelt, fear of
Black militancy in 1969 in his campaign against Bradley.
And each time he has benefited by another fear—that of the
unknown. Many people feel they know Sam Yorty, at least
in a vague way. Despite (and apparently at times because of)
his traveling, querulousness, constant political ambition, radio and television antics, and other activities, he is their
Mayor and they feel a closeness to him.' A political new-
comer in the mayoralty arena, merely by being new, probably poses a threat for many people to the comfort of things-
as-the-are. Sam Yorty has won partly because he is the
familiar incumbent, the Mayor of Los Angeles.

Although southern California is well known as a hotbed
of right-wing politics, the city of Los Angeles has shown itself on various occasions to be an exception to this conservatism. In every general election for President, Governor,
and United States Senator between 1962 and 1972 the city
voted in favor, usually decisively, of the more liberal major
candidate. A critical difference, however, between those
elections and the Yorty mayoralty contests is that the race
for Mayor of Los Angeles is officially nonpartisan. State law
prohibits political party identification from appearing with
the names of candidates for any local elective office. Yorty
has profited greatly from this nonpartisan condition. Although a conservative, he has been able to extract in mayoralty contests a measure of support from liberals—enough to
put him in City Hall when combined with conservative
votes. If Los Angeles had partisan primaries for Mayor, Sam
Yorty might not have survived the Democratic primary in
1961, 1965, or 1969. Yorty has long been a man without a
party, and the nonpartisan facade has been perfect for him.

The Yorty political style seemingly has also contributed
to his success. Although at times he may seem gauche, he
casts friendly smiles and homely aphorisms at the public;

Sam thus employs a down-to-earth populist approach, much in the manner of George Wallace. Yorty comforts people when it is to his advantage, and when it suits his purpose he feeds their worries. In personal appearances he is purposely folksy, using few if any notes and priding himself on not having staff writers. In dealing with questions, he operates with skill and shrewdness, frequently parrying many of them and showing himself to be a master of the innuendo. In such situations, he often is much like a veteran wrestler trapped in a corner who displays a canny ability to earn a draw or to come out on top. The midwestern, humble beginnings of the Little Giant—however distant in the past —may be partially responsible for the way in which he casts himself as one of the masses. In a day when many politicians reach for glittering images of charismatic perfection, Yorty still thrives on seeming to be the man next door.

This person-to-person approach is similarly evident in the Yorty rhetoric. Sam does not beat around the bush; he goes straight for a jugular vein. He says outrageous things about his opponents and their allies, generally depicting them as losers, radicals, bunglers, trouble makers, or even outright dangers to the country. One example is Yorty's criticism of Earl Warren as an overrated vote-getter, characterizing all of his gubernatorial opponents as losers, from Culbert Olson through Robert Kenny and James Roosevelt. "And even I found out how easy it is to beat [Roosevelt]," said Sam.[1] On a later occasion Yorty termed presidential candidate George McGovern as "anti-American" and one who speaks like "Hanoi."[2] Although Sam does not mince words about others, he bridles at any criticism of himself.

The Yorty attacks are almost always direct and personal. Dick Richards was a purveyor of "double talk." Pat Brown was at first "minor league," and later a "machine" politician. Reagan was an "amateur," and Norris Poulson was pictured as virtually on his deathbed. Tom Bradley, whom Yorty had endorsed in the past, suddenly became a pawn of "Black militants." These Yorty hypercriticisms have become so predictable that it is fascinating how often they work.

Yorty is adept and persistent at sloganeering, always preferring to utilize catchy phrases and gimicky alliterations. "Double Dick Richards," "President Eisenhoover," "wired, packed, rigged, and stacked," and the "Fulbright Triplets" are typical Yortyisms stretching out over many years. He is also fond of finding scapegoats after both partisan electoral defeats and losing battles with the City Council. For instance, he has blamed some of his partisan losses on the performance of another candidate on the statewide ticket and the liberalism of the California Democratic Council. And members of the City Council are often termed "obstructionists" and "parochial" when they oppose him.

Ever since December, 1939, Sam Yorty's favorite campaign issue has been anti-communism. He has used this theme like a two-edged sword. If an opponent is more liberal than he is, Yorty can credibly paint him as "backed by radicals." If the opponent is more conservative, the Yorty ultraliberalism of the 1930's may be presented again, with Sam responding that he is a victim of a "communist smear attack." In reality, of course, communism is a ridiculous issue in Los Angeles municipal politics. But if voters are comfortable with simplistic examinations of city affairs, the communist issue can be utilized to considerable advantage by a politician.

This observation about the simple approach to city affairs brings us to a consideration of the depth of interest generated in Los Angeles by the issues of local politics. The city voters are not totally disinterested, as they have been turning out in increasing numbers for recent mayoralty elections. In 1961, when Yorty won his first term, the turnout at the general election was less than 50 percent; in 1969, more than 75 percent voted. No reliable way exists to measure the amount of thought that a Los Angeles voter devotes to local issues. In this city, mayoralty elections always come a few months after presidential campaigns. Following months of charges and countercharges in a national election, a voter is understandably tired of political speeches and talk. Many Angelenos may close their ears to mayoralty campaigns, listening in (out of a sense of duty) only at the last minute and then voting.

Also, local communications media are spotty in their coverage of local government. The *Los Angeles Times* is providing more ample treatment and comment about the local public scene, but most of this coverage is buried in part two, and many readers skip from part one to the sports or social pages. The local television and radio stations, both network and independent, are notoriously weak in their coverage of local government. Although some of these stations are improving, they all still spend more time on sports, weather, and insignificant local items than on issues concerning city government. At city election time local television and radio coverage grows markedly, but this simply illustrates journalism's present-orientedness. An election, but not the day-to-day government of the city, is "news." City government is a year-round operation that cannot be adequately covered by extensive reporting of campaign verbiage. Citizens who are treated to this scanty and disorganized reporting are susceptible to politicians who take credit for what is good and disclaim responsibility for what is bad.

Sam Yorty has thrived on this weak coverage and poor knowledge of municipal affairs. He is able to win elections with simplistic rhetoric and glittering generalities. As a transplanted midwesterner, Yorty is well suited to a constituency that in part is (literally or psychologically) similarly derived. A character in a newspaper comic strip is plagued by a constantly pursuing thunderhead; wherever he travels, rain falls in his face. Citizens of Los Angeles are similarly followed by a sense of the small town life, circumscribed by the limits of visibility. Like a runner who travels in the eye of a hurricane and is unaware of the surrounding storm, an Angeleno goes to and fro in the metropolis, seeing only a limited stretch of civilization. Only on a rare, marvelous, crystal-clear day can one actually see the city of Los Angeles. And the population is scattered over more than 460 square miles. The people are isolated from one another and from their City Hall. They either live indoors, watching television, or venture outside, walled up in their automobiles on the freeways, listening to the radio. Their weekends are spent in front of the television or on visits to the many recreational areas in southern California; Los Angeles is less a city of neighbors than a city of strangers.

The veil of smog and haze and the separation of local residents by miles of freeways may have political overtones. The people may be anesthetized by their remoteness from City Hall, and they may consider themselves to be residents of Canoga Park, Pacific Palisades, or San Pedro—not of Los Angeles. They may see Sam Yorty as a Mayor who does not really affect them and thus they do not have much interest in city affairs.

In this atmosphere Sam Yorty has flourished as "America's Most Decorated Mayor." Despite his frequent partisan embarrassments, he has been Mayor for three full terms and is set to run for a fourth. He is a totally political man, probably as much as any other recent American figure. He has given the lie to two longtime political maxims—a person should never run for public office unless he has a good chance of winning, and political defeats are certain tickets to oblivion. Sam Yorty has ignored the first of these rules and indeed if he had followed it he never would have become Mayor. The underdog role has served him well. And notwithstanding the disdain of his enemies and the contempt of those who made the rules Sam breaks, the Little Giant still seems to be a long way from political oblivion.

NOTES

CHAPTER 1

1. James Phelan, "Trouble in Happyland," in William M. Leiter, *California Government: Issues and Institutions* (Pacific Palisades, Calif.: Goodyear Publishing Company, Inc., 1971), p. 84.

2. Ed Ainsworth, *Maverick Mayor* (Garden City, New York: Doubleday & Company, 1966), p. 26.

3. *Ibid.*, p. 92.

4. Russell H. Fletcher, *Who's Who in California, 1942–1943* (Los Angeles: Who's Who Publications, 1941), p. 1019.

5. *Ibid.*

6. Ainsworth, *op. cit.*, pp. 62–3.

7. *Ibid.*, p. 60.

8. Eugene P. Dvorin and Arthur J. Misner, *California Politics and Policies* (Reading, Mass.: Addison-Wesley Publishing Co., 1966), p. 10.

9. Ainsworth, *op. cit.*, p. 72.

10. *Ibid.*, p. 62.

11. Arthur H. Samish and Bob Thomas, *The Secret Boss of California* (New York: Crown Publishers, Inc., 1971), p. 74.

CHAPTER 2

1. Ainsworth, *Maverick Mayor*, p. 77.

2. State of California, *California Statutes, 1931*, p. 286.

3. Ainsworth, *op. cit.*, pp. 77–8.

4. Statement by Samuel Yorty, KNBC News, July 7, 1972.

5. Ainsworth, *op. cit.*, p. 79.

6. *Ibid.*

7. State of California, *Statement of Vote*, Primary Election, August 25, 1936.

8. William Goodman, *Culbert Olson and California Politics* (M. A. thesis, University of California, Los Angeles, 1948), p. 122.

9. Ainsworth, *op. cit.,* p. 83.

10. *United Progressive News,* October 26, 1936.

11. State of California, *Statement of Vote,* General Election, November 3, 1936.

CHAPTER 3

1. State of California, *Journal of the Assembly,* 53rd Session, p. 2819. (The resolution was signed by Yorty and four others.)

2. *United Progressive News,* October 11, 1937.

3. *United Progressive News,* July 12, 1937.

4. Samish, *Secret Boss,* pp. 57–8.

5. John B. Tenney, *Jack B. Tenney, California Legislator* (Los Angeles: University of California, Los Angeles, Oral History Program, 1969), p. 320.

6. State of California, *Journal of the Assembly,* 53rd Session.

CHAPTER 4

1. John Anson Ford, *Thirty Explosive Years in Los Angeles County* (San Marino, Calif.: The Huntington Library, 1961), p. 14.

2. Jerry S. Caplan, *The C.I.V.I.C. Committee in the Recall of Mayor Frank Shaw* (M. A. thesis, University of California, Los Angeles, 1947), p. 1.

3. Robert W. Kenny, *My First Forty Years in California Government* (Los Angeles: University of California, Los Angeles, Oral History Program, 1968), p. 111.

4. Caplan, *op. cit.,* p. 19.

5. Kenny, *op. cit.,* p. 112.

6. Guy W. Finney, *Angel City in Turmoil* (Los Angeles: Amer Press, 1945), p. 164.

7. *Ibid.,* p. 165.

8. *Los Angeles City Charter,* Article 27, sec. 290(a), 1937 ed., p. 199.

9. *The Communist,* November 1938, pp. 1020–3.

10. *Los Angeles Independent Review,* July 28, 1938.

11. *Los Angeles Independent Review,* August 4, 1938.

12. *Los Angeles Examiner,* August 5, 1938.

13. *Los Angeles Times,* August 4, 1938.

14. *Los Angeles Examiner,* August 9, 1938.

15. *Ibid.*

16. *Ibid.*

17. *The Communist,* November 1938, p. 1022.

18. *Los Angeles Independent Review,* August 11, 1938.

CHAPTER 5

1. *Los Angeles Independent Review,* June 30, 1938.
2. Tenney, *California Legislator,* pp. 509–10.
3. *Ibid.,* p. 532.
4. Robert E. Burke, *Olson's New Deal for California* (Berkeley and Los Angeles: University of California Press, 1953), p. 45.
5. *Los Angeles Examiner,* August 9, 1938.
6. H. R. Philbrick, *Legislative Investigative Report,* 1938.
7. Ainsworth, *Maverick Mayor,* p. 98.
8. Tenney, *op. cit.,* pp. 601–2.
9. State of California, *Journal of the Assembly,* 53rd Session, p. 2955.
10. Burke, *op. cit.,* p. 118.

CHAPTER 6

1. Jacobus Tenbroek and others, *Prejudice, War, and the Constitution* (Berkeley and Los Angeles: University of California Press, 1954), p. 4.
2. Dorothy S. Thomas and Richard Nishimoto, *The Spoilage* (Berkeley and Los Angeles: University of California Press, 1946), p. 366.
3. Carey McWilliams, *Prejudice* (Boston: Little, Brown & Co., 1945), p. 25.
4. *Ibid.*
5. Tenbroek and others, *op. cit.,* p. 32.
6. Ainsworth, *Maverick Mayor,* p. 89.
7. State of California, *Text of Assembly Bill 336 (1939).*
8. Ainsworth, *op. cit.,* p. 88.
9. *Los Angeles Illustrated Daily News,* April 21, 1939.
10. Eldon R. Penrose, *California Nativism: Organized Opposition to the Japanese* (M. A. thesis, California State College, Sacramento, 1969), p. 156.
11. *Japan-California Daily News,* March 12, 1939.
12. Kanichi Kawasaki, *The Japanese Community of East San Pedro* (M. A. thesis, University of Southern California, Los Angeles, 1931).
13. United States Department of the Interior, *Myths and Facts About the Japanese* (Washington: War Relocation Authority, 1945).
14. Ainsworth, *op. cit.,* pp. 88–9.
15. State of California, *Journal of the Assembly,* 54th Session, p. 3435.

16. Dennis M. Ogawa, *From Japs to Japanese* (Berkeley: Mc-Cutchan, 1971), p. 15.

17. McWilliams, *op. cit.,* p. 22.

18. *Los Angeles Times,* April 1, 1939.

CHAPTER 7

1. *Los Angeles Times, April* 6, 1939.

2. Caplan, *The C.I.V.I.C. Committee,* p. 58.

3. *Los Angeles Times,* March 22, 1939.

4. *Los Angeles Times,* April 19, 1939.

5. *Los Angeles Times,* March 22, April 2, and April 25, 1939.

6. *Los Angeles Illustrated Daily News,* May 2, 1939.

7. *Los Angeles Times,* May 1, 1939.

8. City of Los Angeles, *Official Election Results,* City Clerk's Office, (Election Division).

CHAPTER 8

1. *Los Angeles Times,* May 2, 1939.

2. *Los Angeles Illustrated Daily News,* May 2, 1939.

3. Ainsworth, *Maverick Mayor,* p. 96.

4. *Los Angeles Times,* May 3, 1939.

5. *Los Angeles Times,* December 20, 1939.

6. *Ibid.*

7. *Los Angeles Independent Review,* February 1, 1940.

8. Ainsworth, *op. cit.,* p. 100.

9. *Los Angeles Illustrated Daily News,* December 30, 1939.

10. Goodman, *Olson and California Politics,* p. 122.

11. *Los Angeles Illustrated Daily News,* January 5, 1940.

12. *Los Angeles Illustrated Daily News,* January 8, 1940.

13. *Los Angeles Illustrated Daily News,* February 2, 1940.

14. *Ibid.*

15. *Los Angeles Illustrated Daily News,* February 3, 1940.

16. *Ibid.*

17. Ainsworth, *op. cit.,* pp. 101–2.

18. *Ibid.,* p. 100.

19. *Los Angeles Independent Review,* February 29, 1940.

20. Ainsworth, *op. cit.,* p. 101.

21. *Los Angeles Independent Review,* Febraury 22, 1940.

22. *Los Angeles Times,* December 28, 1939.

23. Tenney, *California Legislator,* p. 783.

24. *Congressional Record,* 82nd Cong., 1st sess., 97:12 (May 9, 1951), pp. A2634–41.

25. *Los Angeles Times,* March 17, 1940.

CHAPTER 9

1. Peter G. Boyle, *The Study of an Isolationist: Hiram Johnson* (Ph. D. thesis, University of California, Los Angeles, 1970), p. 395.
2. *Los Angeles Times,* August 6, 1940.
3. *Los Angeles Independent Review,* February 29, 1940.
4. *Los Angeles Independent Review,* February 8, 1940.
5. *Los Angeles Independent Review,* February 1, 1940.
6. *Los Angeles Independent Review,* June 27, 1940.
7. *Los Angeles Examiner,* August 25, 1940.
8. *Ibid.*
9. *Ibid.*
10. Reuben W. Borough, *Reuben Borough and California Reform Movements* (Los Angeles: University of California, Los Angeles, Oral History Program, 1968), p. 138.
11. *Los Angeles Examiner,* August 26, 1940.
12. John Anson Ford, *John Anson Ford and Los Angeles County Government* (Los Angeles: University of California, Los Angeles, Oral History Program, 1967), p. vii.
13. Statement by Samuel W. Yorty, *News Conference,* KNBC News, May 21, 1972.
14. *Los Angeles Times,* August 12, 1940.
15. Boyle, *op. cit.,* p. 438.
16. *Los Angeles Times,* August 3, 1940.
17. State of California, *Statement of Vote,* Direct Primary Election, August 27, 1940.

CHAPTER 10

1. *Los Angeles Times,* November 11, 1940.
2. *Los Angeles Times,* February 1, 1941.
3. *Los Angeles Times,* April 3, 1941.
4. *Los Angeles Times,* February 6, 1941.
5. *Ibid.*
6. *Los Angeles Times,* February 20, 1941.
7. Tenney, *California Legislator,* p. 1002.
8. Ainsworth, *Maverick Mayor,* pp. 108–9.
9. *Los Angeles Times,* March 7, 1945.
10. *Los Angeles Times,* July 28 and September 14, 1948.
11. Tenney, *op. cit.,* p. 1436.
12. *Ibid.,* p. 1568.
13. *Los Angeles Times,* April 25, 1949.

14. *San Francisco Call-Bulletin,* June 30, 1949.
15. *Los Angeles Times,* June 4, 1949.
16. Samish, *Secret Boss,* p. 132.
17. Tenney, *op. cit.,* p. 1577.
18. Samish, *op. cit.,* p. 133.
19. *Ibid.*
20. *Los Angeles Times,* April 28, 1949.
21. Tenney, *op. cit.,* p. 1574.
22. *Ibid.,* p. 1569.

CHAPTER 11

1. State of California, *Statement of Vote,* General Election, November 2, 1948.
2. Walt Anderson, *Campaigns: Cases in Political Conflict* (Pacific Palisades, Calif.: Goodyear Publishing Company, Inc., 1970), p. 136.
3. *Ibid.,* p. 137.
4. *Ibid.,* pp. 141–2.
5. David Farrelly and Ivan Hinderaker, *The Politics of California* (New York: The Ronald Press Company, 1951), p. 257.
6. *Ibid.,* pp. 275–6.
7. *Los Angeles Times,* January 27, February 27, March 10, August 28, and November 10, 1952; January 8, 1953.
8. *Los Angeles Times,* February 8, 1952.
9. Ainsworth, *Maverick Mayor,* pp. 116–7.
10. *Congressional Record,* 82nd Cong., 1st sess., 97:4 (May 7, 1951), pp. 5008–15.
11. *Congressional Record,* 82nd Cong., 1st sess., 97:12 (May 9, 1951), pp. A2634–41.
12. Gladwin Hill, *Dancing Bear: An Inside Look at California Politics* (Cleveland and New York: World Publishing Company, 1968), p. 94.
13. Samish, *Secret Boss,* pp. 77–8.
14. Hill, *op. cit.,* p. 243.
15. Committee to Abolish Cross-Filing in California, Campaign Pamphlet, General Election, 1952.
16. State of California, *Journal of the Assembly,* 1949 Session, p. 4611.
17. Hill, *op. cit.,* p. 117.

CHAPTER 12

1. Tenney, *California Legislator,* p. 1801.
2. *New York Times,* January 31, 1954.
3. *New York Times,* December 13, 1953.

4. *New York Times,* March 3, 1953.

5. Leonard Rowe, *Preprimary Endorsements in California Politics* (Berkeley: Bureau of Public Administration, University of California, Berkeley, 1961), p. 48.

6. *Frontier,* 5 (February, 1954), pp. 24–5.

7. Francis Carney, *The Rise of the Democratic Clubs in California* (New York: Henry Holt, 1958), pp. 12–3.

8. Rowe, *op. cit.,* p. 48.

9. *Los Angeles Times,* February 8, 1954.

10. *Ibid.*

11. *New York Times,* February 8, 1954.

12. *Los Angeles Times,* February 8, 1954.

13. *Los Angeles Examiner,* February 8, 1954.

14. *Los Angeles Times,* January 25, 1954.

15. *Los Angeles Times,* January 27, 1954.

16. *Los Angeles Times,* January 29, 1954.

17. *Los Angeles Times,* May 7, 1954.

18. *Los Angeles Times,* January 27, 1954.

19. *Your Democratic Nominees,* Campaign Pamphlet, 1954.

20. *Los Angeles Times,* June 24, 1949.

21. *Los Angeles Examiner,* May 19, 1949.

22. *Los Angeles Times,* May 10, 1954.

23. Democrats for Kuchel, *An Open Letter to Registered Democrats,* Campaign Pamphlet, May 1954.

24. *Los Angeles Times,* January 4, 1940.

25. *Los Angeles Times,* June 4, 1954.

26. *New York Times,* May 30, 1954.

27. *Los Angeles Daily News,* June 3, 1954.

28. *Los Angeles Times,* June 3, 1954.

29. *Los Angeles Times,* June 4, 1954.

30. *Ibid.*

31. *Ibid.*

32. *Ibid.*

33. *Ibid.*

34. *Los Angeles Times,* October 3, 1954.

35. *Los Angeles Times,* June 4, 1954.

36. *Los Angeles Daily News,* June 4, 1954.

37. Hill, *Dancing Bear,* p. 244.

38. *New York Times,* September 9, 1954.

39. *Los Angeles Times,* May 23 and May 30, 1954.

40. State of California, *Statement of Vote,* Direct Primary Election, June 8, 1954.

41. Totton J. Anderson, "Mainstream Politics," in Leiter, *California Government,* p. 232.

42. *New York Times,* September 9, 1954.

43. *Congressional Record,* 82nd Cong., 2nd sess., 98:9 (February 26, 1952), p. A1454; 83rd Cong., 1st sess., 99:9 (March 9, 1953), p. A1337.

44. Ronald E. Chinn, *Democratic Party Politics in California* (Ph.D thesis, University of California, Berkeley, 1958), p. 169.

45. *New York Times,* September 9, 1954.

46. *Los Angeles Times,* October 3, 1954.

47. *New York Times,* September 9, 1954.

48. *Los Angeles Times,* September 23, 1954.

49. *Ibid.*

50. Herbert L. Phillips, *Big Wayward Girl: An Informal Political History of California* (Garden City, New York: Doubleday & Company, Inc., 1968), p. 173.

51. State of California, *Statement of Vote,* General Election, November 2, 1954.

52. Ainsworth, *Maverick Mayor,* p. 121.

53. *Los Angeles Times,* December 6, 1954.

CHAPTER 13

1. Phillips, *Big Wayward Girl,* p. 174.

2. *New York Times,* October 21, 1955.

3. *Los Angeles Times,* December 4, 1955.

4. *New York Times,* October 30, 1955.

5. Ainsworth, *Maverick Mayor,* p. 121.

6. State of California, *Statement of Vote,* General Election, November 2, 1954.

7. Rowe, *Preprimary Endorsements,* p. viii.

8. *Ibid.,* p. 49.

9. *New York Times,* January 31, 1954.

10. *Los Angeles Times,* November 11, 1955.

11. *Los Angeles Times,* January 19, 1956.

12. *Ibid.*

13. John R. Owens and others, *California Politics and Parties* (New York: The Macmillan Company, 1970), p. 207.

14. *Los Angeles Times,* February 4, 1956.

15. *Los Angeles Times,* January 23, 1956.

16. *Los Angeles Times,* January 27, 1956.

17. State of California, *Statement of Vote,* General Election, November 2, 1954.

18. *Sacramento Bee,* February 1, 1956.

19. *Los Angeles Times,* February 1, 1956.

20. *Los Angeles Times,* February 5, 1956.

21. *Ibid.*

22. *Ibid.*

23. *Los Angeles Times,* February 6, 1956.

24. *Sacramento Bee,* February 3, 1956.

25. *Sacramento Bee,* February 6, 1956.
26. *Los Angeles Times,* March 16, 1956.
27. *Sacramento Bee,* February 6, 1956.
28. *Los Angeles Times,* February 6, 1956.
29. *Sacramento Bee,* February 6, 1956.
30. *Ibid.*
31. *Los Angeles Times,* March 29, 1956.
32. *Los Angeles Times,* May 2, 1956.
33. *Fortnight,* 19 (June, 1956), p. 20.
34. *Los Angeles Times,* March 9, 1956.
35. *Los Angeles Times,* April 14, 1956.
36. *Ibid.*
37. *Los Angeles Times,* May 28, 1956.
38. *Ibid.*
39. *Los Angeles Times,* May 13, 1956.
40. *Council Newsletter* (Organ of the Congress of Industrial Organizations Political Action Council), February 15, 1956.
41. *Time,* 63 (April 5, 1954), p. 8.
42. *Los Angeles Times,* May 4, 1956.
43. *Sacramento Bee,* June 1, 1956.
44. State of California, *Statement of Vote,* Direct Primary Election, June 8, 1956.
45. *Fortnight,* 19 (June, 1956), p. 20.
46. *Frontier,* 5 (February, 1954), p. 22.
47. *Frontier,* 5 (August, 1954), p. 13.
48. *Newsweek,* 48 (October 8, 1956), p. 27
49. State of California, *Statement of Vote,* General Election, November 6, 1956 and November 2, 1954.

CHAPTER 14

1. *Los Angeles Times,* June 25, 1961.
2. Dean R. Cresap, *Party Politics in the Golden State* (Los Angeles: The Haynes Foundation, 1954), p. 93.
3. *New York Times,* January 18, 1953.
4. *New York Times,* May 19, 1953.
5. City of Los Angeles, *Official Election Results,* City Clerk's Office, (Election Division).
6. Frank P. Sherwood and Beatrice Markey, "The Mayor and the Fire Chief", in Edwin A. Bock, *State and Local Government: A Case Book* (University, Ala.: University of Alabama Press, 1963), pp. 109–134.
7. Robert Conot, *Rivers of Blood, Years of Darkness* (New York: Bantam Books, 1967), pp. 263–4.
8. *Evening Outlook* (Santa Monica), June 16, 1972.
9. James V. Martindale, *Martindale-Hubbell Law Directory* (Sum-

mit, New Jersey: Martindale-Hubbell, Inc., 1959), p. 184.

10. Joseph P. Harris, *California Politics* (San Francisco: Chandler Publishing Company, 1967), p. 65.

11. *Los Angeles Times,* October 8, 1957.

12. *Los Angeles Times,* June 29, 1960.

13. Ainsworth, *Maverick Mayor,* p. 124.

14. Samuel W. Yorty, *I Can't Take Kennedy,* Campaign Pamphlet, 1960.

15. *Ibid.*

CHAPTER 15

1. *Los Angeles Times,* May 4, 1960.

2. *Los Angeles Times,* May 5, 1960.

3. Herbert M. Baus and William B. Ross, *Politics Battle Plan* (New York: The Macmillan Company, 1968), p. 20.

4. Charles G. Mayo, "The 1961 Mayoralty Election in Los Angeles: The Political Party in a Nonpartisan Election," *Western Political Quarterly* 17 (June, 1964), p. 328.

5. Ainsworth, *Maverick Mayor,* p. 129.

6. *New York Times,* June 2, 1961.

7. Baus and Ross, *op. cit.,* p. 20.

8. *Los Angeles Times,* November 2, 1960.

9. Phelan, "Trouble in Happyland," p. 83.

10. *Ibid.,* p. 82.

11. *Ibid.*

12. *Valley News and Green Sheet* (Van Nuys), January 3, 1961.

13. City of Los Angeles, *Official Election Results,* City Clerk's Office, (Election Division).

14. Mayo, *op. cit.,* p. 325.

15. Francis M. Carney, "The Decentralized Politics of Los Angeles," *The Annals of the American Academy of Political and Social Science,* 353 (May, 1964), p. 111.

16. Mayo, *op. cit.,* p. 334.

17. *Ibid.,* p. 333.

18. *Ibid.,* p. 334.

19. Carney, *op. cit.,* p. 111.

20. *Los Angeles Times,* May 18, 1961.

21. *Los Angeles Times,* May 6, 1961.

22. *Los Angeles Times,* May 2, 1961.

23. *Los Angeles Times,* May 16, 1961.

24. *Sacramento Bee,* June 1, 1961.

25. *Los Angeles Times,* May 15, 1961.

26. *Ibid.*

27. *Time,* 77 (June 9, 1961), p. 15.

28. Mayo, *op. cit.*, p. 332.

29. Phelan, *op. cit.*, p. 84.

30. Ainsworth, *op. cit.*, p. 131.

31. *Los Angeles Times,* April 24, 1961.

32. *Los Angeles Times,* May 9, 1961.

33. Ainsworth, *op. cit.*, p. 133.

34. *Los Angeles Times,* May 9, 1961.

35. *Newsweek*, 57 (June 12, 1961), p. 38.

36. *Los Angeles Times,* May 17, 1961.

37. Mayo, *op. cit.*, p. 333.

38. *Ibid.*, pp. 331–333.

39. *Los Angeles Times,* April 30, 1961.

40. *Ibid.*

41. *Los Angeles Times,* May 21, 1961.

42. *Los Angeles Times,* May 8, 1961.

43. *Ibid.*

44. *Los Angeles Times,* May 5, 1961.

45. *Los Angeles Times,* May 24, 1961.

46. *Los Angeles Times,* April 26, 1961.

47. *Los Angeles Times,* May 26, 1961.

48. *Los Angeles Times,* May 25, 1961.

49. *Los Angeles Times,* May 28, 1961.

50. *Los Angeles Times,* May 16, 1961.

51. Baus and Ross, *op. cit.*, p. 20.

52. *Sacramento Bee,* June 1, 1961.

53. *Los Angeles Times,* June 2, 1961.

54. Richard B. Harvey, *The Dynamics of California Government and Politics* (Belmont, California: Wadsworth Publishing Company, Inc., 1970), p. 211.

55. *Los Angeles Times,* May 31, 1961.

56. City of Los Angeles, *Official Election Results,* City Clerk's Office, (Election Division).

57. *Los Angeles Times,* June 2, 1961.

58. Baus and Ross, *op. cit.*, p. 20.

59. *The Enterprise* (Los Angeles), June 9, 1961.

60. City of Los Angeles, *Official Election Results,* City Clerk's Office, (Election Division).

61. *Newsweek*, 57 (June 12, 1961), p. 38.

62. Mayo, *op. cit.*, p. 337.

63. Phelan, *op. cit.*, p. 87.

64. *Los Angeles Times,* June 25, 1961.

CHAPTER 16

1. Ainsworth, *Maverick Mayor,* p. 181.

2. *Los Angeles Times,* November 8, 1962.

3. *Congressional Quarterly* (Weekly Report), XXI (June 21, 1963), pp. 1023–24.

4. *Los Angeles Times,* March 24, 1964.

5. *Ibid.*

6. *Los Angeles Times,* March 26, 1964.

7. *Frontier,* 16 (March, 1965), p. 5.

8. *Los Angeles Times,* May 27, 1964.

9. *Los Angeles Times,* May 22, 1964.

10. *Los Angeles Times,* May 28, 1964.

11. *Ibid.*

12. *Los Angeles Times,* May 30, 1964.

13. State of California, *Statement of Vote,* Primary Election, June 2, 1964.

14. *Los Angeles Times,* June 3, 1964.

CHAPTER 17

1. *Los Angeles Times,* March 28, 1965.

2. *Frontier,* 16 (March, 1965), p. 6.

3. *Los Angeles,* 9 (March, 1965), p. 29.

4. *Los Angeles Herald Examiner,* September 27, 1963

5. *Frontier,* 16 (March, 1965), p. 6.

6. *Los Angeles Times,* March 3, 1965.

7. *Ibid.*

8. *Los Angeles Times,* March 19, 1965.

9. *Los Angeles Times,* March 24, 1965.

10. City of Los Angeles, *Official Election Results,* City Clerk's Office, (Election Division).

CHAPTER 18

1. *Christian Science Monitor,* November 1, 1965.

2. *Los Angeles Times,* July 13, 1964.

3. Curt Gentry, *The Last Days of the Great State of California* (New York: Ballantine Books, 1968), pp. 202, 222.

4. *Time,* 86 (August 20, 1965), p. 14.

5. *Report of the National Advisory Commission on Civil Disorders* (New York: E. P. Dutton & Co., 1968), p. 308.

6. *Time,* 86 (August 27, 1965), p. 10.

7. *Christian Science Monitor,* November 1, 1965.

8. *Los Angeles Times,* June 2, 1961.

9. O. W. Wilson, ed., *Parker on Police* (Springfield, Ill.: C. C. Thomas, 1957), p. 141.

10. *New Republic,* 153 (September 4, 1965).

11. *U. S. News and World Report,* 59 (August 23, 1965), p. 6.

12. *Time,* 86 (August 27, 1965), p. 11.

13. *New York Times,* December 12, 1965.

14. *Time,* 86 (August 20, 1965), p. 13.

15. Ainsworth, *Maverick Mayor,* pp. 207–8.

16. *Time,* 86 (August 20, 1965), p. 19.

17. *U. S. News and World Report,* 59 (August 30, 1965), p. 16.

18. *Ibid.*

19. *Ibid.*

20. *New York Times,* December 12, 1965.

21. Governor's Commission on the Los Angeles Riots, *Violence in the City—An End or a Beginning* (Sacramento: State of California, 1965), p. 3.

22. Robert Conot, *Rivers of Blood, Years of Darkness* (New York: Bantam Books, 1967), p. 415.

23. Robert Blauner, "Whitewash on Watts," *Trans-action,* 3 (March/April, 1966), p. 4.

24. *New York Times Magazine,* June 12, 1966, p. 80.

25. *Time,* 86 (August 27, 1965), p. 10.

26. Gentry, *op. cit.,* p. 230.

27. Bill Boyarsky, *The Rise of Ronald Reagan* (New York: Random House, Inc., 1968), p. 116.

28. *Time,* 86 (August 13, 1965), p. 17B.

CHAPTER 19

1. Boyarsky, *The Rise of Ronald Reagan,* p. 8.

2. *Ibid.,* p. 60.

3. Kathy Randall Davis, *But What's He Really Like?* (Menlo Park, Calif.: Pacific Coast Publishers, 1970), p. 58.

4. Boyarsky, *op. cit.,* p. 146.

5. *Los Angeles Times,* February 8, 1966.

6. *Los Angeles Times,* February 2, 1966.

7. *Ibid.*

8. Boyarsky, *op. cit.,* p. 116.

9. Totton Anderson, "Mainstream Politics in California," in Leiter, *California Government,* p. 235.

10. Walt Anderson, *Campaigns,* p. 203.

11. Gentry, *The Last Days,* p. 135.

12. *Ibid.*

13. Lou Cannon, *Ronnie and Jesse: A Political Odyssey* (Garden City, New York: Doubleday & Company, Inc., 1969), p. 83.

14. Winston Crouch and others, *California Government and Politics* (5th ed.; Englewood Cliffs, N.J.: Prentice-Hall, Inc., 1972), p. 51.

15. Gentry, *op. cit.,* p. 159.

16. State of California, *Statement of Vote,* Primary Election, June 7, 1966.

17. Boyarsky, *op. cit.,* p. 118.
18. Phillips, *Big Wayward Girl,* p. 241.
19. Boyarsky, *op. cit.,* p. 40.
20. *Ibid.,* p. 155.
21. *Los Angeles Times,* April 11, 1967.
22. *Sacramento Bee,* March 29, 1967.
23. *New York Times Magazine,* September 17, 1967, p. 114.
24. *Los Angeles Times,* April 11, 1967.
25. *Sacramento Bee,* March 29, 1967.
26. *The Enterprise* (Los Angeles), March 29, 1968.
27. Cannon, *op. cit.,* p. 292.

CHAPTER 20

1. Ainsworth, *Maverick Mayor,* p. 186.
2. *Los Angeles Herald Examiner,* January 2, 1969.
3. James Q. Wilson and Harold R. Wilde, "The Urban Mood," *Commentary,* 48 (October, 1969), p. 52.
4. *New York Times,* February 9, 1969.
5. *New York Times Magazine,* September 17, 1967, p 114.
6. *Los Angeles Times,* March 29, 1969.
7. City of Los Angeles, *Official Election Results,* City Clerk's Office (Elections Division).
8. *Los Angeles Times,* April 3, 1969.
9. *The Enterprise* (Los Angeles), April 4, 1969.
10. *Ibid.*
11. Richard L. Maullin, "Los Angeles Liberalism," *Trans-action* 8 (May, 1971), p. 44.
12. *Ibid.*
13. *Los Angeles Times,* April 12, 1969.
14. *Ibid.*
15. *Ibid.*
16. *Los Angeles Times,* April 27, 1969.
17. *Newsweek,* 73 (June 9, 1969), p. 31.
18. Maullin, *op. cit.,* p. 43.
19. *Newsweek,* 73 (June 9, 1969), p. 32.
20. *Ibid.,* p. 31.
21. John W. Caughey, *California* (3rd. ed.; Englewood Cliffs, N. J.: Prentice-Hall, Inc., 1970), p. 558.
22. *Los Angeles Times,* April 23, 1969.
23. Wilson and Wilde, *op. cit.,* p. 59.
24. *Los Angeles Times,* April 29, 1969.
25. Wilson and Wilde, *op. cit.,* p. 59.
26. *New York Times,* May 25, 1969.
27. Maullin, *op. cit.,* p. 45.

28. *Ibid.*
29. *Ibid.*, p. 46.
30. Wilson and Wilde, *op. cit.*, p. 59.
31. City of Los Angeles, *Official Election Results*, City Clerk's Office (Elections Division).
32. Maullin, *op. cit.*, p. 48.
33. Wilson and Wilde, *op. cit.*, p. 53, and *Newsweek*, 73 (June 9, 1969), p. 32.
34. *John Birch Society Bulletin*, July, 1969.
35. *Newsweek*, 73 (June 9, 1969), p. 24.

CHAPTER 21

1. *Los Angeles Times*, January 31, 1970.
2. *Ibid.*
3. *Ibid.*
4. *Congressional Quarterly* (Weekly Report), XXVIII (February 27, 1970), p. 650.
5. *Los Angeles Times*, March 18, 1970.
6. *Los Angeles Times*, March 4, 1970.
7. *Los Angeles Times*, March 18, 1970.
8. *Ibid.*
9. *Sacramento Bee*, May 27, 1970.
10. *Los Angeles Times*, March 18, 1970.
11. *Sacramento Bee*, April 3, 1970.
12. *Los Angeles Times*, April 3, 1970.
13. *Sacramento Bee*, April 3, 1970.
14. *Sacramento Bee*, May 27, 1970.
15. *Los Angeles Times*, May 26, 1970.
16. *Los Angeles Times*, April 24, 1970.
17. *Sacramento Bee*, April 28, 1970.
18. *Los Angeles Times*, May 30, 1970.
19. *Los Angeles Times*, April 3, 1970.
20. *Los Angeles Times*, May 25, 1970.
21. State of California, *Statement of Vote*, Primary Election, June 2, 1970.

CHAPTER 22

1. Ainsworth, *Maverick Mayor*, p. 1.
2. *Newsweek*, 78 (November 29, 1971), p. 18.
3. *Los Angeles Times*, August 26, 1971.
4. Ralph H. Clark, "A Million Laughs with Mayor Sam," *LA* (newspaper), August 26, 1972, p. 5.
5. *The Enterprise* (Los Angeles), September 22, 1972.

6. *Los Angeles Times,* November 20, 1969.

7. *Los Angeles Times,* August 6, 1970.

8. *A Study of the Los Angeles City Charter* (Los Angeles: Town Hall, December, 1963), p. 151.

9. *Ibid.,* pp. 40–41.

10. *City Government for the Future* (Los Angeles: Los Angeles City Charter Commission, July, 1969).

11. City of Los Angeles, *Official Election Results,* City Clerk's Office, (Election Division).

12. *Ibid.*

13. *The Enterprise* (Los Angeles), August 26, 1966.

14. *Ibid.*

15. *Ibid.*

16. *New York Times,* June 25, 1961.

17. *Los Angeles Times,* February 19, 1969.

18. *Los Angeles Times,* January 31, 1964.

19. Phelan, "Trouble in Happyland," p. 86.

20. *TV Guide,* December 9, 1967, p. 22.

21. *Los Angeles Times,* May 12, 1970.

22. *Los Angeles Times,* June 30, 1971.

23. *Ibid.*

24. *Los Angeles Times,* November 17, 1971.

25. *Ibid.*

26. *Los Angeles Times,* September 27, 1967.

27. *Ibid.*

28. *Los Angeles Times,* December 7, 1971.

29. *Los Angeles Times,* July 7, 1969.

30. KNBC News, July 7, 1972.

31. *The Yorty Years,* Campaign Booklet, 1969.

32. Martin and Susan Tolchin, *To the Victor* (New York: Random House, 1971), p. 31.

CHAPTER 23

1. *Manchester Union Leader,* February 23, 1972.

2. *Manchester Union Leader,* March 3, 1972.

3. *Congressional Record,* 82nd Cong., 1st sess., 97:3 (April 11, 1951), p. 3683.

4. *Ibid.*

5. *Manchester Union Leader,* March 3, 1972.

6. *Manchester Union Leader,* February 17, 1972.

7. Wilson, *Parker on Police,* p. 141.

8. *The Enterprise* (Los Angeles), June 30, 1972.

9. *Manchester Union Leader,* February 9, 1972.

10. Clark, "A Million Laughs," p. 6.

11. *Los Angeles Times,* April 17, 1971.

12. *Los Angeles Times,* May 15, 1971.

13. *Los Angeles Times,* July 27, 1971.

14. *Ibid.*

15. *Los Angeles Times,* October 16, 1971.

16. *Ibid.*

17. *Ibid.*

18. *Los Angeles Times,* October 26, 1971.

19. *Los Angeles Times,* November 30, 1971.

20. *Manchester Union Leader,* February 15, 1972.

21. *Manchester Union Leader,* February 10, 1972.

22. *Manchester Union Leader,* February 1, 1972.

23. *Manchester Union Leader,* February 29, 1972.

24. *The Enterprise* (Los Angeles), March 3, 1972.

25. *Manchester Union Leader,* February 23, 1972.

26. *Manchester Union Leader,* February 4, 1972.

27. *The Enterprise* (Los Angeles), January 14, 1972.

28. *Manchester Union Leader,* February 17, 1972.

29. *Manchester Union Leader,* March 3, 1972.

30. *New York Times,* March 5, 1972.

31. *Manchester Union Leader,* March 7, 1972.

32. State of New Hampshire, *Official Primary Election Results, Summary by Counties,* March 7, 1972.

33. *The Enterprise* (Los Angeles), March 10, 1972.

34. *Manchester Union Leader,* March 1, 1972.

35. *Los Angeles Times,* February 23, 1972.

36. *Lincoln Evening Journal,* April 3, 1972.

37. *Ibid.*

38. *Omaha World-Herald,* May 5, 1972.

39. *Ibid.*

40. *Manchester Union Leader,* March 3, 1972.

41. *Omaha World-Herald,* April 30, 1972.

42. *Baltimore Sun,* May 11, 1972.

43. State of Nebraska, *Results of Primary Election of May 9, 1972,* Board of State Canvassers.

44. *Lincoln Evening Journal,* April 27, 1972.

45. *New York Times,* June 2, 1972.

46. *The Enterprise* (Los Angeles), May 19, 1972.

47. *Los Angeles Times,* June 1, 1972.

48. *The Enterprise* (Los Angeles), May 19, 1972.

49. *Los Angeles Times,* June 5, 1972.

50. *Omaha World-Herald,* May 8, 1972.

51. *Los Angeles Times,* June 6, 1972.

52. *Ibid.*

53. State of California, *Statement of Vote,* Primary Election, June 1972.

54. *Evening Outlook* (Santa Monica), June 8, 1972.

55. *Ibid.*
56. KNXT News, July 11, 1972.
57. These figures are compiled from the official records of the five states cited.
58. *Los Angeles Times,* June 1, 1972.
59. *California Journal,* January, 1972, p. 33.
60. *Los Angeles Times,* March 9, 1972.
61. *Los Angeles Times,* June 4, 1972.

CHAPTER 24

1. Baus and Ross, *Politics Battle Plan,* p. 159.
2. *Omaha World-Herald,* May 3, 1972; *Los Angeles Times,* May 27, 1972.

APPENDIX:
THE YORTY POLITICAL RECORD

Year	Announced/Discussed Running	Ran	Won/Lost (Finish)	% of Vote Primary	% of Vote General
1934	Assemblyman	No			
1934	Congressman	No			
1936	Assemblyman	Yes	Won	20.1	60.9
1938	Mayor	No			
1938	Assemblyman	Yes	Won	49.6*	59.8
1939	City Councilman	Yes	Lost (2)	33.0	47.1
1940	U. S. Senator	Yes	Lost (4)	7.4*	
1941	Mayor	No			
1942	Governor	No			
1942	State Senator	No			
1942	Lieutenant Governor	No			
1942	Assemblyman	Yes	Lost (2)	28.5*	41.1
1945	Mayor	Yes	Lost (6)	3.7	
1949	Assemblyman	Yes	Won		42.9**
1950	Congressman	Yes	Won	59.0*	48.3***
1952	Congressman	Yes	Won	55.1*	87.9
1954	U. S. Senator	Yes	Lost (2)	52.4*	45.5
1956	U. S. Senator	Yes	Lost (3)	20.4*	
1961	Mayor	Yes	Won	27.3	51.5
1964	U. S. Senator	No			
1964	Presidential Delegate Slate	Yes	Lost (2)	32.0	

Year	Announced/Discussed Running	Ran	Won/Lost (Finish)	% of Vote Primary	% of Vote General
1965	Mayor	Yes	Won	57.9	
1966	Governor	Yes	Lost (2)	38.1	
1968	Presidential Delegate Slate	No			
1968	U. S. Senator	No			
1969	Mayor	Yes	Won	26.1	53.3
1970	Governor	Yes	Lost (2)	26.3	
1972	President (N. H. Primary)	Yes	Lost (3)	6.1	
1972	President (Neb. Primary)	Yes	Lost (6)	1.8	
1972	President (Calif. Primary)	Yes	Lost (6)	1.4	

*Also cross-filed in the Republican primary; the percentage shown is for the Democratic party primary only.

**A special election (and thus not preceded by a primary contest) to fill an unexpired term.

***A candidate for the Independent-Progressive party received about 13 percent of the vote, which along with the Republican total, denied the winner a majority of the votes.

INDEX

and the viewpoint of the observer, the innovations were either liberating, treasonable, uplifting or corrupting, and for this reason it is not surprising that it was the first great crisis of the industrializing society, acting in conjunction with major improvements in the production and distribution of literature,[29] which generated the transformation in the availability of the written word to which the autobiographers referred. The "War of the Unstamped" reached a new pitch of intensity which between 1830 and 1836 saw at least 562 newspapers and journals, containing every sort of prose and poetry, written, printed, published and bought by working men.[30] By 1836 about 200,000 papers a week were on sale at prices of 1d. or 2d.[31] At a literary level, the middle class response was twofold. The religious publishing organizations redoubled their efforts and although it is impossible to measure the full extent of their output, some idea of its size can be gauged from the fact that between 1840 and 1850 the Religious Tract Society issued 23,290,301 publications in the British Isles, and by 1850 the S.P.C.K. was distributing about four million items a year.[32] Alongside these now traditional means of attempting to elevate the reading matter of the working class, a group of middle class radicals under the leadership of Henry Brougham launched the Society for the Diffusion of Useful Knowledge in 1827. The prices of the volumes in its early Libraries of Useful and Entertaining Knowledge were, at 3s. and 4s. 6d. respectively, still too high for the pockets of most working men, but in 1831 it made a determined effort to reach the homes of the working class by sponsoring Charles Knight's *Penny Magazine*,[33] the fortunes of which will be discussed in more detail in the following chapter.

The flood of cheap literature produced in response to the growing political, social and economic conflict not only encouraged the emergence of related ventures, such as, in particular, the Chambers brothers highly successful *Chambers Edinburgh Journal*, but also stimulated the circulation of the entire publishing industry. The price of the two or three volume novel, which stood at about 3s. a volume in the 1780s, had been pushed up by the increasing cost of labour and raw materials, particularly during the Napoleonic Wars, as well as by the failure of the industry to modernize its machinery, until by 1830 it had reached a standard 10s. 6d. a volume.[34] At the respectable end of the market there was little further movement in prices, with the average cost of a volume over the ten years between 1831 and 1849 remaining as high as 8s. 6d., but the introduction of single volume reprints, which sold at 5s. or 6s. each, caused the average price of a complete book to fall from 16s. in 1828 to 8s. 4½d.

[29] S. H. Steinberg, *Five Hundred Years of Printing* (Harmondsworth, 1974), pp. 277–288; F. A. Mumby and Ian Norrie, *Publishing and Bookselling* (5th edn., London, 1974), pp. 187–203.
[30] Joel H. Wiener, *A Descriptive Finding List of Unstamped British Periodicals, 1830–1836* (London, 1970).
[31] Estimation by *Weekly Times*, quoted in Patricia Hollis, *The Pauper Press* (Oxford, 1970), p. 124.
[32] William Jones, *The Jubilee Memorial of the Religious Tract Society* (London, 1850), pp. 246–7; W. O. B. Allen & Edmund McClure, *Two Hundred Years: The History of the Society for Promoting Christian Knowledge. 1698–1898* (London, 1898), p. 98. These are domestic sales only. Over the half century the R.T.S. claimed an overall circulation, domestic and foreign, of 500 million.
[33] Charles Knight, *Passages of a Working Life During Half a Century* (London, 1865), vol. II *passim*; Charles Knight, *The Old Printer and the Modern Press* (London, 1854), pp. 243–4.
[34] R. English, "The Price of the Novel, 1750–1894", *The Author*, vol. V (1894), pp. 94–99; Marjorie Plant, *The English Book Trade* (London, 1965), pp. 414–418.

in 1853,[35] and from 1836 onwards, with the publication of *Pickwick Papers*, reputable literature could also be obtained in 1*s*. numbers. The drop in prices both reflected and furthered a rapid acceleration in the output of the industry. The average number of books published each year during the last decade of the eighteenth century was 372, which represented a fourfold increase over the average for the first half of the century. By 1828 the number of new books published had climbed to 842, by 1853 it had reached 2,500. At the end of 1831 there were 177 monthly publications, in the next two years another 59 were launched and by 1853 there were 362 for sale.[36] These figures relate only to the higher end of the market and can give only an indication of the general trend. It is impossible to calculate the size of the industry as a whole, but it is perhaps worth noting that in addition to the respectable areas of publishing, the Religious Tract Society reckoned that in 1850, "there is a yearly issue in London of nearly thirty million copies of infidel and licentious works".[37] And what was published in London was distributed to the provinces with increasing facility. Lovett observed that, "In 1830, the great majority of our country booksellers seldom had more than one parcel per month from London, and now most of them have a parcel weekly, and many of them in large towns, three or four weekly, showing great increase".[38]

The proliferation of books, newspapers and periodicals imparted an essential buoyancy to the pursuit of knowledge. Partly as a result of the efforts of the working class community, and partly as a result of the actions of middle class publishers and of the innovations in printing and distribution brought about by industrialization and urbanization, the sheer presence of the printed word increased dramatically over the life-time of the autobiographers. If much of what was published was still expensive, there was now a much greater incentive to make the necessary sacrifices, and if a high proportion of what could be afforded was rejected, there was so much more opportunity to exercise discrimination. This apparently limitless expansion in the world of literature fired the ambition of working class readers. In this respect, if in no other, history appeared to be on their side.

The autobiographers' sense of progress lay in the comparisons they made between the situation at the beginning of the nineteenth century and that which prevailed one and two generations later, yet as their appetite increased with each new development, their capacity to appease their hunger remained as limited as ever. At every turn the reader continued to face enormous difficulties in his pursuit of books. A witness to the 1849 Select Committee on Public Libraries summarized the relationship between the working class community and the book trade after two decades of growing production and falling prices: "Are you able to state how the lower classes in London are supplied with literature?—By accident altogether . . .".[39] A survey of the methods adopted by the autobiographers to obtain their literature reveals a pattern consistent only in its diversity. We might look, for instance, at the means by which Thomas Carter, a Colchester tailor, gained access to the

[35] This figure was calculated by Edward Edwards, and includes all new works and new editions and reprints of old books published in this period, but excludes pamphlets and periodical publications. Public Libraries Committee, p. 30; Knight, *The Old Printer*, p. 261.
[36] Knight, *The Old Printer*, pp. 238, 260-1, 263.　　[37] William Jones, op. cit., p. 634.
[38] Public Libraries Committee, p. 179.　　[39] *Ibid.*, p. 81.

world of books. He learnt to read with the aid of the basic religious library owned by his parents:

> When I first began to read for amusement, I had, as has been hinted, access to but few books that were likely to be useful as well as entertaining. My parents' stock consisted of two Bibles, a Common Prayer Book, a Universal "Spelling Book", Watt's "Divine and Moral Songs", with some tattered and odd volumes of sermons and other theological disquisitions.[40]

His first opportunity to get hold of secular literature was provided by an old woman who ran a local sweetshop:

> About this time I also gained the good-will of an aged woman who sold cakes, sweetmeats, and fruit, and was moreover a dealer in little books. With her, as with my aunt, I was quite at my ease, as she freely gave me much that tickled the palate, and also allowed me ample scope for amusing my childish fancy. I had even then a taste for reading, which was here gratified by my being permitted to read all the little stories which she kept on sale.[41]

Carter's father had enlisted as a private soldier in the Napoleonic Wars, and to provide herself with an income, his mother opened a small dame school. Thomas joined the class, and contact with other children provided more books: "I also gained some profit as well as pleasure by there coming under my mother's care, being thereby enabled to peruse several small books belonging to the children, which otherwise would not have come in my way".[42] From there he went to a day school run by a congregation of Protestant Dissenters. One of the two masters at the school favoured the talented boy, and let him have the run of his own small library:

> On my asking him he readily granted my request, nor did he ever revoke his grant: the books were chiefly old and odd volumes of the "Arminian" and the "Gentleman's" Magazines; these, though of but little intrinsic value, were to me a treasure, as they helped to give me a wider and more varied view of many more things than I had previously been able to command. I perused them very much in the way of those undiscriminating readers who devour "The total grist unsifted, husks and all".[43]

His next step up in life was becoming apprenticed to a tailor. Here he benefited from the paternalistic concern of his employer's family:

> . . . several books which I had not before seen now fell in my way. This was through the courtesy of my young master, whose kindly feelings I have already noticed. He now gave me free access to his little library, in which were Enfield's "Speaker", Goldsmith's "Geography", an abridged "History of Rome", a "History of England", Thomson's "Seasons", "The Citizen of the World", "The Vicar of Wakefield", and some other books the titles of which I do not now remember.[44]

[40] Carter, *Memoirs*, p. 28. Carter was born in 1792. [41] *Ibid.*, p. 20.
[42] *Ibid.*, p. 40.
[43] *Ibid.*, pp. 57–58. Few elementary schools possessed their own libraries, as distinct from the private collections of masters. As late as 1880 only 2,000 school libraries existed in England (J. Lawson and H. Silver, op. cit., p. 327).
[44] *Ibid.*, pp. 74–5. The smaller and more isolated the unit of production, the more significant was the potential role of the employer. James Hogg, for instance, employed as a farm hand

The workshop employed a shopman, two apprentices, a foreman, and six journeymen, a sufficient number of individuals to combat the then high price of radical literature and to introduce Carter to contemporary politics: ". . . they clubbed their pence to pay for a newspaper, and selected the 'Weekly Political Register' of that clever man the late William Cobbett".[45] Later he moved to London, and was able to avail himself of two more methods of extending the scope of his reading matter. He made a habit of taking his breakfast at one of the coffee shops, "which were just then becoming general", on his way to work, where he would read the previous day's newspapers, the contents of which he would later relay to his fellow workmen.[46] And in his spare time he found an opportunity for supplementing his own small library: "At home I acquired increased facilities for reading, by means of a small book-club, consisting of my landlord and a few of his friends. Of this I became a member; and thus had the means of becoming a little acquainted with works which I had not before seen".[47]

No two of the autobiographers followed the same course, and Carter's career is representative only in that the variety of the methods he used encompassed the main groups of sources: the home, commercial outlets such as shops and circulating libraries—although the practice of buying a new book from a shop which sold nothing but books was the least common of all—educative and religious institutions and their libraries, teachers and pupils, economic and social superiors, fellow working men, whether inside or outside the workplace and whether organized or not, and places of recreation such as public houses and coffee shops. The multitude of devices were each attempts to reduce the influence of the high price of literature. Some were more successful than others, but except in the occasional instance of an extremely efficient book-club, the working man was never in a position to exert complete control over his supply of reading matter. Willie Thom bleakly summarized his situation and its effect on his pattern of reading: " 'My Books'—I have a few of my own—pick up a loan where it can be had; so of course my reading is without choice or system".[48] The consequences of the lack of control are to be seen in the booklists of all the autobiographers. Take the diverse collection of literature that Christopher Thomson, a sometime shipwright, actor and housepainter, worked his way through. It included adventure stories such as *Robinson Crusoe* and the imitative *Philip Quarll*, books of travel, such as Boyle's *Travels*, some un-named religious tracts, a number of "classics" including Milton and Shakespeare, some radical newspapers, particularly Cobbett's *Register* and Wooller's *Black Dwarf*, mechanics' magazines, and some occasional items of contemporary literature,

in a remote area of the Borders, was absolutely dependent on the farmer and his wife for his early reading matter (Hogg, pp. 9–10).

[45] *Ibid.*, p. 90. This was in 1807, just after Cobbett's paper had begun to espouse the cause of radical politics; *The Register* cost 10*d.* at this time. G. D. H. Cole, *The Life of William Cobbett* (3rd edn., London, 1947), pp. 126–30. M. L. Pearl, op. cit., p. 67. See also Dunning's and Farish's accounts of artisan workshops clubbing together to buy the 8½*d. Weekly Dispatch* during the reform bill crisis. (Dunning, p. 123; Farish, *Autobiography*, p. 11.)

[46] *Ibid.*, pp. 186–7. The first of the new type of coffee shops which stocked newspapers and sometimes had small libraries was Potter's, which opened in 1811 at 35 High Street, Bloomsbury. By the end of the period there were at least 2,000 in London alone. Claxton, p. 17; Public Libraries Committee, pp. 172, 177.

[47] *Ibid.*, p. 187.

[48] Thom, p. 30.